THE NEW
PATTERNS IN THE SKY

THE NEW
PATTERNS IN THE SKY

Myths and Legends of the Stars

Julius D. W. Staal

The McDonald and Woodward Publishing Company
Blacksburg, Virginia
1988

The McDonald and Woodward Publishing Company
P. O. Box 10308
Blacksburg, Virginia 24062–0308

THE NEW PATTERNS IN THE SKY
Myths and Legends of the Stars

All rights reserved. First Printing, 1988
Composition by Marathon Typesetting, Roanoke, Virginia
Printed in the United States of America
by Southern Printing Company, Inc., Blacksburg, Virginia

95 94 93 92 91 90   10 9 8 7 6 5 4 3 2

Library of Congress Cataloging-in-Publication Data

Staal, Julius D. W.
    The new patterns in the sky.

    Rev. ed. of: Patterns in the sky. 1961.
    Includes index.
    Summary: Provides astronomical data on the constellations and relates
myths and legends associated with each one.
    1. Stars—Juvenile literature.   2. Stars—Mythology—Juvenile literature.
3. Stars—Folklore—Juvenile literature.   4. Constellations—Juvenile
literature. [1. Stars. 2. Stars—Folklore.   3. Constellations]   I. Staal, Julius D. W.
Patterns in the sky.   II. Title.
QB801.7.S72 1988   523.8   87–92030
ISBN 0-939923-10-6; ISBN 0-939923-04-1 (pbk.)

Contents

Editor's Preface

Julius D. W. Staal (1917–1986), British planetarian, astronomer, and Fellow of the Royal Astronomical Society of London, was well known within his profession as an authority on myths and legends of the constellations. During his lifetime of work as lecturer, teacher, astronomer and administrator at planetariums in The Netherlands, Great Britain, South Africa and the United States, Mr. Staal entertained and enlightened audiences with hundreds of star stories collected from throughout the world. Many of these stories were printed in Staal's book *Patterns in the Sky*, originally published in Great Britain in 1961. When Mr. Staal retired from full time responsibilities at the Fernbank Science Center planetarium, Atlanta, Georgia, in 1978, he started preparing a revision of *Patterns in the Sky* that was to include star stories from throughout the world for all 88 of the constellations. Mr. Staal had nearly completed this revision when he died in 1986.

When we were offered the nearly finished manuscript for *The New Patterns in the Sky*, we immediately recognized that this would be a book of interest to a wide audience and certainly should be published. Since Mr. Staal would not be able to approve or otherwise respond to our editorial suggestions, our policy in editing this manuscript was to make only the minimum number of changes necessary to bring the manuscript around to publishable form. Our alterations consisted of standardizing the order in which information is presented in the various chapters, removing repetitive information, making modest stylistic changes, and revising distances and other physical data pertaining to individual stars to correspond with information in the *Observers' Handbook* for 1988. All of the illustrations were redrafted, and four appendices (III, IV, VI, VII) were added. Throughout, however, we attempted to preserve faithfully Mr. Staal's scope, pitch, and raconteurish style of presentation.

For assistance in evaluating and editing the manuscript for this book, we extend our sincere appreciation to Edward F. Albin (Louisiana Arts and Science Center Planetarium, Baton Rouge, Louisiana), John W. Burgess (Fernbank Science Center, Atlanta, Georgia), M. Rikk Harris (Center of Science and Industry, Columbus, Ohio), and Dr. Richard M. Williamon (Fernbank Science Center, Atlanta, Georgia).

Jerry N. McDonald

Author's Preface

In 1961, when I lived in Great Britain, I wrote a book titled *Patterns in the Sky*—a collection of myths and legends about the constellations and other celestial objects that were visible from the British Isles. Since 1961, *Patterns in the Sky* has been reprinted three times—once in Sweden and twice in the United States—and has enjoyed steady circulation. During the years since 1961, however, I have collected many additional star stories from throughout the world. Upon my retirement from full time lecturing at the Fernbank Science Center in Atlanta, Georgia, in 1978, I decided to incorporate my new information in a revised and enlarged edition of *Patterns in the Sky*—hopefully for publication in 1986, the 25th anniversary of the first edition. The present book—*The New Patterns in the Sky*—is the result of my recent efforts.

The first edition of *Patterns in the Sky* was concerned almost exclusively with Greek and Roman myths about the constellations that were visible from the latitude of London, England. The present book, however, incorporates myths, legends and other information about all 88 of the officially recognised constellations that adorn the canopy of Heaven. The star lore of not only the Greeks and Romans, but of many other cultures from throughout the world, is included in this book.

The constellations are arranged in this book according to the season of best visibility from the middle latitudes of the Northern Hemisphere. With but few exceptions, each constellation is discussed separately. Examples of the known mythology for each constellation are provided, as are notes on the history of constellation names and astronomical objects of interest. A reasonably complete list of current meteor showers, including all major showers and most important minor showers, has been derived from Norton's *Star Atlas*.

The illustrations in this book are entirely new, and represent an important addition to the material presented in the earlier version of this book. At least one figure is provided for each constellation; more than one is provided for most and some constellations are represented by several figures. These illustrations show the most prominent stars in the constellation; mythical, legendary or other imaginative figures projected against the stars of the constellation; and the location of the constellation in the sky. The primary illustration of each constellation is shown against the celestial coordinate grid, which is illustrated and explained in Appendix VI. Appendix VII contains star maps showing the location of all of the constellations. (A planisphere, available at planetariums, museums of natural history, and many bookstores, would be a useful companion to this book.) Bibliographic information about the illustration is provided parenthetically in the caption for each figure. This information includes (1) the alphanumeric catalog identification of figures in the Zeiss library of planetarium projections (prefixes A through F) and my personal library of figures (prefix JS); (2) the author of the figure upon which my illustration was based; (3) the nationality of the author of the reference figure; and (4) the approximate date the reference figure was prepared or published.

I wish to thank the optical firm of Carl Zeiss, Oberkochen, West Germany, for allowing me to use their beautiful collection of illustrations of the constellations. These illustrations were created by the late Dr. Helmut Werner, who also provided me with articles about his research on many of these constellations. Most of the figures in this book are based upon illustrations from the Zeiss collection. The cooperation of Dr. Werner and the Carl Zeiss firm contributed greatly to the successful completion of this book.

The University of Waikoto, New Zealand, kindly provided information about the star lore of Tamarereti's Canoe. Mary Larsen, librarian at the Fernbank Science Center, Atlanta, Georgia, obtained this information for me from the University of Waikoto, and I thank her for this service.

Mr. Rahlf Hansen, a student in physics and the history of science at the University of Hamburg, and an assistant at the planetarium in Hamburg, West Germany, provided me with information about many constellations and their lore that simply was not available to me in the United States.

I praise Mozelle Funderburk for the excellent artwork on the cover of this book. The painting depicts a scene from the ride of Phaethon—the moment when Zeus knocked Phaethon out of the Sun Chariot in order to save the Earth from total destruction by conflagration.

I could not have prepared the illustrations in this book without the able assistance of Mr. Guadelupe Torres. Mr. Torres made the rolls of film for me showing all the Zeiss illustrations, and he also loaned me his enlarger so that I could project these illustrations around the star fields.

Lastly, I must give thanks to the publishers of Norton's *Star Atlas* which I have used as a basis for the star fields in this book. Three different editions of Norton's *Star Atlas* have been my companions through my more than 30 years as a planetarium lecturer.

Why did not somebody teach me
the constellations and make me
at home in the starry heavens which
I don't half know to this day.

Thomas Carlyle

Introduction

How often, during a peaceful walk in the night, have you paused a while and looked up at the stars? And, seeing the stars, were you not captured by their beauty? Were your senses of imagination and wonder not piqued? Did you ever think about how many other eyes have been directed skyward during human history, what thoughts passed through the minds of these observers, and what meaning these sky watchers found in the stars and their motion?

Ancient man lived much closer to nature than we do, and knowledge of the stars and other celestial bodies was essential to his existence. The stars were the calendar and clock of early man; the Sun and the Moon were the hour and minute hand on the celestial dial. To read this dial, early humans grouped certain stars together into recognisable patterns so that the host of stars and its regular movement in the heavens could be followed with greater ease. The brighter stars were selected and connected with imaginary lines. The resulting figures were imagined to be animals, heroes, heroines and objects which were closely related to daily and annual rhythms and religious beliefs. And so, out of observation, correlation, uncertainty and necessity, the constellations were born. Thus early man learned to mark time by watching the predictable procession of the stars. The appearance and disappearance of certain stars was correlated with the seasons of the year, and reminded observers when to plough, sow, reap, hunt, fish and celebrate other annual events.

The stories associated with the constellations were told by farmers, sailors, soldiers and shepherds alike. Over the years and throughout the world, these stories were repeated from generation to generation, and developed into distinctive traditions in most of the world's cultures. We of European culture are most familiar with those stories of the stars that are derived from the Greeks, Romans, Arabs and Persians. Less familiar, but every bit as fascinating, are star stories of other cultures; star lore from the people of Africa, northern Europe, the four corners of Asia, North and South America, and the Pacific Islands. A sample of the rich body of celestial lore that has developed among the world's cultures is presented on the following pages.

Names of the Constellations and Stars

In the descriptions that follow, Greek and Latin names are used for the constellations and other celestial objects, and English equivalents are included for clarity. The Latin and English names for the constellations are listed in alphabetical order in Appendix II.

The stars of the constellations usually are ranked in order of decreasing brightness using letters of the Greek alphabet. Thus the brightest star in a constellation is designated by α (alpha), the first letter of the Greek alphabet. The second brightest star in the constellation is designated by β (beta), the second letter in the Greek alphabet, and so on. To illustrate, Regulus, the brightest star in the constellation of Leo, is designated α-Leonis. Algol, the second brightest star in Perseus, is designated β-Persei. Occasionally, however, the brightest star in a constellation is designated by a letter other than α. Rigel, or β-Orionis, for example, is brighter than Betelgeuse, or α-Orionis. Star names are given in the genitive case which indicates possession, so α-Leonis means "star alpha of the Lion." The Greek alphabet is presented in Appendix I, and genitives of the constellation names are given in Appendix II.

The Stars of the Seasons

The saying "the stars of Autumn, Winter, Spring and Summer" is somewhat misleading as it erroneously implies that the stars of Autumn are visible only in the Autumn, the stars of Winter in Winter, and so on. This, of course, is not absolutely true. The use of seasonal terms has come into practice because the majority of people living in any given latitude that are interested in star and constellation hunting do so at a convenient hour, say sometime between nightfall and midnight. Only certain stars are visible to these observers at any one time. The constellations are arranged in this book according to the season that they can be seen between about 8:00 P.M. and midnight in the middle latitudes of the Northern Hemisphere. Each successive month the same constellations will be seen about two hours earlier in the same place in the sky. For instance, if a planisphere is set for September 10 at midnight, one can see at a glance that the constellations can be observed in the same position in the sky on October 10 at 10:00 P.M., and on November 10 at 8:00 P.M. After a while, when you begin to grasp the movement of the stars, you will know when to look for your favourite constellations of a certain season at any time of the night. You will know that if you look before midnight you will have to search for your favourites a little more to the east, and if you are keen and look in the early hours of the morning you will have to direct your eyes more to the west.

The Open Window of the Celestial Dome

In addition to describing some of the rich body of star lore that has developed around the constellations, I hope that this book will serve as

2

an enticement to the reader to look into the sky—to find the constellations described herein and thereby come to know the stars more intimately. If you are new to sky watching, and if at first you find it difficult to locate the stars, persevere and try again another night. Do not, to begin with, look for longer than about half an hour at a time. Begin by locating a few of the more easily recognised constellations; success at this will lead to greater ease in finding and remembering the more difficult constellations later.

When you can trace the outline of the constellations yourself, you might be led to indulge in some of the more astronomical facets of the constellations. If so, see if you can find and separate a double star with your telescope, whether you can see a nebula or a star cluster, or detect the mysterious light changes of a variable star. This will be a sure way to reinforce an appreciation for the stars.

Omnia vincit amor, "love conquers all things," is a saying that also applies to the stars. If you have patience and do persevere, some of the most beautiful facets of astronomy can provide you with an immensely rewarding and inexpensive hobby. All you need is love for the stars; with it, pictorial astronomy is yours for the taking.

The Stars of Autumn

In the Autumn then, when over much of the Northern Hemisphere the leaves on the trees turn to gold and brown, when the evenings fall earlier and the nights become longer, the starry host both invites and deserves all the attention the sky watcher can spare. Vacation season is over, the mellowness of the summer is passing rapidly, and the skies are becoming resplendent with the gems of Heaven which have many a story to tell.

The great square of Pegasus is the dominating constellation for Autumn. Intertwined with the story of Pegasus are those of Andromeda, Cassiopeia, Cepheus, Perseus and Cetus—so the stories of these constellations will be told first. Following these are the stories of Aries, Triangulum, Aquarius and the other constellations that are most conveniently observed from the Northern Hemisphere during Autumn nights.

The Legend of Princess Andromeda
Andromeda, the Princess

Andromeda was the daughter of King Cepheus and Queen Cassiopeia of Ethiopia. Cassiopeia was a very beautiful queen, but she was also extremely proud and boastful. One day she boasted of being fairer than the Nereids, the water nymphs, who were renowned for their exquisite beauty. The Nereids overheard this boast and complained to their father Poseidon, the God of the Seas.

Poseidon, infuriated, shook the brine with his trident and so created a flood and a monster called Cetus. Poseidon sent Cetus to the waters of Ethiopia, where the monster appeared from the waves at unexpected moments to devour people and their herds. There did not seem to be any means of rendering the monster harmless. In despair, King Cepheus consulted the oracle of Ammon to see what could be done to rid his country of this plague. One can imagine the horror that filled Cepheus' heart when the oracle said that the land could only be saved if he were to sacrifice his daughter, Andromeda, to the monster.

What could Cepheus do? He had to choose between saving his own flesh and blood or his people, and as king he had no alternative. So Andromeda was led to the water's edge where she was to be chained to a rock and left to the mercy of the monster.

Perseus, mounted on the winged horse Pegasus, was passing by Ethiopia just as the unfortunate Andromeda was being chained to the rock. Perseus offered to rescue Andromeda on the condition that King Cepheus allow him to marry her. Cepheus agreed immediately and Perseus took up his position by the rock not very far from Andromeda. Perseus told Andromeda to keep her eyes firmly closed. As soon as the monster crawled out of the water and lumbered towards the place where Andromeda was waiting in great fear with closed eyes, Perseus jumped from his hiding place, pulled Medusa's head out of the leather bag and dangled it in front of Cetus. The monster instantly changed into a great rock which, it is said, can still be seen on the Levantine shore of the Mediterranean Sea.

Perseus quickly put the head back in the bag and freed Andromeda from her chains. A wonderful wedding followed combined with festivities to celebrate the riddance of the monster. There was, however, one ugly incident at the wedding. Phineus, a brother of King Cepheus, to whom Andromeda had been promised in marriage, caused a violent quarrel at the banquet. Once again, however, fate was sealed by the demonic power of Medusa's head. After the wedding, Perseus and

Andromeda went to Argos to live. Medusa's head was given to Minerva, who put it in the coat of arms on her shield.

Mythology is not a rigid subject, so one may find various renderings of the Andromeda story, and other stories as well, in different sources. Here follows a free translation of the story of Andromeda that is found in Book IV of the *Metamorphoses* of Publius Ovidius Naso—or simply Ovid—a Roman poet who lived from 43 B.C. to about A.D. 18.

After Perseus completed his assignment of decapitating Medusa, he put on his winged sandals, girded on his sword, and took off through the air. After some time he saw the Egyptian shores below him. Here Cepheus was king. Andromeda had just been chained to the rocks because the poor maiden had a foolish mother who talked too much. When Perseus saw her, tears running down her cheek and hair fluttering in the wind, she seemed to be as beautiful as a work of art, hewn out of the very rocks.

Perseus landed near the girl and said, "You should never have to wear those chains. Wear the manacles that lovers cherish as they sleep in each other's arms. Please tell me your name. Why are you in this plight? Where were you born?"

Being shy and modest she did not immediately answer. She was afraid to talk to any bold young gentleman and if her hands had not been chained, she probably would have covered her face.

Finally she overcame her shyness and spoke. She told Perseus who she was and how her mother had bragged of her own beauty. While she was talking, great splashing could be heard coming from the sea where a huge monster was riding the waves. As it clambered clumsily ashore and moved towards Andromeda, she screamed in terror while her harried parents rushed to her side, weeping and beating their breasts, realising the danger facing the girl.

Then Perseus spoke and said, "There will be time enough for weeping later. Time for rescue, however, is short. Would you give your daughter in marriage to me, Perseus, son of Jove and Danae, who conceived me in a shower of golden rain when she was locked up in a bronze chamber by her father? To me, Perseus, who flies the air with winged sandals and killed the Gorgon Medusa with the snake-curled hair?"

What else could the parents do? They accepted his terms, pleaded for Andromeda's rescue and promised rich lands and a daughter's dowry. Meanwhile the monster sped towards the shore like a ship that ploughs through the waves, driven by the arms of galley slaves. The water was churning and broke into showers of spray all around the monster.

Perseus leapt into the air. The monster saw Perseus' shadow on the sea and plunged toward it in an attempt to tear it apart. At that moment Perseus dived upon the furious monster and thrusted his sword up to the hilt into its shoulder. The beast reared with the gaping wound bleeding but, with his agile wings, Perseus dodged the snapping jaws of the creature. Then, as the monster rolled over and exposed its soft belly, Perseus struck. The beast started to vomit purple spittle. Perseus' wings, damp with the spray of brine, began to grow heavy. He saw a protruding rock and leapt onto it to safety. From here he continued the fight, thrusting his sword three more times into the monster's bowels.

Then it was all over and, from the canopies of heaven whence the gods looked down on Perseus, great cheers rang out. Cepheus and Cassiopeia called to the hero who had saved the honour of their house. With chains removed, Andromeda stepped forward so that Perseus could receive his promised reward.

Perseus brought suitable offerings as thanks to the gods who had helped him. Then he took Andromeda as his bride. Hymen and Cupid brandished the wedding torch. Fires were lit. The odor of burning incense wafted through the air. The houses and streets were decorated with garlands. Music could be heard everywhere and the palace gates stood open, revealing golden banquet halls made ready for a sumptuous wedding feast.

Historians believe that the Andromeda story is very old and might have originated in Mesopotamia, the land between the Tigris and Euphrates rivers in what is today Iraq. This story seems to be linked to the creation story of Marduk and the dragon Tiamat, described below under Ophiuchus and Serpens. This origin would place the original setting rather a long way from the Levant, the setting of our stories. The Ethiopia in the first legend given above was most likely the African coast along the Red Sea. This location would very likely mean that Andromeda was a dark skinned girl such as was alluded to by Ovid in his description of her as *fusca colore patriae suae*, "of the dusky colour of her country." On the other hand, Gaius Manilius, a Roman poet of the First Century A.D. used the description *nivea cervice*, "of snow-white neck," when referring to Andromeda.

The story of Princess Andromeda is well represented in the heavens. Andromeda is a long line of fairly bright stars; her head coincides with the star Alpheratz of Pegasus and her feet lie near Perseus. Fainter stars represent the outstretched arms of Andromeda while she is chained to the rock (Figures 1, 2).

Perseus towers protectively over Andromeda, standing with one foot on the Pleiades, often seen as the nymphs who gave him the winged sandals and showed him the way to Medusa. In his hand hangs the awful head of Medusa. An interesting star in the head of Medusa is Algol (Alghul), "Demon of the Woods." This star changes its brightness every three days and is easily observed doing this with the naked eye. Ancient people believed that even in death this horrible head still had demonic power and winked its evil eye from time to time. The sword of Perseus

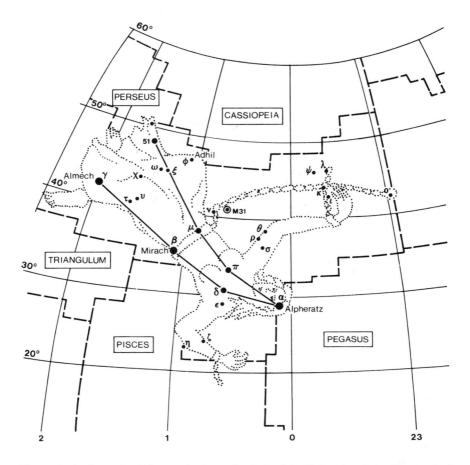

Figure 1. Andromeda. Princess Andromeda chained to the rocks along the coast of Ethiopia, being sacrificed to the sea monster Cetus. (A1; Argelander, German, ca. A.D. 1843.)

has in its tip the famous double cluster of Perseus, which also can be seen with the naked eye on a clear night.

Pegasus is an outstanding square of stars near Andromeda, whereas Cetus looms low over the southern horizon in the Autumn. Cepheus and Cassiopeia lie north of Andromeda.

The Chinese saw in this part of the sky Koui-siou, the House of the Sandal, the first house of the White Tiger. The constellation Koui-siou is made up of the middle section of Andromeda's stars and the stars of the northerly part of Pisces, the Fishes (Figure 3). The appearance of this constellation in the Autumn sky was a reminder that it was time to see to the manufacture of foot wear. The Chinese did not have an equivalent for the Andromeda figure in the form of a woman.

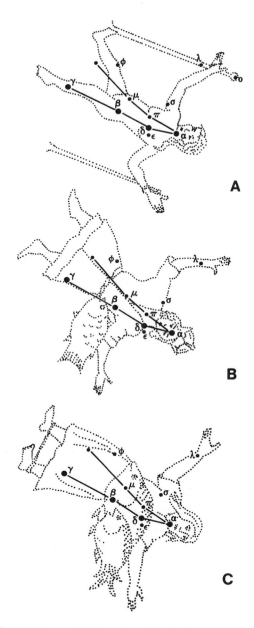

Figure 2. Andromeda. A. Princess Andromeda, without clothing, bound as a sacrifice to Cetus. (A2; al-Sufi, Persian, 10th Century A.D.) **B.** Princess Andromeda wearing her crown, with one of the Fishes at her waist. (A3; al-Sufi, Persian, 10th Century A.D.) **C.** Princess Andromeda, bound at the ankles, as a sacrifice to Cetus. Some interpretations of the Andromeda story identify the Fishes as the monster to which Andromeda was to be sacrificed. (A4; al-Sufi, Persian, 10th Century A.D.)

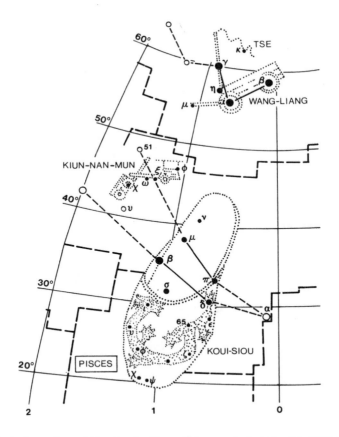

Figure 3. Andromeda and Cassiopeia. Three Chinese asterisms in this region of the sky include Koui-siou, the House of the Sandal; Kiun-nan-mun, the Southern Camp Gate; and Wang-liang and Tse, the Chariot and Whip. (Staal, British, A.D. 1986.)

Another interesting little Chinese asterism is Kiun-nan-mun, the Southern Camp Gate, made up of the stars φ, ξ, ω, χ in Andromeda's skirt (Figure 3). When camp was made, the chariots and carts were drawn up in a large circle. The entrance to this circle was closed by drawing together the tongues of two chariots. The chariots were pulled apart to open the entrance.

Points of Interest in Andromeda

A little northeast from the stars μ and ν is the famous Andromeda Galaxy, calculated to be 2.4 million light years from Earth. On a clear and dark night this galaxy, barely visible to the naked eye, looks like a misty streak. A pair of binoculars will help one find this gem. Other than the Milky Way, the Andromeda Galaxy is probably the best known of all galaxies. Being near the Milky Way, the Andromeda Galaxy is a favourite photographic object. Time lapse photographs made through large telescopes reveal and record the spiral nature of this galaxy, which appears as an oval because it is tilted about 15° from the edge-on position.

γ-Andromedae is a double star. The brighter of the two is golden in colour; the companion is bluish-green. The distance between the pair is approximately 260 light years. γ-Andromedae is also the radiant point of an annually recurring meteor shower called the Andromedids. The Andromedids are believed to be the remains of the comet Biela, which split into two before the eyes of observing astronomers during the middle part of the 19th Century. Seven years later the comet was expected to return and indeed it was punctual in its arrival, but the distance between the two parts had increased considerably. On its estimated return in 1872 no comet appeared. Instead a heavy shower of meteors took place. Again in 1885 a similar display took place and now every year from 17–27 November, when the Earth is at or near the intersection of its own orbit and that of the former comet Biela, a good display of shooting stars can be observed. This display will not be as dense as the 1872 shower, but during some years several scores of flashes per hour may be counted as the meteors streak through the sky.

Although we say that the radiant point of the Andromedids is in γ-Andromedae, this is only an illusion. The streams of meteors really move in lines that are nearly parallel but, just as railroad tracks seem to diverge from a distant point of apparent origin, so does the stream of parallel meteors seem to diverge from γ-Andromedae. In fact, the meteor display takes place about 100 miles above our heads when small meteoric fragments plunge into our atmosphere. These fragments then vaporise due to friction with the molecules of rarefied air. Depending on their size and on the angle of entry into our atmosphere, these particles usually disintegrate some 40 to 60 miles above our heads. Bigger particles sometimes survive their passage through our atmosphere and land on the Earth's surface. Such particles are known as meteorites. Our eyes cannot of course see the difference in perspective between 100 miles and the much more distant stars of Andromeda. So to us on Earth it appears that these showers originate in a certain constellation and hence they are given the name of that constellation. In this case, the shower is named the Andromedids after its apparent radiant point against the background stars of the constellation Andromeda.

Cepheus and Cassiopeia
Cepheus, the King, and Cassiopeia, the Queen

Cepheus and Cassiopeia were king and queen of Ethiopia, and the parents of Princess Andromeda. King Cepheus can be seen clearly in the stars. Cepheus is often portrayed with his arms upheld as a supplicant, presumably beseeching the gods to spare the life of his daughter, but some interpretations picture him as a more regal, authoritarian king (Figure 4).

Cassiopeia was condemned by the gods to swing forever around the North Celestial Pole because of her offensive boasting. When Cassiopeia is above the North Celestial Pole, the stars β-, α-, η-, γ-, δ-, ε-Cassiopeiae form the letter M. When below the North Celestial Pole, these same stars form the letter W. This change in aspect is symbolic of the punishment Cassiopeia received for her bragging. When below the Pole, Cassiopeia has to hang on for dear life lest she fall off her throne (Figure 4). Twelve hours later she gets some respite while sitting in an upright position again.

The Persian astronomer al-Sufi, who lived during the Tenth Century A.D., portrayed Cassiopeia as a queenly figure with a crown on her head and a staff in her right hand. In al-Sufi's figure, Cassiopeia's staff is surmounted by the crescent of the moon (Figure 4). In 1679 Augustin Royer, a French astronomer, represented in Cassiopeia a female figure holding a palm leaf in her left hand while seated on a rather hard looking marble throne. She is drawing a robe over one shoulder with her right hand (Figure 5). The palm leaf has been interpreted as that of a Judean palm tree. Usually a palm leaf is a symbol of victory, but this does not fit well with the Classical story of Queen Cassiopeia. Her predicament can hardly be seen as a victory. However, the palm was also a symbol of Christian martyrdom that appeared in figures drawn for religious purposes during the 17th Century. Such persons as Mary Magdalene; Bathsheba, the mother of Solomon; and Deborah, a prophetess who dwelt under a palm tree on Mount Ephraim were depicted in the stars of Cassiopeia during the 17th Century.

While the constellation Cassiopeia was usually adorned with the figure of a woman in Greco-Roman mythology, other cultures associated different mythical forms to this constellation. Quite often, in fact, these cultures recognised mythical figures that incorporated parts of more than one of the 88 constellations recognised today.

Some Arab groups recognised a mythical Tinted Hand in the constellations Cassiopeia and Perseus. The idea of the Tinted Hand might have

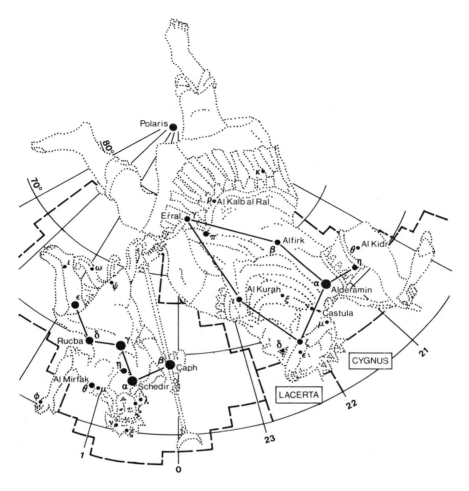

Figure 4. Cassiopeia and Cepheus. King Cepheus as an authoritarian figure (B12; Royer, French, ca. A.D. 1679) and Queen Cassiopeia on her endless circuit of the high northern sky (B1; al-Sufi, Persian, 10th Century A.D.).

derived from the practice of Arab women painting their hands and feet with henna, a reddish dye. The author was told that this was a cosmetic precaution to protect the skin from the heat. Another source says that the Tinted Hand is the hand of Fatima, daughter of Mohammed, stained with blood. The hand lies around the stars of the W of Cassiopeia, whereas the arm is in line with the stars ϵ-, ν-, δ-, α-, γ-, η-Persei (Figure 6A).

It is only natural that people like the Arabs and other Middle Eastern nations, who depended heavily upon the camel as a mode of transport, would give this animal a place of honour in the stars. One Arab rendition of the camel has the animal's head around the stars λ-, κ-, ι-, ψ-Andromedae

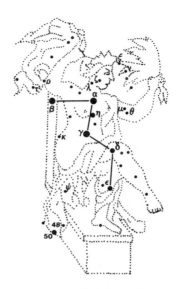

Figure 5. Cassiopeia. Female figure holding a palm branch and drawing a robe over her right shoulder. (B2; Royer, French, ca. A.D. 1679.)

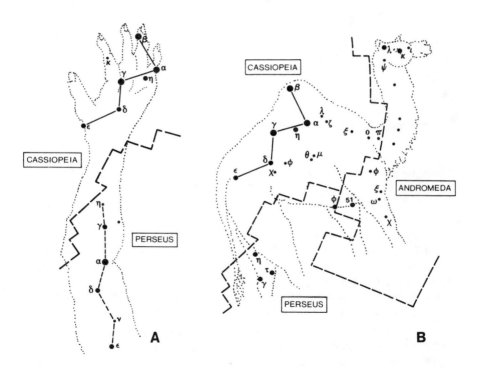

Figure 6. Cassiopeia. A. The Tinted Hand: Middle East (B3). **B.** The Camel: Middle East (B4).

(Andromeda's right hand), the hump around β-Cassiopeiae, the legs around some of the stars of Perseus and Andromeda, while most of the body lies within Cassiopeia (Figure 6B).

The Lapps of northern Europe see the antler of a moose (called elk in Europe) around the W stars of Cassiopeia and other stars of Andromeda and Perseus (Figure 7A). The Chukchee, hunters and gatherers native to Siberia, see five reindeer stags around the M stars of Cassiopeia (Figure 7B).

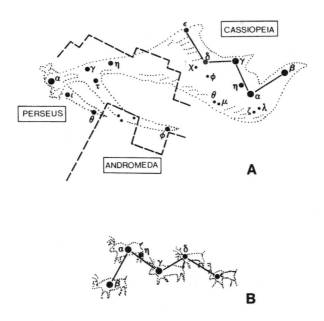

Figure 7. Cassiopeia. A. The Moose Antler: Lapplanders; northern Scandinavia (B6). B. The Five Reindeer Stags: Chukchee; Siberia (B7).

Natives of the Marshall Islands in the Pacific Ocean see a porpoise in the sky, a fitting asterism for people living amidst the sea. This porpoise stretches across four modern constellations, from Cassiopeia through Andromeda and Triangulum to Aries. The W stars of Cassiopeia form the tail of this porpoise while α-, β-, γ-Arietis represent the head. Many of the bright stars of Andromeda form the body of the porpoise (Figure 8).

As with Andromeda, the Chinese recognised no female figure in the stars of Cassiopeia. Instead, they saw here a great chariot called Wang-liang (Figure 3). Actually Wang-liang means Bridge of the Kings, but this applies only to the stars κ-, η-, μ-Cassiopeiae. The camp of the emperor was surrounded by a moat and visiting vassals had to cross a bridge,

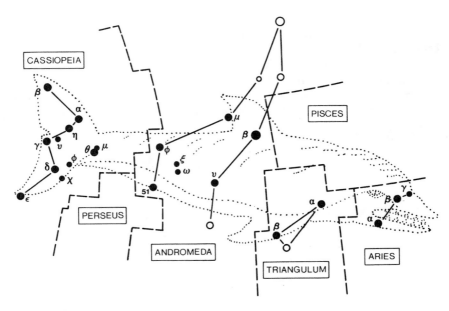

Figure 8. Andromeda, Aries, Cassiopeia and Triangulum. The Porpoise, as recognised by the Marshall Islanders (B8).

hence the name Bridge of the Kings. When, however, the stars α-, β-Cassiopeiae were added, the figure became a Chariot, representing the chariots in which the vassals came to the court of the emperor. There was also in Chinese mythology a famous charioteer called Wang-liang, a contemporary of another famous charioteer named Tsaou-fou. Tsaou-fou was the charioteer of King Mou, who reigned from 1001 to 947 B.C. These two charioteers were so strong that they could check horses in full gallop and simply pick up chariots and turn them upside down with the greatest of ease. To complete the scene there was also a whip, Ts'e, γ-Cassiopeiae.

Perseus

Perseus, the Hero

In the land of Argos lived two princes, Acrisius and Proteus. These men should have divided their kingdom equally between themselves, but instead they were jealous of each other and each continually strived to obtain more than his rightful share. Finally, following a violent quarrel, Proteus was driven out of Argos by Acrisius.

Everything now appeared peaceful for Acrisius. He controlled all of Argos. What more could he wish for? Perhaps peace of mind. Acrisius was greatly troubled by a prophecy which foretold his death by the son of his daughter Danae.

Driven to near insanity by this gnawing knowledge he finally decided to prevent Danae from marrying, and he gave orders to lock her up in a brass-lined tower. But Jupiter had seen all this, and was so attracted by the beauty of Danae that he wished to lie with her. He found entry into the apparently impregnable tower by changing himself into a shower of gold coins. From Jupiter's union with Danae was born Perseus. When Acrisius heard about this miracle he became so frightened and angry that he ordered Danae to be cast out, in an open chest, into the sea.

But he should have known that a mortal cannot combat the gods! Danae drifted for several days while the gods kept a watchful eye on her. She finally arrived at the island of Seriphos where she was found by a fisherman, called Dictys, who took her into his home and adopted her as his own daughter. Dictys had a brother, Polydectes, who was the chieftain of the island.

For a while all was peaceful. Danae's son, Perseus, grew up into a strong and tall man, whom the gods loved because of his versatility and skill in many manly arts. Then one day, Polydectes' wife died. Danae was a beautiful woman and a daughter of a king, so Polydectes asked her to marry him. But Danae told him that she did not love him, and was interested only in raising her son Perseus. In Polydectes' anger at Danae's refusal to be his wife, he made her his slave.

Unfortunately, all this happened while Perseus was away on an errand in Samos, one of the neighbouring islands. One afternoon, when he was resting a while in a forest, Perseus fell asleep and had a wondrous dream. A beautiful woman, wearing a helmet and carrying a spear and a great brass shield, seemed to hover over his head. She seemed to be trying to tell him something. At first her message was not at all clear. Then in the highly polished shield appeared the image of a woman whose beauty was marred by an ugly head with coiling snakes for hair and a devilish grin on her mouth. She also had great flapping wings and hooked claws on her feet. Perseus turned restlessly in his sleep as he shuddered at this sight, but the vision would not fade. Then the goddess of his dream told him that he would have to kill this monster in the near future. Perseus could still hear the voice of the dream goddess clearly as he awakened from his uncomfortable sleep. He pondered the dream, but he could not find its meaning and tried to forget about it.

Perseus returned home and discovered that his mother had been made a slave to Polydectes. He stormed in anger to the palace where he would have slain the king had not Dictys pleaded with Perseus to spare Polydectes' life. Perseus controlled his rage, but he took his mother to the temple of Aphrodite, where she would be safe because nobody would violate this holy shrine.

Polydectes, realising that Perseus would always stand in his way, decided to get rid of him. To do this he organised a banquet and, according to the custom of the times, every guest brought a gift. He also invited Perseus, well knowing that the poor man could not afford any gifts. All the nobles laughed at and taunted Perseus, making him very angry. Then he remembered his dream and, jumping up, he spoke, "I will bring you a gift you have never had before—I will bring you Medusa's head, and you will be sorry for ridiculing me." The peers and chieftains scoffed at, and further ridiculed, Perseus. Polydectes told him to leave the palace and the island, and not to dare to set foot on it again until he could present him with this wonderful gift.

Perseus left the palace and went into seclusion in order to think out a plan and to pray to Minerva, Goddess of Wisdom, to tell him what he should do. Suddenly he saw the same apparition he had seen in his dream, and he realised that the beautiful woman in his dream had been none other than Minerva herself. There she stood accompanied by Mercury, the swift Messenger of the Gods.

Minerva once again told Perseus his task and gave him directions for finding the horrible Gorgons, three sisters called Stheno (the Mighty One), Euryale (the Wandering One), and Medusa (the Queen), who were daughters of the aged sea god, Phorcys, and Keto. These ugly beings lived far away in the land of the Hesperides, the Daughters of the Night and Eternal Darkness. Perseus was instructed not to look directly at Medusa but to catch her reflection in the shining shield which Minerva had lent him. If he did not take this precaution, he would be turned to stone by the gaze of Medusa. Minerva also gave Perseus a magic sword, and Mercury gave him his winged sandals which would carry him over land and sea. When Perseus was all prepared and had memorised his instructions, Minerva and Mercury bade him farewell and good luck, and then disappeared from view. Perseus leapt up, the winged sandals began to flap, and he floated away like a bird.

Perseus flew on, leaving Greece behind him. The winged sandals guided him towards the North Star, to the dim wastes where the Sun never shines, where mist prevails and the cold wind blows over the ice-covered fields. Here he found three sisters sitting in the snow, singing under the light of the pale yellow moon. They had but one eye and one tooth between them and he could see how they passed these on to each other while they sang. He asked if they could direct him to the land of the Hesperides, but they took no notice of him. In despair Perseus threatened that he would take their one eye and throw it away. Fearing that he would, the sisters told him that he was on the wrong track and that he should turn southward and find Atlas.

Perseus, only too glad to leave these dismal barren wastes, flew towards the sunlight. When the fog lifted, he saw the mountain where Atlas lived. Perseus told Atlas his task. Atlas warned Perseus never to go near the Gorgons unless he was wearing a helmet which would make him invisible. Atlas then sent a messenger to Hades, the Underworld, to fetch the helmet. Before he handed over the helmet, however, Atlas made Perseus promise that he would show him Medusa's head if he were successful in his mission. At first Perseus was reluctant to make this promise. However, after Atlas beseeched him because he was old and tired from supporting the celestial sphere, and because he wanted a perpetual rest from all this, Perseus swore that he would grant him this last wish.

Atlas then handed over the helmet. Perseus put it on and immediately became invisible. He flew back to the north and eventually neared the land of the Hesperides. He could hear the flapping of the Gorgons' wings and the clanging of their metal claws. As ordered by Minerva, he manoeuvered his shield in such a way that he could only see the reflection of these horrible sisters. After a while he saw his chance, swooped down and, with one mighty blow of his sword, severed Medusa's disgusting head from her body (Figure 9). Perseus quickly put it into a leather bag and flew off as rapidly as he could. The other two sisters pursued him for quite a while but his winged sandals put him well ahead of them.

When Perseus arrived back in Atlas' country, as he had promised, he showed the gruesome head to Atlas. Atlas instantly turned into a huge mountain which we can still see today as the Atlas Mountains in North Africa.

Eager to go home, Perseus did not delay any longer and, changing course, crossed over the kingdom of King Cepheus. Here he performed his epic and heroic deed of rescuing Andromeda from the monster Cetus, as was told above under the legend of Princess Andromeda.

Perseus, laden with gold and silver, and accompanied by Andromeda, whom he had married, sailed at last to Seriphos. One can imagine the delight of his mother, Danae, upon seeing him again after seven long years of separation.

Perseus' next task was to go to the palace of Polydectes, who was just having another banquet. The king grew pale when he recognised

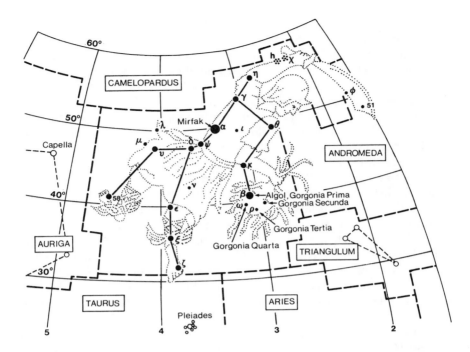

Figure 9. Perseus. Perseus with the head of Medusa. Algol, once seen as the evil blinking eye of Medusa, is actually one of a pair of eclipsing stars with a period of about 69 hours. (D19; al-Sufi, Persian, 10th Century A.D.)

Perseus, who said to him, "I have come to pay my debt and give you what I have promised you." With these words Perseus pulled Medusa's head out of the leather bag and the entire company of nobles and peers changed into stone. Perseus declared Dictys king and he then took Andromeda and his mother back to Argos, where he had been born.

Circumstances on Argos had changed. Proteus, who had been driven out by Acrisius, had come back with many warriors and driven Acrisius from his kingdom. Once on the island, Perseus revealed who he was. The islanders took his side in the battle which ensued between Perseus and Proteus. Proteus was killed in this battle, and so Perseus became King of Argos.

All was peaceful for a time, but as Danae grew older she longed to see her father again in spite of what he had done to her. Perseus promised he would fetch Acrisius and allow him to live in peace to the end of his days on the island of Argos. Perseus sailed to the land of the Palasgians and found Acrisius taking part in a great banquet. There were various games and contests and Perseus took part in many of these to test his skill with his rivals. In one such contest he threw a discus with all his might and it would have hit its target had not a sudden gust of wind

22

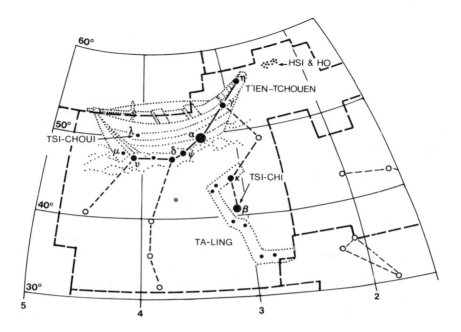

Figure 10. Perseus. Chinese asterisms in Perseus include T'ien-tchouen, the Celestial Boat; Tsi-choui, the Swollen Waters; Ta-ling, the Great Trench; and Tsi-chi, the Heaped-up Corpses. The unfortunate imperial astronomers Hsi and Ho are represented by the double cluster hχ. (Staal, British, A.D. 1986.)

pushed it off its course. The discus hit Acrisius and killed him. And so, what the oracle had foretold came true!

It is interesting to note again that the Chinese had no equivalent of a Perseus hero figure in this part of the sky. Instead they had four asterisms in the stars of Perseus, namely T'ien-tchouen, the Celestial Boat; Tsi-choui, the Swollen Waters; Ta-ling, the Great Trench; and Tsi-chi, the Heaped-up Corpses (Figure 10).

T'ien-tchouen, the third paranatellon of the third house of the White Tiger, was a reminder that the flood season would arrive toward the end of August and the beginning of September. The boats were to be made ready in case dikes burst and other forms of communication were temporarily disrupted.

Tsi-choui, the fourth paranatellon of the third house of the White Tiger, was a reminder that the annual flood waters could crest at unusual heights.

Ta-ling, the fifth paranatellon of the third house of the White Tiger, commemorated the great trench in which criminals would be buried. During Autumn, mass executions of criminals took place. The corpses from these executions were cast in a common grave because the Chinese felt that these criminals were not entitled to an honourable burial. Tsi-chi, sixth paranatellon of the third house of the White Tiger, is represented by the star Algol. This star marks the place where the corpses of the executed criminals were piled.

The ancient Chinese believed that the Sun, Moon and planets influenced the lives of man. Chinese astronomers diligently studied the movements of these bodies and anything else that might happen to them from time to time. For example, changes in the colour of these bodies were seen as an omen that war or some other peril was imminent. Changes in the appearance of the Sun were a sure sign that misfortune or calamity might befall the reigning monarch. Should the Moon turn red or deathly pale, it was augured that unlucky tidings were around the corner.

With so much at stake, the emperor wished to be forewarned of perils originating within the heavens. Consequently, Chinese astronomers residing at the imperial courts never had it so good. The court astronomers were coddled, pampered, and provided with luxurious living quarters; they enjoyed the best of food and drink, and were given a liberal sprinkling of the most beautiful girls for their amusement. Astronomers Hsi and Ho, who worked at the court of Emperor Tsung-k'ang during the third millenium B.C., did not, however, always seem to take things too seriously. On occasion, these men enjoyed so much lavish partying, eating, drinking, and other frivolities with the ladies that they did not have enough time to perform their duties as astronomers properly. They neglected to check the movements of the stars. Timekeeping was in confusion. Then, the unexpected struck. The Sun was suddenly eclipsed, and the emperor and his nation had not been forewarned.

The people were terrified and started to riot because everybody believed that the end had come and that the Sun was being devoured by a gigantic dragon. On previous occasions the people had been warned in advance of the coming of the Sun-eating dragon, and they had prepared themselves to scare away the monster by blowing trumpets, clanging cymbols, striking drums, shouting, crying, and whistling. At totality, it looked to the Chinese as if the Sun's disk shone through the dragon's stomach wall. Miraculously, the Chinese always succeeded in chasing away the demon. After a while, the dragon always had regurgitated the Sun.

On this occasion, however, Hsi and Ho were the cause of the near death of the Sun, and one can imagine the ire of the Chinese people and Emperor Tsung-k'ang. When the sun shone again, the Emperor summoned Hsi and Ho to the palace and, according to Chinese custom, they were beheaded. Their heads were cast into the sky where they can be seen to this day as two fuzzy patches in the Milky Way near T'ien-tchouen, the Celestial Ship of the prehistoric Chinese sky. Today we know these two fuzzy patches as the double cluster in Perseus (Figures 9, 10). Although the heads of Hsi and Ho have since served as a warning to other astronomers that they carry out their duties with the utmost diligence, it is a gratifying thought that modern astronomers no longer have to fear such a fate.

Points of Interest in Perseus

Perseus is an easy constellation to find (Figure 9). Beginning with one foot, ζ-Persei, just above the Pleiades, Perseus towers in a huge arc towards two beautiful clusters called the "double cluster of Perseus." α-Persei, or Mirfak, "the Elbow," is in Perseus' chest near where his elbow would rest. β-Persei, or Algol, is an eclipsing binary and represents the winking eye in Medusa's head. Algol has a companion star and the two stars revolve around each other. We see this binary system edge-on from Earth. So sometimes we see the companion to the left, sometimes to the right, sometimes behind, and sometimes in front, of Algol. This latter position is when the companion star eclipses Algol. This eclipse is the reason why Algol appears dimmer for a while. Ancient people explained this phenomenon as the winking of the demon's eye, still blinking even after the head had been decapitated.

John Goodricke, in 1782, was the first to explain correctly this phenomenon of dimming. Algol is normally a star of about magnitude 2.2 but fades to about 3.4 when it is eclipsed by its companion. Its brightness is thus diminished by 1.2 magnitudes every 69 hours. The actual dimming lasts only 10 hours and the whole process can be observed easily in one and the same evening. If, for example, the minimum magnitude occurs at 10:00 P.M., begin to look at approximately 5:30 P.M. when Algol will still shine at full brilliance. Shortly after, as the companion begins to intercept Algol's light, one can see the brilliance diminish until at 10:00 P.M. it is at its minimum. After that, the brightness increases gradually and by about 3:00 A.M. all is back to normal. The process will repeat itself approximately 60 hours later.

In an eclipsing system the two stars are sometimes very close together—so close that telescopes cannot separate them. How then do we know that there are two stars? Like a crystal magic wand, the spectroscope comes to the aid of the astronomer. We all know the beautiful colours that are created when sunlight is refracted by a mirror or window. The spectroscope has a prism which also splits light into a band of colours called a spectrum. On one side of the spectrum we can see the reds in various nuances, from dark to light red, changing to orange, yellow, green, blue and violet on the other side. Also present in these spectra are dark lines discovered by Joseph von Fraunhofer (A.D. 1787–1826) and, after him, called the Fraunhofer lines. These lines, by their position in the spectrum, reveal the presence of certain elements in the far away star. The astronomer can therefore tell whether a star contains calcium, hydrogen, helium, carbon, iron, or other elements. These same Fraunhofer lines have also given away another secret. Sometimes these lines showed a shift towards the blue end and sometimes towards the red end of the spectrum. It was discovered that if the lines moved toward the red end of the spectrum it meant that the stars under consideration were moving away from Earth; if the lines moved toward the blue end, the stars were moving nearer to Earth. The radial velocities at which these stars approach or recede from Earth could be determined by considering the amount of line shift, the time over which a shift takes place, and the speed of light. This very same line shift betrays the existence of a companion star in a binary system. As the companion star moves towards Earth, the spectrum lines can be observed moving toward the blue end of the spectrum. As the star moves away from us, the lines shift toward the red end of the spectrum. Eclipsing binaries, so close to each other that telescopes cannot detect them, are revealed by the spectroscope and consequently are called spectroscopic binaries. From detailed study of eclipsing binaries and their spectroscopic data, the mass of the stars can be determined as well as their dimensions, temperature, atmospheric conditions and distance from each other.

Each year, from 10–12 August, we may expect the Perseids meteor shower, which is seen best after midnight. Another shower, called the ε-Perseids, is always expected between 7–15 September. The radiant point of this shower is near ε-Persei.

Finally there is the double cluster of Perseus, sometimes designated hχ-Persei, more accurately NGC 869 (h) and NGC 884 (χ), an excellent object for viewing with a telescope of moderate aperture. This cluster was known as far back as the times of Tsung-k'ang, the fourth reigning monarch of the Hsia Dynasty of ancient China (ca. 2585–2146 B.C.).

Pegasus
The Winged Horse

Pegasus was a winged horse born from the blood of Medusa's head and the foam of the sea. Pegasus usually is shown as half a horse, upside down (Figure 11). The great square formed by α-Pegasi, or Markab, "the Saddle," β-Pegasi, or Scheat or Menkhib, "the Horse's Shoulder," γ-Pegasi, or Algenib, "the Wing" or "the Side," and α-Andromedae, or Sirrah, from *Al Surrat al Faras*, "Navel of the Horse," form the body of the horse. The nose lies in ε-Pegasi, or Enif. H-Pegasi, or Matar, is the knee of the horse. Sirrah, also called Alpheratz, is actually the first star of Andromeda, the princess' head.

In Arabia, the demihorse is seen upright. The fact that it is only half a horse means perhaps that the horse is just rising from the ocean, the other half being still submerged.

Pegasus was a jolly and kind horse. It is said that one day he pranced around so frivolously that his hooves created a spring called Hippocrene, which was alleged to have magic power in its waters. If one were to drink water from this spring, one would be gifted with the art of poetry.

After Perseus delivered the head of Medusa to King Polydectes, Pegasus flew away to Olympus, where he became the bearer of thunder and lightning for Jupiter. Pegasus did, however, return to Earth to become the trusted steed of Bellerophon, son of Glaucus, King of Ephyra (Corinth). Bellerophon was a brave and handsome young man who had received his name after he had killed a Corinthian named Bellerus. After this deed he went to Proteus, King of Tiryns. Sthenaboea, the king's wife, tried to attract Bellerophon but he scorned her advances. In seeking revenge Sthenaboea told her husband a totally different story, namely that Bellerophon had tried to seduce her. Proteus knew that it would not conform to etiquette to kill a guest at his palace, so he sent Bellerophon on an errand to Iobates, Proteus' father-in-law, with a sealed message. The message told Iobates to scheme Bellerophon's death.

Iobates, therefore, imposed various nigh impossible tasks on Bellerophon from which no normal man could return alive. Bellerophon was commanded to conquer the Chimaera, a malicious monster with the head of a lion, the body of a goat and the tail of a snake. Minerva, the Goddess of Wisdom, helped Bellerophon complete his tasks. When one night Bellerophon prayed fervently in Minerva's temple for her guidance, he found to his astonishment a golden bridle lying nearby. He realised that this must be a sign from Minerva. Bellerophon picked up the bridle and, as he left the temple, he saw a beautiful and unusual horse calmly

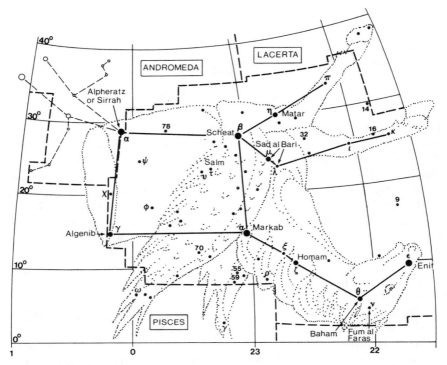

Figure 11. Pegasus. Pegasus as an inverted demihorse, facing west—the typical representation of this playful creature. (D12; Aratus, Greek, ca. 270 B.C.)

grazing the surrounding meadow. The horse was quite tame; he came to Bellerophon and let himself be harnessed with the golden bridle. So Bellerophon, riding Pegasus, set out on his mission. When at last the Chimaera was found it was Pegasus, with his deft wing movements, who kept Bellerophon out of harm's way. Bellerophon stuffed lead in the monster's fiery mouth which instantly melted in the flames, suffocating the monster.

Iobates next ordered Bellerophon to subjugate the savage tribes of the Solymia and the Amazons, at which Bellerophon also succeeded. Iobates, in despair, next tried to ambush Bellerophon but the young hero survived this attack without a scratch. Iobates thereafter gave up and, in fact, became filled with admiration for Bellerophon. Iobates allowed Bellerophon to marry his daughter, by whom Bellerophon had two children, Laodameia and Isandrus. But the end of Bellerophon's life was tragic for both his children were killed by the gods.

All this time Pegasus remained Bellerophon's good friend, and although there was nothing to hold Pegasus on Earth he stayed for a while to be with Bellerophon. But sadness about the death of his children and arrogance due to the success in his various tasks went to Bellerophon's head and, in time, he demanded that Pegasus take him to Olympus to become the equal of the gods. Pegasus shot up through the sky with Bellerophon clinging on to his back. The gods on Olympus watched Pegasus approach the heavenly palace with his mortal rider. Jupiter could not tolerate this arrogance. Some say that Jupiter slung a thunderbolt at Pegasus and Bellerophon. Others say that Jupiter dispatched a stinging fly which stung Pegasus and made him rear suddenly and throw off his rider. Whatever the cause of his unseating, Bellerophon ignominiously plunged headlong to Earth, where he landed with a terrific crash which blinded him for life. Thereafter, Bellerophon wandered in misery, alone and fleeing the haunts of men. A warning for the presumptous! Some believe that Jupiter eventually showed pity and put Bellerophon amongst the stars, and as such he is sometimes seen in the constellation of Auriga, the Charioteer.

Pegasus has always been a symbol of ecstasy and élan which could inspire poets and make heroes perform wonderful deeds. He was always seen as a light hearted creature, a sort of emissary between Earth and Olympus. Pegasus loved to gambol around, sometimes in the heavenly fields, sometimes on the earthly plains, and sometimes skimming over the waters from which he had been born.

The Greek poet-astronomer Aratus (ca. 270 B.C.) described Pegasus in his famous *Phaenomena:*

> Beneath (Andromeda's) head is spread the huge horse, touching her with his lower belly. One common star (Alpheratz: α-Andromedae) gleams on the horse's navel and the crown of her head.
>
> Three other stars (α-, β-, γ-Pegasi), large and bright at equal distances set on flank and shoulder, trace a square upon the horse.
>
> His head is not so brightly marked, nor his neck, though it be long. But the farthest star on his blazing nostril (Enif: ε-Pegasi) could fitly rival the former four, that invest him with such splendour.
>
> Nor is he four footed. Parted at the navel, with only half a body, wheels in Heaven the Sacred Horse. He it was, men say, that brought down from lofty Helicon the bright water of bounteous Hippocrene. For not yet on Helicon's summit trickled the fountain's springs. But the horse smote it and straight away the gushing water was shed abroad at the stamp of his forefoot and herdsmen were the first to call that stream "the Fountain of the Horse." From the rock the water wells and never shalt thou see it far from men of Thespiae; but the horse himself circles in the Heaven of Zeus and it is there for thee to behold.

In the Tenth Century A.D., the Persian astronomer al-Sufi deviated from the classical demihorse by showing Pegasus as a complete horse, upright and facing eastwards. The entire horse is shifted west from the location of the Greek horse, and its head lies in the stars of Lacerta, The Lizard. The right foreleg passes through β-Pegasi. The left foreleg is outlined by η-, μ-, λ-Pegasi, while the back is in π-Pegasi and μ-Cygni. The belly and flank are indicated by ι-, κ-Pegasi and the rear legs pass through 9-Pegasi (Figure 12). It is not known why al-Sufi represented Pegasus this way; perhaps he wanted to commemorate the famous Arabian stallions.

The Hindus saw in the square of Pegasus a bedstead representing the 26th and 27th Hindu lunar stations (Figure 13A). The Hindus and other people of India often used a bedstead for lunar stations, to provide a proper resting place for the fast traveling Moon. Each day the Moon is located at another station.

The Arawak and Warrau Indians of Guiana, in tropical South America, saw the square of Pegasus as a huge barbecue grill resting on high stilts (Figure 13B).

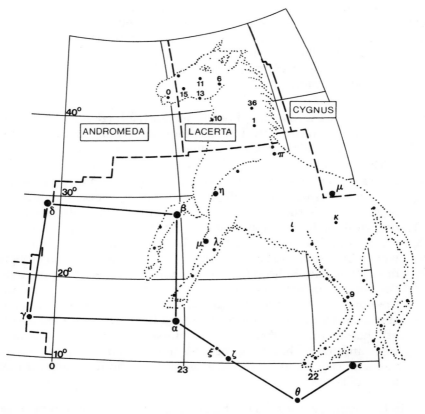

Figure 12. Lacerta and Pegasus. Pegasus as a complete horse, upright, facing east and extending into Lacerta. (D16; al-Sufi, Persian, 10th Century A.D.)

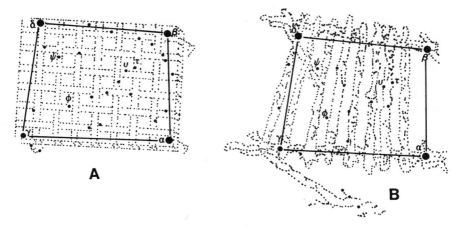

Figure 13. Pegasus. A. A bedstead: Hindu; India (D17). **B.** A barbecue grill: Arawak and Warrau; northern South America (D18).

Points of Interest in Pegasus

Although the square of Pegasus is devoid of bright stars which can be seen with the naked eye, an ordinary pair of binoculars will disclose many faint stars. Over 160 nebulae have been discovered in Pegasus at distances of 100 and more light years from Earth. Within the square, it is said, 17 faint stars can be seen with the naked eye; finding them is a test for one's eyesight.

The Pole star (α-Ursae Minoris), Alpheratz (α-Andromedae), and Algenib (γ-Pegasi) all lie approximately on the zero-hour circle. A line drawn through these stars points to the Vernal Equinox, about 15° below γ-Pegasi. The Vernal Equinox is the point where the ecliptic, or Sun's highway, intersects the Celestial Equator, the point where the Sun stands on the first day of Spring (see Appendix VI). Some 2,000 years ago this point of intersection was seen against the background of the stars of Aries, the Ram. Since that time this point has always been referred to as "the First Point of Aries," although this title sounds contradictory today when the Vernal Equinox is seen against the background stars of Pisces, the Fishes. This change of background constellations is due to a movement called the precession of the equinoxes, caused by a top-like wobble of the Earth's axis of rotation. Every 2,100 years or so the First Point of Aries moves into another segment of the zodiac. From Pisces, the First Point will move to Aquarius, then to Capricornus, and so on all around the zodiac until, after 25,800 years, the point will be back at its present location. Precession will also cause different stars to become

Pole stars in centuries to come. But, every 25,800 years, Polaris again becomes the North Celestial Pole Star.

The signs of the zodiac are the same today as they were 2,000 years ago, but these signs do not now coincide with the background stars for which they were named, and will not do so again until an entire cycle of precession has been completed. In the year A.D. 24,100 the zodiacal sign of Aries, the Ram, will once more be seen against the background of the constellation of Aries, the Ram. In the year A.D. 11,200 the First Point of Aries will be seen against the stars of Libra, the Scales. At that time Pegasus will be a Spring constellation instead of an Autumn constellation.

On 30 May, in the early hours of the morning, the η-Pegasids meteors are visible, with the radiant point being near the star η-Pegasi.

Cetus
The Whale or Sea Monster

During September and October we in the Northern Hemisphere can see Cetus crawling low in the sky over the southern horizon. Cetus is a large sprawling figure: its clumsy and bulky body lies south of the Celestial Equator while its ugly head protrudes above the Equator. Cetus is usually translated as Whale, although there were no whales in the region where this constellation originated. Cetus more likely was based on some big, fictitious creature that supposedly lived in the sea than on any real form of life. The nearest thing to the mythical creature was a whale, about which the people of Mesopotamia and the Mediterranean region had heard. With this in mind, it is possible that the origin of the myth lies ultimately with whales, but graphic representations of Cetus are more like fanciful, fictitious monsters than whales.

Cetus is amphibious and, in the story of Argo Navis, it appears as the Dragon. Cetus is also the monster that would have devoured Andromeda had it not been for Perseus' intervention. Cetus is the personification of everything bad, such as hatred, envy, and egotism. Cetus was pictured as something ugly, living deep in the dark waters of the ocean, and, when from time to time it came above the surface, it was seen as an evil, lumbering creature, smelly and dripping with seaweeds. Equivalents of Cetus can be found in the myths of many cultures, such as those of India and China, where it is often a Dragon. The theme is the same in all of these stories; a beautiful young woman is abducted by a monster and finally rescued by a handsome young hero.

A glance at a star map shows that Cetus lives in an area of the sky where all of its neighbouring constellations have some connection with water. East of Cetus is Eridanus, the Great River; north of it is Pisces, the Fishes; west of it are Aquarius, the Water Carrier, and Capricornus, the Seagoat; and to the south lies Piscis Austrinus, the Southern Fish. Ancient people often called this part of the sky The Sea because of the many water-related constellations located here.

The German astronomer Johannes Bayer (A.D. 1572–1625) visualised a dragon fish in the stars of Cetus (Figure 14). In 1661 the German, Cellarius, created a representation of a whale-like animal (Figure 15A) similar to one that had appeared earlier on a celestial globe made by the Dutch globe maker Willem Jansson Blaeu (A.D. 1571–1638). Other renditions have represented Cetus as having a fish-like body attached to the head of a lion, a dog, or a horse, or as an elephant fish complete with trunk and one tusk.

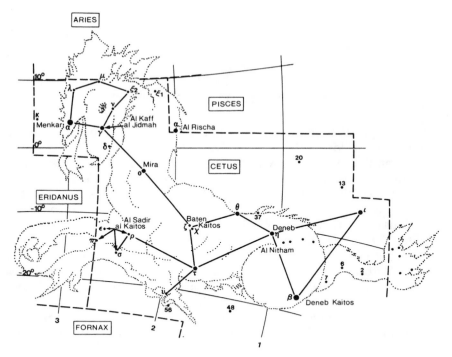

Figure 14. Cetus. Cetus as the Dragon Fish. (B21; Bayer, German, ca. A.D. 1603.)

Non-western cultures have seen entirely different figures in Cetus. The Tukano and Kobeua Indians of northern Brazil saw Cetus as a Jaguar (Figure 15B). To these people, the Jaguar is the personification of the God of Violent Storms and Hurricanes. To the Chinese, the head of Cetus was a circular celestial grain storehouse called T'ien-k'iun—the second paranatellon of the third house of the White Tiger. The back part of Cetus is a square celestial grain storehouse called T'ien-ts'ang. This is the third paranatellon of the second house of the White Tiger.

Points of Interest in Cetus

Cetus has one very remarkable star, o-Ceti, or Mira, "the Wonderful Star." Mira is a long-period variable star with a cycle of about 332 days from one period of maximum brightness to the next. This period is sometimes a little erratic and can be off by as much as 30 days either way. For about five months Mira is invisible, then in the next six months it gradually increases in brilliance, until finally it shines with the beautiful sparkle of a star of the second magnitude. This peak of brilliance lasts for about a fortnight, after which time it again starts slowly to fade.

It was David Fabricius who discovered the impressive light change in Mira in 1596. Just as for the Cepheids, the reasons for this change are still not fully understood. The star pulsates and, as it grows in size, it increases its brilliance. When Mira contracts, its brilliance diminishes. Ancient people believed this pulsating action to represent the beating heart of the monster Cetus.

Mira can be found easily when it is at or near full brilliance. Early in Autumn, in the Northern Hemisphere, Mira can be found by drawing a line from Polaris through γ-Andromedae (Andromeda's foot) to near the horizon (about 20° above the horizon for an observer at about 40° N) where the sparkling Wonderful Star should be located. If Mira cannot be located, it is probably because the star is at minimum brightness and the naked eye cannot detect it.

Mira is about 200 light years distant from Earth. It is a huge star with a diameter of about 350 million miles—about 400 times the diameter of the Sun. At maximum brightness, when Mira has swollen to its maximum size, the star can attain a diameter about 500 times that of the Sun.

α-Ceti, or Menkar, is a star of magnitude 2.5 and marks the head of the monster. β-Ceti, or Deneb Kaitos, is the tail of the monster.

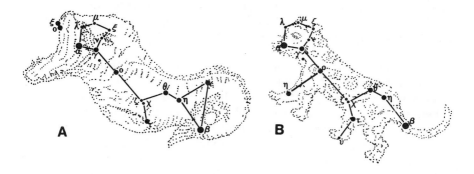

Figure 15. Cetus. A. Cetus as the Whale. (B21; Cellarius, German, ca. A.D. 1661.) **B.** The Jaguar: Tukano and Kobeua; Brazil (B17).

Aries
The Ram

The ram has played an important role in the religion and mythology of many different cultures. In ancient Egypt, Ammon Ra—the God of Fertility and Creative Life—was depicted with the body of a man and the head of a ram. From about 1730 B.C. until A.D. 420 Aries was the *Princeps Signorum Coelestium*—the background constellation of the first day of Spring, "the Indicator of the Reborn Sun" (Figure 16). After A.D. 420, due to the precession of the Equinoxes, Aries relinquished this honour to Pisces, the Fishes, but around A.D. 24,100 the Vernal Equinox will again enter Aries.

King Athamas of Boeotia, in Asia Minor, had for a queen a goddess named Nephele, the Nebulous Cloud. Although marriage between mortals and gods very often occurred, the god or goddess was never allowed to stay on Earth forever. So the time came when Nephele had to leave Earth, and to leave her son Phrixos and daughter Helle in the care of Athamas.

Not long after Nephele left Earth Athamas chose another wife, Ino, whom he hoped would also be a good mother for his two children. But, after a while, the stepmother turned against the children and started scheming to rid herself of them. She managed to have disease spread amongst the crops of the land, and when the whole harvest failed, she spread the rumor that the gods were angry with Phrixos and Helle. The only solution was to have the children sacrificed to the gods. King Athamas would not hear of it, but Ino had corrupted even the priests of the land and, when they advised the king to sacrifice his children, he had to give in.

But mortals forget that they cannot scheme against the will of the gods. Nephele, of course, had seen all this from Olympus and, in the depth of night, she descended from Heaven to solace her poor children and devise a plan to rescue them. At the critical moment she would send to them a ram with a golden fleece. The children were to jump on the back of the ram and hang on to its golden curls. The ram would do the rest. There was, however, one warning; Phrixos and Helle must not, under any circumstance, look down!

When the morning of the sacrificial execution came, the children were led to the altar. Suddenly, the golden ram, having descended from Heaven, landed in front of the children. They instantly jumped on the ram's back, and it bounded into the air before any of the astonished onlookers could recover. The children, elated and happy, enjoyed their ride, but Helle could not resist the temptation to look down. That was, of course, fatal. She became giddy, fell off of the ram, and fell into the sea. The place where she landed has been called Hellespont ever since.

Phrixos fared better and arrived, very much saddened, at Colchis in the kingdom of Aeëtes. At Colchis, Phrixos sacrificed the ram to Jupiter and gave its golden fleece to King Aeëtes, who had it nailed to a tree and guarded by a dragon who never slept. Jupiter placed the noble ram in the heavens where we can see it still amongst the stars. How the golden fleece was recovered can be read in the story of Argo Navis and Jason.

Another story of the ram takes us back to the time of Odysseus, who also had a ram to thank for saving his life. Homer described the episode beautifully in Book IX of the *Odyssey*. Briefly the story is as follows.

Odysseus, King of Ithaca, had played a leading role in the war against Troy, a nearly impregnable city which had been captured by the Greeks only with a cunning trick. After a siege of many months the Greeks

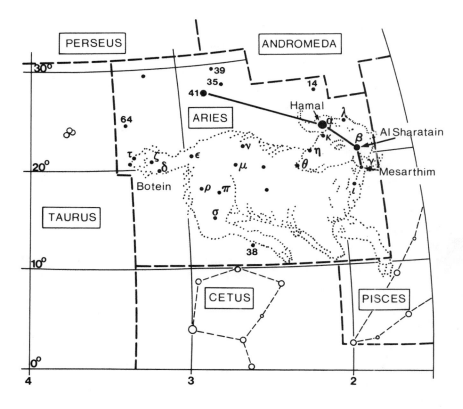

Figure 16. Aries. Aries in the recumbent position. (A17; Flamsteed, English, ca. A.D. 1729.)

37

feigned departure by sailing away in their ships. The Trojans, who saw them go with a sigh of relief, found a huge wooden horse on the beach. The Trojans dragged the horse inside the city walls as a spoil of war. Little did they know that they had drawn in their own destruction. During the night some Greek soldiers crept out of the hollow belly of the horse. Meanwhile the Greek navy had returned under cover of darkness and, choosing their time well, they made a coordinated attack on the town with the help of the Greeks already inside. So Troy was occupied before the Trojans had even realised what was happening.

The war over, Odysseus started for home. During his wanderings he came to the island occupied by the Cyclops, a race of one-eyed giants. While exploring the island, Odysseus and several of his men were captured and kept in the cave of one of the Cyclops, Polyphemus. Odysseus tried, without success, to make friends with the hostile Polyphemus who, every day, ate two of Odysseus' men. Polyphemus had locked the Greeks in his mountain cave with an enormous boulder that was too heavy for anybody to move. As strength could not prevail, cunning was the only answer. So Odysseus, during the daytime while Polyphemus was watching over his herd of sheep, called his men together and drew up a plan for their escape. They found a tree trunk in the cave. They cut a sharp point on one end of this trunk, hardened it in the fire, then hid the trunk under some dung heaps. When Polyphemus came home that evening he slew two more of Odysseus' companions. After Polyphemus' hunger was sated, Odysseus spoke to him. "Cyclop, take and drink this wine after thy feast of man's meat, that thou mayest know what manner of drink our ship held."

Polyphemus drank the wine and asked for more. Three times he had his bowl refilled with the dark strong wine. Polyphemus asked Odysseus for his name. Very shrewdly Odysseus answered, "Cyclops, thou askst me my renowned name, and I disclose it unto thee. 'No Man' is my name." Polyphemus answered, "Then No Man will I eat last in the number of his fellows. That shall be thy gift."

Then Polyphemus sank back, drunk and satisfied. When the Cyclops was fast asleep, Odysseus and his company dug up the pointed tree trunk and reheated the point. With one mighty heave, they plunged the stake into the giant's eye; his eyelid singed, his eyeball sizzled, and the roots of his eye crackled. Mad with pain, the giant roared so loudly that the hillsides trembled. All the neighbouring Cyclops came running to his cave to ask, "What hath so distressed thee, Polyphemus, that thou criest thus aloud through the night and makest us sleepless?"

And Polyphemus answered, "No Man is slaying me!" So his friends answered, "Well, if no man is slaying thee, do not keep us from our sleep." And they went away again.

The giant was helpless, but Odysseus had yet to get out of the cave. He tied each of his companions and himself underneath a ram. Next morning, the giant opened the cave and checked each ram by stroking its back as it left the cave. And so Odysseus escaped from the terrible Polyphemus, and he had a ram to thank for saving his life.

The astronomical meaning of this myth is simple to see. That Odysseus was brought by a ram from the dark cave to the light symbolises that when the Sun is in Aries, the long dark Winter months are over and Spring has begun. Everywhere people, other animals and plants rejoice at the return of light and warmth as the Sun begins to shine longer and longer every day.

A third story of a ram in Classical mythology relates to primordial times when the Olympic gods were still battling with the Titans for the supremacy of the Universe.

On one occasion the Olympic gods had to flee to Egypt as they were pursued by Typhon, the scourge of mankind. The Olympic gods, thinking they were safe in Egypt, were holding a feast by the river Nile when Typhon suddenly came upon them. To save their lives they changed themselves into all sorts of animal figures. It was said that Jupiter altered himself into a ram, which Typhon overlooked completely. Jupiter thought the ram to be such a good disguise that he immortalised it in the constellation of Aries, as a memento of his own cunning (Figure 16).

Aratus provided a figure of Aries (Figure 17A) and said:

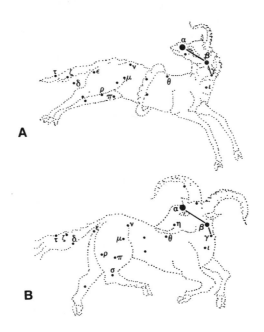

Figure 17. Aries. A. Aries running, bearing an equinoctial colure symbolising the Vernal Equinox. (A18; Aratus, Greek, ca. 270 B.C.) **B.** Aries running. (A19; al-Sufi, Persian, 10th Century A.D.)

There too are the most swift courses of the ram, who
Pursued through the longest circuit, runs not a whit
Slower than the Bear Cynosura . . . himself weak and
Starless as on a moonlit night, but yet by the belt of
Andromeda, thou canst trace him out.
For a little below her is he set. Midway he treads
The mighty heavens, where wheel the tips of the
Scorpion's claws and the belt of Orion.

John Flamsteed (A.D. 1646–1719), an English astronomer, saw in
Aries a ram lying down with its head turned sideways. The star α-Arietis
sits in the forehead at the root of the right horn, β-Arietis on the root of
the left horn, γ-Arietis in the left horn itself, ε-Arietis in the root of the
tail, and τ-, ζ-, δ-Arietis in the tail itself (Figure 16). Earlier, the Persian
astronomer al-Sufi had depicted the ram running with its head turned
backwards, possibly admiring its golden fleece (Figure 17B).

The Chinese saw in the stars of Aries the House of the Reapers, called
Leou-siou. Figure 18 shows a woman carrying a basket on her head
containing some of the harvest. Leou-siou is the second house of the
White Tiger. This asterism is also a reminder that it is now time to reap
the fruits of Autumn. The Reaper is flanked by a left and a right inspector,
Tso-kang and Yeou-kang, respectively, the first and second paranatellon
of the second house of the White Tiger. Tso-kang was the Inspector of
Marshes and Ponds. Yeou-kang looked after the distribution of pasture
land.

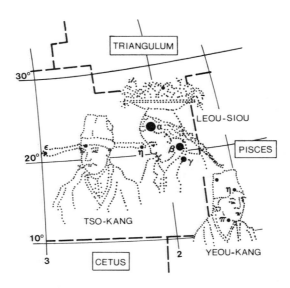

Figure 18. Aries. Chinese asterisms in Aries include Leou-siou, the House of the Reapers,
and the two inspectors, Tso-kang and Yeou-kang. (Staal, British, A.D. 1986.)

40

The Ram is not a very outstanding constellation. It has one bright star, α-Arietis, or Hamal, in the head of the animal. All the other stars are faint and inconspicuous. The ε-Arietids meteor shower gives its display each year from 12–23 October.

Aquarius
The Water Carrier

West of Pisces and below the neck of Pegasus lie the stars of Aquarius, the Water Carrier. Aquarius is always depicted as a man carrying a jar, the contents of which he is pouring out. The stream of water from this jar flows into the mouth of Piscis Austrinus, the Southern Fish (Figure 19).

When in Classical times the Sun passed in front of the stars of Aquarius, it used to be the rainy season. The Egyptians used to say that the Nile would overflow its banks when Aquarius dipped his great jar into the waters of the Nile. This was the beginning of the Egyptian Spring.

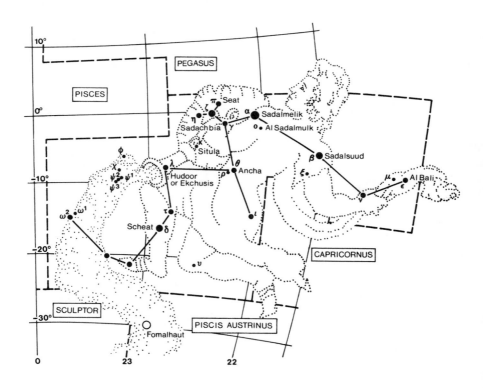

Figure 19. Aquarius. Aquarius, the Water Carrier. (A6; Bayer, German, ca. A.D. 1603.)

Aquarius was also seen as the cup-bearer of the gods. Water carrying was a very common and important occupation in ancient times. It was the custom to offer people water to refresh themselves after long journeys and to clean their tired feet. Water carriers also acted as terrestrial and celestial waiters at banquets in the houses and palaces of kings and noblemen, as well as at the festivities in the halls of the Olympic gods. Ganymede, a handsome young mortal, was abducted by order of Jupiter, who sent an eagle to carry him away from the Earth, so that he might serve as cup bearer to the gods. Ganymede had a place next to Jupiter's throne on Olympus and, whenever he accompanied Jupiter elsewhere, he was seated on the eagle. Aquarius and Ganymede are usually seen as one and the same being, although Ganymede was sometimes considered to be the god who gave rain to the Earth. After the apotheosis of Ganymede, a clear division between Aquarius and Ganymede cannot be given. Ganymede was made into the constellation Aquarius by astronomers of old.

In practically all countries of the world the story of the great flood is told in some version or another. Ancient mythology personified this event in Aquarius; it was he that poured out the waters that nearly terminated life on Earth. Only Deucalion and Pyrrha—a man and a woman—survived this ordeal and reestablished the human population.

Aquarius is the central figure of that region of the sky often referred to as The Sea. To the east of Aquarius is Eridanus, the Great River, Cetus, the Whale, and Pisces, the Fishes; to the west lies Capricorn, the Seagoat; and to the south is Piscis Austrinus, the Southern Fish—all members of the watery elements. Two thousand years ago Aquarius coincided with the month of February, which has its derivation from *februare*, "to cleanse." In those far off days it was during the time of Aquarius that people cleaned their homes, farms and barns after the long dark Winter. Even in modern times housewives still do their Spring cleaning after the long Winter months, except that this now takes place in March, due to the precession of the equinoxes.

Aquarius was entirely unknown to the Chinese. Rather, to the Chinese, the water stream and its many droplets of faint stars have become soldiers, namely Yu-lin-kiun, the Army of Yu-lin (Figure 20). These soldiers are under the command of Pe-lou-sse-moun, General of the Northern Districts. Their encampment is close to a line of ramparts known as Loui-pi-tchin. In their midst is Fou-youe, the Axes, indicative of an armoury or the weapons used to execute hostages if ransom was not forthcoming. Yu-lin means literally "Feathers" and "Forests," the name of a special unit of soldiers that were as light and swift as feathers and as numerous as the trees in a forest. Today this would be a unit of light infantry. Yu-lin-kiun was the special palace and temple guard, soldiers held in readiness for extraordinary duties and unforeseen eventualities.

43

Aquarius is a very elaborate constellation and one difficult to visualise because of its abundance of stars. The easiest way to locate Aquarius is to remember the two shoulder stars α and β. A line drawn to ε on one side and the characteristic triangle of stars π, η and γ (with ζ in the centre) on the other side, represents the water jug. Fomalhaut, in Piscis Austrinus, is the end of the water flow. Between the jug and Fomalhaut is a multitude of faint stars representing the spatters and droplets of water (Figure 19).

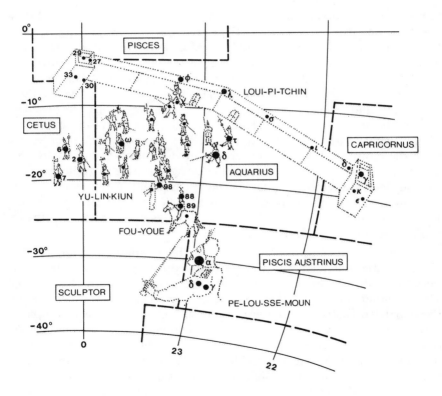

Figure 20. Aquarius. The Chinese asterisms in Aquarius include Yu-lin-kiun, the Army of Yu-lin; Pe-lou-sse-moun, the General of the Northern Districts; Fou-youe, the Axes; and Loui-pi-tchin, the Line of Ramparts. (Staal, British, A.D. 1986.)

Pisces
The Fishes

West of Aries and below Pegasus and Andromeda lies the constellation of Pisces, the Fishes. This is an inconspicuous, scattered constellation and careful observation is needed to find the component stars.

There are two fishes in Pisces, each shaped like an irregular diamond. These fish are widely separated; one lies near the head of the Ram and just below β-Andromedae, the other near and below Markab, α-Pegasi. Both Fishes are tied together by a fishing line, and the knot of this line is in α-Piscium or Al-Rischa, "the Cord."

The Fishes are now the first constellation of the zodiac. The First Point of Aries has now shifted from Aries to the background stars of the Fishes, due to the precession of the equinoxes.

The Romans believed that one day Venus and her son, Cupid, were startled by Typhon, the monster-dragon, who could live in flames and fire but not in water. Venus, however, had been born out of the foam of the sea. She could therefore escape through water. So both Venus and Cupid changed into fishes and disappeared into the dark blue waters of the sea. In order not to lose each other they tied themselves together with a long line. In this way they escaped Typhon. This escape is commemorated in Pisces, which is also popularly known as "Venus and Cupid."

It is said, too, that fishes were seen as powerful, secretive creatures, able to bestow wealth because the hidden treasures of the ocean beds were available to them. They could glide over the sunken ships laden with gold and precious gems, pearls, corals and other wealth. Yet fishes seem completely oblivious as they swim around, over and under these treasures out of reach of the grabbing, greedy hands of mankind.

A German story illustrates the wealth-giving power of fishes and points out a moral for greedy humans. This story describes how Antenteh and his wife lived in very poor circumstances in a cabin by the sea. Their only possessions were a crude cabin and a tub. They had filled the tub with down and feathers from swans and geese so that they might, at least, have a place to sit and rest. One day Antenteh caught a fish, which pulled and tugged so vehemently at the net that he decided to let the fish go back to the sea again. To the amazement of Antenteh, the fish started to speak to him. The fish told Antenteh that he was an enchanted prince and, in return for his release, Antenteh could ask for anything he desired. But Antenteh was a simple soul and felt so honoured at having rescued a person of such nobility that he would not accept anything. However, when his wife heard the story, she became extremely angry with him for letting such an opportunity pass. She nagged Antenteh until he went back to the shore, where he called for the fish, who instantly came swimming towards him. Rather embarrassed, Antenteh told the fish of his wife's wish for a house with furniture in it. The fish told him to leave everything to him and to return to his cabin. Antenteh did so where, instead of his cabin, he found a splendid house. If Antenteh's wife had not been so greedy, all might have ended well, but after a while she wanted more. She wished to be a queen and have a palace. Her wish was granted. Still not satisfied, she demanded to become a goddess. And that was the end of it all. The fish was furious at the insatiable desires of this woman. With one flip of his mighty tail he made everything Antenteh had been given disappear, and in its place there stood again the tub with feathers in the little cabin by the sea. A warning for those who have plenty, not to dare the gods and be too greedy!

The tub is sometimes seen in the great square of Pegasus. Cygnus, the Swan, flies not far from this tub and can be related to the story of Antenteh easily in connection with the down and feathers which he and his wife had gathered. The Fishes represent the enchanted prince.

The Persian astronomer al-Sufi represented the story of Venus and Cupid in Pisces. Venus and Cupid were tied together by a cord so that they would not lose each other in the dark waters of the Euphrates, where they had taken refuge when they were unexpectedly attacked by the fire-breathing Typhon (Figure 21). The German engraver and painter Albrecht Dürer (A.D. 1471–1528) represented Pisces as the Monster Fish (Figure 21). In some mythologies the more northerly of the two fishes is often seen as the monster in the Andromeda story. Usually, however, the monster in the Andromeda story is Cetus.

In the year 7 B.C. there occurred a triple conjunction among the planets Jupiter and Saturn and some stars in the Fishes. This triple conjunction has often been regarded as the star that shone at the birth of Christ. The Greek word for fish is $IX\Theta Y\Sigma$. Taking the first letter of each word in the sentence $I\eta\sigma\sigma\varsigma$ $X\rho\iota\sigma\tau\sigma\varsigma$ $\Theta\epsilon\sigma\upsilon$ $Y\iota\sigma\varsigma$ $\Sigma\omega\tau\eta\rho$ one does obtain the word $IX\Theta Y\Sigma$. The meaning of the sentence is "Jesus Christ son of God, the Redeemer." The fish has always been considered a religious symbol in the Christian faith. The triple conjunction between Jupiter (Star of David) and Saturn (Protector of Israel) against the background stars of Pisces, the Fishes, is therefore a strong contender for the Star of Bethlehem.

The Chinese saw in the stars α-, ξ-, ν-, μ-, ζ-, ϵ-, δ-Piscium a fence, which they called Wai-ping, the Outer Enclosure. It is the fence which prevents the farmer from accidentally falling into the marshes (ϕ^1-, ϕ^2-, ϕ^3-, ϕ^4-Ceti) and prevents the pigs, who wallow in the marshes, from wandering away. The more northerly of the two fishes was absorbed in the Chinese constellation of Koui-siou, the House of the Sandal (Figure 3).

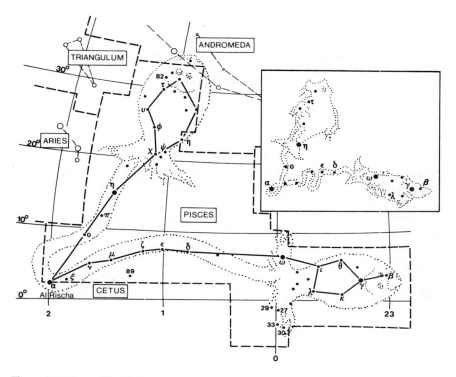

Figure 21. Pisces. The Fishes depicted as Venus and Cupid. (D23; al-Sufi, Persian, 10th Century A.D.) **Inset:** Pisces as monster fishes. (D24; Dürer, German, ca. A.D. 1515.)

47

Triangulum
The Triangle

Gods, humans, other animals and plants are not the only figures that have been commemorated in the constellations. Sometimes, inanimate objects have been placed in the stars to commemorate a certain event or accomplishment. Most probably, therefore, the Triangle symbolises the accomplishments of the Greeks in the science of mathematics. Originally pictured as an equilateral triangle, Triangulum has subsequently come to be viewed as a scalene triangle (Figure 22A).

Another meaning attached to this little triangle is that it represents the island of Sicily. Ceres was the Roman Goddess of Agriculture, and agriculture was very important in Sicily during and after the early Classical period. Many temples honouring Ceres were erected in Sicily, which pleased Ceres a great deal. Mythology tells that Ceres asked Jupiter to honour the island by placing a likeness of it in the stars (Figure 22B).

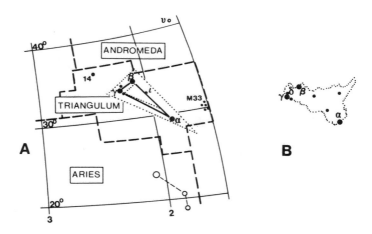

Figure 22. Triangulum. A. The Triangle. (JS81; Staal, British, A.D. 1986.) **B.** The Triangle as Sicily. (JS81a; Staal, British, A.D. 1986.)

The Chinese saw in the stars of Triangulum and a few stars of neighbouring constellations the Great Celestial General, called T'ien-ta-tsiang-kiun. This was the fifth paranatellon of the second house of the White Tiger. The star γ-Trianguli represented the General. The stars 14-Trianguli and υ-Andromedae on either side of him were the General's personal standards. The remaining stars were his officers. The General was responsible for the administration of the vassal states, territories and principalities. When judicial verdicts were pronounced, the General was the one who authorised the punishment or execution.

The stars of Triangulum are not very conspicuous. They can be found between Andromeda and Aries.

Points of Interest in Triangulum

The French astronomer Charles Messier (A.D. 1730–1817) searched the heavens for nebulous patches; he found many, gave each a number, and listed them in his famous catalog. Nebulae recorded by Messier are identified by number, such as Messier 19 or, simply, M19. Not far from α-Trianguli lies the galaxy M33, believed to be at a distance of 2,184,000 light years from Earth.

Lacerta
The Lizard

Professor Richard Hinckley Allen in his book *Star Names* says that the Polish astronomer Johannes Hevelius (A.D. 1611–1687) formed the inconspicuous constellation Lacerta from stars lying between Cygnus and Andromeda. Apparently Hevelius originally created a weasel-like creature with a long curly tail which later was modified into a lizard (Figure 23).

Before the Lizard was created by Hevelius, Augustin Royer invented quite a different constellation in this region of the sky, namely Sceptrum et manus iustitiae, "the Sceptre and Hand of Justice," in commemoration of King Louis XIV of France. The stars of this constellation extended into the neighbouring constellations of Andromeda, Cassiopeia, Cepheus and Cygnus (Figure 24A). This constellation is no longer recognised.

A century after Royer, the German astronomer Johann Ellert Bode (A.D. 1747–1826) changed Royer's asterism to Honores Frederici (sometimes called Gloria Frederica) in honour of his king, Frederick the Great of Prussia, who died in 1786. Bode described the new constellation as follows: "Below a nimbus, the sign of Royal dignity, hang wreathed with imperishable laurel of fame, a sword, pen and olive branch to distinguish this ever to be remembered monarch as hero, sage and peace-maker." Bode's figure of Honores Frederici does not, however, show any of the above attributes. Instead, it depicts a staff and crown. In spite of the wonderful epithet by Bode, Honores Frederici has lapsed into oblivion. The stars of the crown infringe on Cassiopeia and those of the head of the staff or sceptre extend into Andromeda (Figure 23B).

The ancient Chinese saw in Lacerta the coiling T'ang-chie, the Awakening Serpent (Figure 24B). When this asterism culminated at the end of January it announced the end of the Winter. The serpents which had been hibernating through the Winter now began to stir again; when one could see them leave their burrows it was a sure sign that Spring was around the corner. T'ang-chie is the 10th paranatellon of the sixth house of the Black Tortoise.

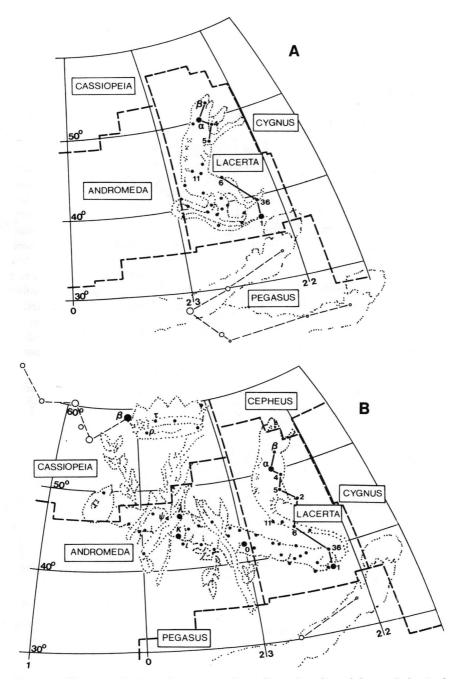

Figure 23. Lacerta. A. The Lizard as conceived initially—a long-legged, long-tailed animal resembling a small mammal more than a lizard. (C12; Hevelius, Polish, ca. A.D. 1690.) **B.** Lacerta and neighbouring constellations as Honores Frederici. (C13; Bode, German, ca. A.D. 1800.)

51

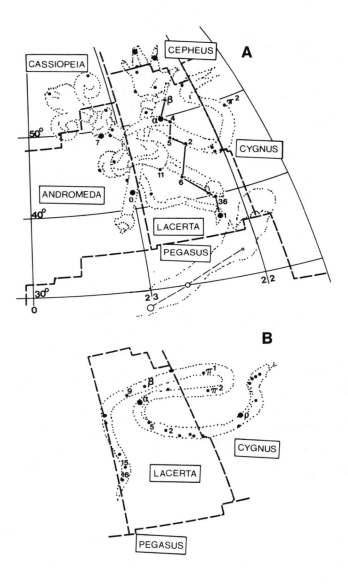

Figure 24. **Lacerta.** **A.** The Sceptre and Hand of Justice, an antecedent of Lacerta. (C14; Royer, French, ca. A.D. 1679.) **B.** T'ang-chie, the Awakening Serpent. (Staal, British, A.D. 1986.)

52

Grus
The Crane

The German astronomer Johann Bayer is credited with creating Grus, the Crane, in 1603. Cranes are long necked birds with great wing spans and long, straight pointed beaks (Figure 25A). As they strut around they give an impression of haughtiness. In flight, they look very sleek and streamlined, neck stretched forward and legs straight out behind them.

Grus has been seen as the Stork of Heaven (Jeremiah VIII, 7). During the Middle Ages, Grus was known sometimes as Phoenicopterus, the Flamingo, and was shown taking a peck at the Southern Fish. People of the Marshall Islands in the western Pacific Ocean saw Grus as a fishing rod, an understandable choice of island people who earned much of their livelihood by various methods of fishing (Figure 25B).

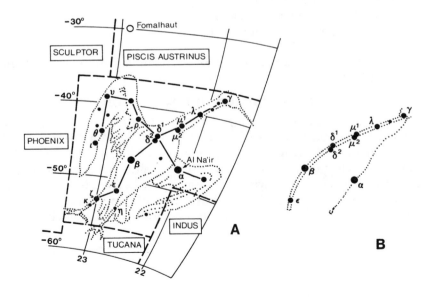

Figure 25. Grus. A. The Crane. (C1; Dopplemaier, ca. A.D. 1742.) **B.** A fishing rod: Marshall Islands (C2).

Piscis Austrinus
The Southern Fish

Piscis Austrinus (or Piscis Australis), the Southern Fish, is sometimes shown with its back towards the north and, at other times, with its back towards the south (Figure 26). The fish's mouth is always taking in the water that pours from the jar of Aquarius. This act is often seen as a symbol of salvation in deluge stories, where a fish saves the world by drinking the waters of the flood. In early legends, the Southern Fish sometimes is seen as the parent of the two Northern Fishes (Pisces).

Under Orion is the story of the Egyptian Osiris, who was killed and cut into pieces by his brother, Set. When Isis, Osiris' sister-wife, tried to reassemble the pieces she could not find the phallus—it had fallen into the river Nile and had been swallowed by the Southern Fish. Thereafter the Southern Fish, known as Oxyrhynchus, became sacred to the Egyptians.

Aratus, in *Phaenomena*, said:

> Below Aegoceros (Capricorn) before the blast of the
> South wind, swims a fish, facing Cetus, alone and apart
> From the former fishes (Pisces)
> And him men call the Southern Fish.

The Arabs knew the Southern Fish as Al Hut al Janubiyy, "the Large Southern Fish."

Points of Interest in Piscis Astrinus

Fomalhaut, α-Piscis Austrini, is the mouth of the fish. The name of this star is derived from Fum al Hut, "the Fish's Mouth." Fomalhaut is a star of magnitude 2 and is some 22 light years distant from Earth. It is sometimes referred to as "the Solitary One," although there is another star (Alphard, in Hydra) with the same epithet. The ancient Persians knew Fomalhaut as one of the four Royal Stars of Heaven; the other three were Aldebaran in Taurus, Antares in Scorpius, and Regulus in Leo.

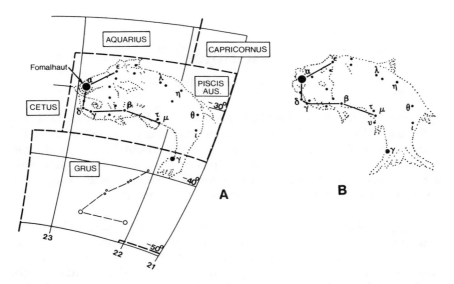

Figure 26. Piscis Austrinus. A. The Southern Fish, with back facing south. (F57; Germanicus, Roman, ca. A.D. 15.) **B.** The Southern Fish, with its back facing north. (F58; al-Sufi, Persian, 10th Century A.D.)

Sculptor
The Sculptor

The French astronomer the Abbé Nicolas Louis de La Caille (A.D. 1713–1762) used the stars between Cetus and Phoenix to create the constellation Sculptor. The Abbé named this constellation L'Atelier du Sculpteur, which in English becomes The Sculptor's Workshop. Today, however, astronomers refer to this constellation as just Sculptor. Sculptor is flanked on the west by Piscis Austrinus and on the east by Fornax (Figure 27).

Sculptor is a rather unspectacular constellation to view, since it contains only four stars of magnitude 4.5; the remaining visible stars being of magnitudes 5 and 6. Sculptor is therefore not very suitable for observation from city confines where the atmosphere is polluted and the night sky blurred by the glow of urban lights. This inconspicuous constellation can be seen best on a moonless night from high up in the mountains, in the desert, or at sea.

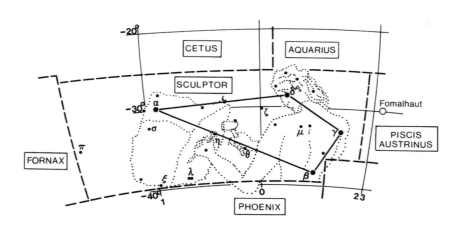

Figure 27. Sculptor. The Sculptor at work on a block of marble. (Staal, British, A.D. 1986.)

Phoenix
The Phoenix

Phoenix was the fabulous bird which could live until it was 500 years old. At the end of its life, it built and settled on a nest of spices, fragrant leaves, and twigs. Then, when the Sun next reached its apex, the heat of its rays set the nest on fire and the Phoenix perished in the flames. From the ashes, however, a little worm crawled forth and, with the heat of the Sun, was transformed into a new Phoenix. This new Phoenix wrapped the remains of the old Phoenix in myrrh, carried these to Heliopolis (City of the Sun), and burned them there as an offering—and a token of its obeisance—to the Sun.

The Phoenix apparently lived alone, without a mate. The Phoenix is a symbol of cyclic patterns and an emblem of solar and fire worship and immortality.

The Dutch globe maker Willem Jansson Blaeu (A.D. 1571–1638) depicted the Phoenix sitting on its fragrant nest at the moment that the nest was ignited by the Sun's rays. In this rendition, the Phoenix extends slightly into some adjacent constellations (Figure 28).

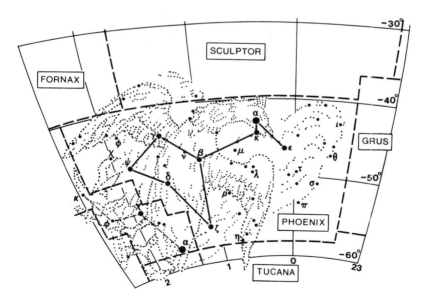

Figure 28. Phoenix. The Phoenix being consumed by the flames of its burning nest. (D21; Blaeu, Dutch, 16th–17th centuries A.D.)

Arabs and other peoples living around the Euphrates River had simple boats that were circular in shape and difficult to steer. The small rudder could be moved side to side to propel the boat, but the river's current was usually the main propellant. The people of Mesopotamia used the stars α-, κ-, μ-, β-, ν-, γ-Phoenicis to form the general outline of a small boat in Phoenix (Figure 29A).

The Chinese of the period after 2700 B.C. also saw a bird in the stars of Phoenix. This was known as Ho-niao, the Firebird (Figure 29B).

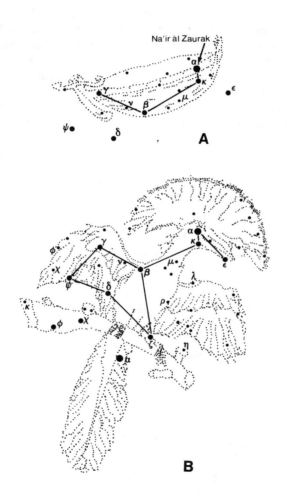

Figure 29. Phoenix. A. The Boat: Middle East (D22). B. Ho-niao, the Firebird. (Staal, British, A.D. 1986.)

The Stars of Winter

Autumn has lapsed into Winter. The Sun stands low in the sky of the Northern Hemisphere and casts its rays obliquely in a feeble attempt to nurse the northern Earth with its warmth. There is not much time in which to do this because in the Winter, after rising, the Sun soon declines again towards the southwest and leaves the Earth to chill as the last rays die out beyond the horizon. Then the night takes over and, as the sky grows darker, thousands of little stars begin to sparkle, inviting us to look up and read their story in the crisp Winter sky as they move majestically from east to west. The clear Winter night has an added lustre as the atmosphere is cold and calm, which makes the stars glitter with even greater beauty.

Master of the Winter skies is the giant Orion, the Hunter. Accompanying Orion on his nightly journey across the heavens are his two dogs, Canis Major and Canis Minor; Taurus, the Bull; Auriga, the Charioteer; Gemini, the Twins; and the dainty cluster of stars known as the Pleiades. The frightened Hare, Lepus, trembles at Orion's feet, while the great river Eridanus thunders by. Directly overhead, the Milky Way gleams as an unfurled silvery sash reminding us of our infinitesimal minuteness within the context of our universe.

The Great Hunting Scene of Orion
Orion, the Hunter

Orion is not difficult to find in the Winter sky (Figures 30, 31). From the middle northern latitudes, look due south in mid-December at midnight, or in mid-January at 10:00 P.M., or in mid-February at 8:00 P.M., and there you will see the three belt stars, lined up like soldiers. The northernmost of the three stars is δ, or Mintaka, "the Giant's Belt." The middle star is ε, or Al Nathin or Alnilam, "String of Pearls." The most southerly of the three stars in the double star ζ, or Alnitak, "the Girdle." The belt of Orion is a wonderful guide to other Winter stars as well. If one draws a line through the belt stars and continues it downwards, the line will lead to the brilliant star Sirius, the eye of one of Orion's dogs. If we draw a line through the belt and continue it upwards, it will take us to the red star Aldebaran, the fiery eye of the Bull.

A good distance above the belt is a reddish glowing star called Betelgeuse, or α-Orionis, the right shoulder of Orion. The left shoulder is in the star γ-Orionis, or Bellatrix. Above the shoulders we can see a faint group of three stars which represent Orion's head. Well below the belt are β-Orionis, or Rigel, a bluish-white star forming Orion's left foot and, on the opposite side, κ-Orionis, or Saiph, Orion's right foot. Between the stars of the belt and the feet are those of Orion's sword. σ, the star nearest the belt, represents the hilt of the sword. Below σ is a hazy string of stars, the lowest of which is ι, or Nair-al-Saif, "the Brightest in the Sword."

In front of Orion, halfway between him and the Bull, is a curve of faint stars depicting either Orion's shield or lion's skin. On a dark night very faint stars can be seen above Orion's right shoulder; these depict his club.

Orion was the son of Neptune and the nymph Euryale and was therefore no ordinary mortal. He was of gigantic size and strength, and of great beauty. Orion was so tall that he could walk through deep water without wetting his head. He had no fear of any animal, and once he even threatened to exterminate all the animals of the Earth. When Gaia, the Goddess of the Earth, heard of this threat she became furious and sent a scorpion to kill Orion. The scorpion bit Orion, and he fell to Earth mortally wounded. In the real sky or on a planisphere, one can see that when the stars of Orion sink below the western horizon, the stars of the Scorpion are just rising in the east. The next night the giant rises again— restored to health and strength by Ophiuchus, the Doctor of Antiquity.

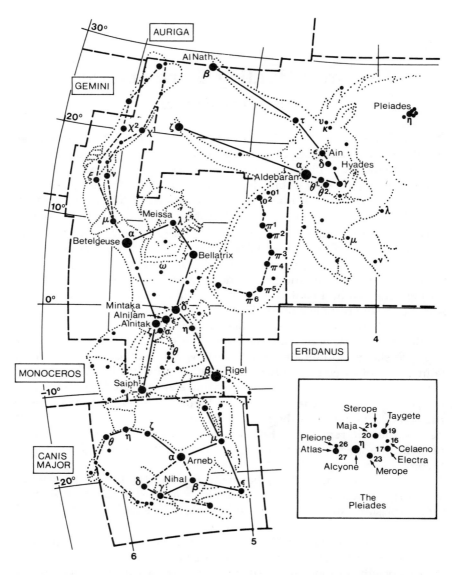

Figure 30. Lepus, Orion and Taurus. The great hunting scene of Orion, with Lepus, the Hare, at Orion's feet. (C42; Bartsch, German, ca. A.D. 1624.) Taurus, the Bull, is above and behind Orion. (A21; Bode, German, ca. A.D. 1800.) **Inset:** The Pleiades.

Ophiuchus gave Orion an antidote for the scorpion's poison which saved the giant's life. This can also be seen in the sky. When the Scorpion sets in the southwest, Ophiuchus stands over him, which means that he tramples him under foot and gives Orion the antidote. Later, when Ophiuchus sets in the west, Orion comes up in the east, fully recovered.

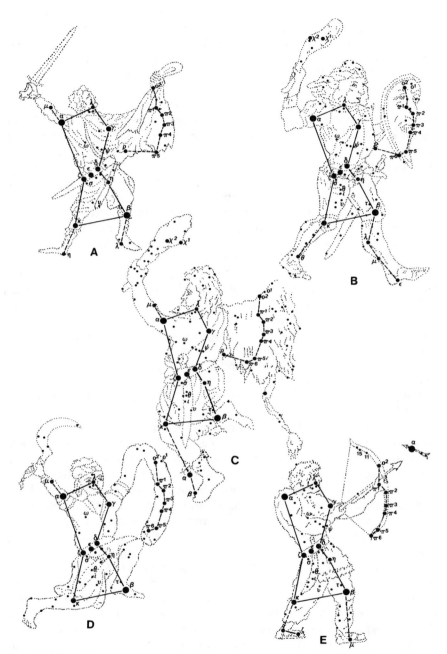

Figure 31. Orion. Orion as a warrior and hunter. **A.** After an illustration by Cicero (106–43 B.C.) (C38). **B.** After an illustration by Hyginus (ca. A.D. 1) (C39). **C.** As a hunter. (C41; Bayer, German, ca. A.D. 1603.) **D.** After an illustration on an Arabian globe. (C45; A.D. 1279.) **E.** As a hunter: Chukchee; Siberia (C49).

Orion was a handsome hunter, and his beauty could not pass unnoticed. Diana, Goddess of the Hunt, fell deeply in love with him and did her utmost to draw him nearer to her. Diana was not, however, the only one competing for Orion's attention. Aurora, the Goddess of the Dawn, also pursued Orion with her love. Orion seems oblivious to the advances of these two goddesses as he moves across the Winter sky. When Orion sets in the west, however, his stars fade very slowly, which means that the Dawn tries to stay by his side as long as possible. When Orion eventually leaves the scene, Aurora weeps bitter tears, which we can see on the flowers, grass, and trees in the morning as glistening drops of dew.

Diana had, of course, seen her rival's actions and, as so often happens, jealousy got hold of her. Rather than let Aurora be at Orion's side, Diana planned to punish him. The next time Orion set in the west, Diana shot him with an arrow and blinded him. Orion's blindness can be imagined if you look at the stars of his head; these stars are very faint, which depict the giant's poor eyesight.

There is, however, another version of this myth which maintains that the arrow fired by Diana was not meant in wrath but was instead an accident. Diana's brother, Apollo, had been displeased for a long time because his sister seemed to neglect her hunting duties. Apollo was alleged to have teased Diana by telling her that she could not even shoot a hare which he thought he saw move in the undergrowth, knowing well that Orion was hunting there. Diana, without thinking, grabbed her bow and arrow and fired a shot, killing Orion. Zeus, at Diana's bidding, placed Orion in the stars so that the illustrious hunter would never be forgotten.

In yet another Greek story, Orion is mentioned as the son of Hyrieus, King of Hyria in Boeotia. One day Zeus, Hermes and Poseidon were traveling on Earth and were entertained royally by Hyrieus. In gratitude for his hospitality, these gods promised to grant Hyrieus whatever he requested. Hyrieus asked for a son. The three gods then took the hide of a cow, urinated on it, and buried it. Nine months later Orion emerged from the ground. From here on, the myth follows the story given first above. The hide has been eternalised in the seven main stars of Orion (Figure 32).

To the ancient Egyptians, Orion was Osiris, God of Light. Set, Osiris' brother and the God of Darkness, tricked Osiris in a sneaky way in an effort to gain the upper hand in their eternal struggle. Set built a beautiful box and invited all his brothers to try out the box for size. He who would fit in it perfectly would be presented with this box. Set, who of course had built the box exactly to Osiris' measurements, slammed the lid shut when Osiris got into the box. Osiris suffocated. Isis, Osiris' wife, found the coffin and discovered what had happened. She went to get help. In her absence Set returned and cut up Osiris into fourteen pieces, which he then scattered in all directions.

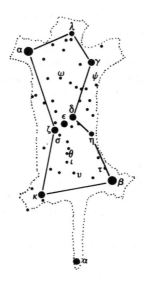

Figure 32. Orion. The cow's hide from which, according to one story, Orion was born nine months after it was urinated on by Zeus, Hermes and Poseidon (C48).

When Isis returned and discovered what had happened, she set about to recover the pieces of her husband's body. Isis managed to find thirteen of the pieces, but the fourteenth—the phallus—she could not find. The phallus had fallen into the river Nile and had been swallowed by a fish. Unless Osiris' body was complete, he would not be able to attain immortality. Isis therefore carved a phallus from a piece of pine wood, the tree sacred to Osiris. She then fixed the phallus onto the body and wrapped the entire corpse in linen. Next Isis breathed into Osiris' nostrils to make his *Ba* (soul) enter the *Sahu* (mummy) so that he would be protected from decay. And so Osiris rose to the sky (Figure 33).

After the Big Dipper, Orion is perhaps the next most celebrated constellation of the Winter sky. Poets have sung its beauty in numerous ways. Aratus wrote in *Phaenomena*:

> Aslant beneath the fore-body of the Bull
> Is set the great Orion. Let none who pass him,
> Spread out on high on a cloudless night, imagine that,
> Gazing on the heavens, one shall see other stars more fair.

Manilius, a Roman, wrote:

> Behold Orion rise! his arms extended
> Stretch over half the skies. His stride
> As large and with a steady pace

He marches on and measures a vast space.
On each shoulder a bright star displayed
And three obliquely grace his hanging blade.
In his vast head, immersed in boundless spheres
Three stars less bright, but yet as great he bears
But farther off removed, their splendour lost
Thus graced and armed he leads the starry host.

In the book *Outer Space* by Gertrude and James Jobes one can read:

Orion, mighty hunter, who warms my dreams,
Drop your trophy, the mangled royal beast;
Unleash your tired hounds;
Release your girdle, set with kingly jewels
That bedazzle at your bend;
Lay away your blood-soiled blade; unlace your buskins;
Loosen your coarse tunic.
Torment me not, transplace your gaze from the Virgin
And let the Butler fill your goblet. Stain my lips
With your wine, pleasure me the pain of your embrace.

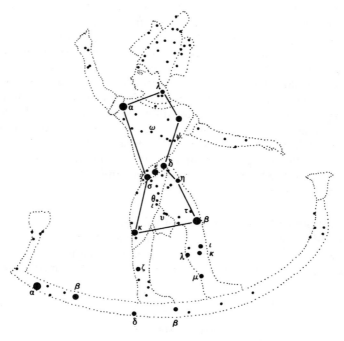

Figure 33. Orion. Osiris, Egyptian God of Light, embarking on his journey up the Nile River to its confluence with the River of Heaven—the Milky Way (C43).

Orion's prominence in the Winter sky has also attracted and inspired the imagination of many non-Western cultures. In most cultures, Orion has been seen as a man with a belt or girdle around his waist, this indicated by the three belt stars (Figure 31). Some people, however, have seen this constellation a little differently. The Taulipang of northern Brazil saw Orion as part of an extensive human figure, but with the belt stars being at the right ankle. This great man is called Zilikawai by the Taulipang. Apparently Zilikawai had a terrible argument with his wife and in a moment of intense fury she hacked off his left leg at the knee. The bloody stump is represented by the red star Betelgeuse (α-Orionis). Bellatrix (γ- Orionis) is in the right hip of this human figure. The shield stars π^1–π^6-Orionis are in the trunk and near the right knee. The body extends over the V stars of Taurus, the Bull, and continues on to the Pleiades, which form its head (Figure 34A).

The Taulipang also talk about the stars of the foot stool, β-Orionis and β-, λ-, ψ-, ω-Eridani. It is an interesting coincidence that these South American Indians would see a foot stool in the same place as did the Arabians. The foot stool of the Taulipang is supposed to be made of an animal's head, although it is not certain what kind of animal.

To the Chimu Indians of Peru, the middle star of Orion's belt, ϵ-Orionis, represents a thief, mischief maker, or criminal whom the Moon Goddess wished to punish. This goddess therefore sent two stars, called Patá (δ-, ζ-Orionis; Patá means "to Hold by the Arms"), to pursue, capture, and restrain the culprit until he could be thrown to the four vultures (α-, β-, γ-, κ-Orionis), who would devour him. These seven stars were placed in the sky as a reminder and warning that anyone who committed a crime would be punished similarly (Figure 35).

The only Chinese asterism that corresponds exactly with the Greek constellation figure of Orion is Tsan (Figure 36). Tsan is in the sixth and seventh houses of the White Tiger. Barbarians—typically nomadic herdsmen who often became hard pressed for food during the winter months—frequently plundered the food reserves of the Chinese farming hamlets. Anticipating these attacks, each Autumn the settled Chinese would come together and choose a commander to organise their defenses against the barbarians. This commander was called Tsan, and he occupied the House of the Supreme Commander—Tsan-siou.

In Hindu tradition, Prajápati had a beautiful daughter named Rohini (the star Aldebaran, in Taurus). Rohini romped around in the guise of an antelope. The father became obsessed with desire for his own daughter so, in order to pursue her without revealing his identity, Prajápati changed himself into a deer called Mriga. Rohini fled across the sky with Mriga in hot pursuit. Lubdhaka, the Hunter, however, saw what was happening and shot an arrow at Prajápati which transfixed him forever to the sky where he now stands helplessly between Rohini and Lubdhaka. Lubdhaka—in honour of this exploit—has since been known as Mrigavyadha, or Deer Slayer (the star Sirius, in Canis Major)(Figure 34B).

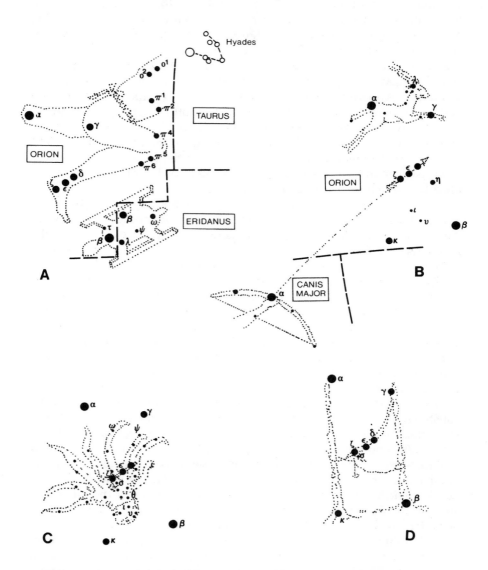

Figure 34. Orion. A. Zilikawai, the Great Man: Taulipang; Brazil (D4). **B.** Lubdhaka, the Deer Slayer, shooting Prajápati: Hindu; India (D1). **C.** The Octopus and the Adze: Marshall Islands (D2). **D.** The Animal Trap: Dayak; Borneo (D3).

People of the Marshall Islands in the Pacific Ocean have placed a fisherman and an octopus in Orion. This fisherman was suddenly attacked by an octopus. The man defended himself with a stone adze,

68

which he drove into the head of the octopus. The octopus immediately opened the sluices of its self defense mechanism and poured out the dark inky fluid behind which it hides or escapes. It is this stage of the action that is commemorated in the stars of Orion. Orion's belt stars form the stone adze. The Octopus has darkened the waters (and the sky), but by looking carefully—perhaps with averted vision—the observer will be able to see a multitude of very faint fifth and sixth magnitude stars outlining the tentacles and suckers of the Octopus (Figure 34C).

The Dayak of Borneo saw Orion as a simple animal trap, the kind they used in hunting (Figure 34D). Two stout trees, represented by α-, κ- and γ-, β-Orionis, were selected for such a trap. A detached branch (ζ-, ε-, δ-Orionis) was then lashed loosely onto a high point of one of the trees (γ-, β-Orionis). A spear point (σ-Orionis) was then strapped to this branch. A piece of thin rope rested in a hook which was itself very loosely poised in a little hole at the lower end of the branch. The whole mechanism was delicately balanced and kept in equipoise by means of a light weight. A small animal blundering into the rope between the two

Figure 35. Orion. Two Patá holding a criminal, who is about to be devoured by four vultures: Chimu; Peru (D5).

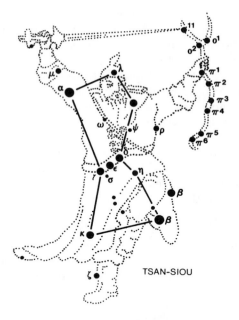

TSAN-SIOU

Figure 36. Orion. Tsan, the Supreme Commander of the defenders of the Chinese farming hamlets. (Staal, British, A.D. 1986.)

trees would knock the hook out of its hole in branch. The branch would then come crashing down and, guided by its lashing to the tree, would drive the spear point into the animal's body. The waiting hunters would then run to the wounded animal and kill it.

The Bororo Indians of central Brazil see a huge cayman in the region of Orion that spreads across several constellations, from Auriga in the north to Lepus in the south (Figure 37). This is a magnificent constellation, worthy of the worship these Indians bestow upon it. The end of the tail of the animal is formed by β-Tauri and nearby stars of Auriga. The middle part of the tail lies in Taurus. The body is formed around the stars of Orion itself, and the head is formed from the stars of Lepus. The cayman is one of the most feared animals of the hot, steamy tropical forests of central Brazil, and is so honoured by its prominent placement in the sky. The Bororo Indians also see Jabuti, the Turtle, in the stars of Orion (Figure 37).

The Maoris of New Zealand see the Canoe of Tamarereti in the stars of Orion (Figure 38). The stern of this canoe is in the belt stars of Orion and the prow is located in the Pleiades. Tamarereti was a mythical ancestor of the Maori people. This personality in his astronomical role indicates when night is about to turn into day. Tamarereti fishes all night, and can be seen doing so in his canoe. As dawn approaches, his canoe

70

draws closer to land (the horizon) until the early morning light reveals that the vessel has touched land. Tamarereti, in violation of established rules, caught a forbidden fish and, during the course of eating this catch, he choked and died. Tamarereti serves as an eternal reminder to the Maori of the need to respect the rules of fishing laid down by the gods. Te Waka o Tamarereti is the Maori name for the Canoe of Tamarereti.

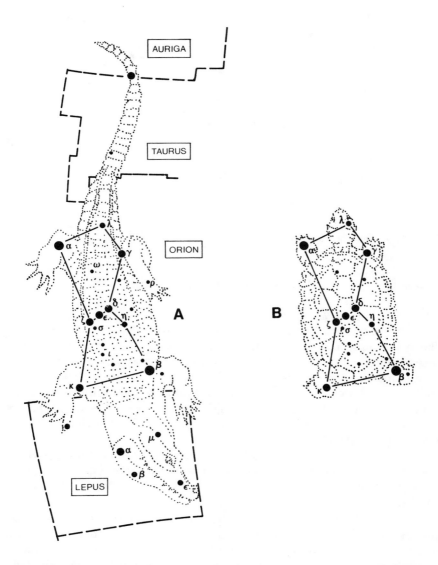

Figure 37. Orion. A. The Cayman: Bororo; Brazil (D8). **B.** Jabuti, the Turtle: Bororo; Brazil (D7).

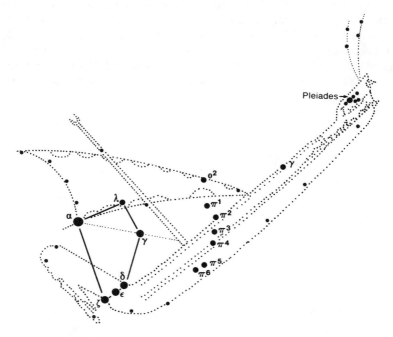

Figure 38. Orion. The Canoe of Tamarereti (D10).

Points of Interest in Orion

Betelgeuse, or α-Orionis, is a reddish coloured star. Its distance from Earth is not accurately known, but is estimated to be about 650 light years. The magnitude of Betelgeuse varies but is approximately 1. This is a giant star whose diameter varies, ranging between 480 and 800 million miles. Betelgeuse is at least 8,000 times more luminous than the Sun, and is the 12th brightest star in the sky. Betelgeuse is spectral type M2, which means that its temperature is in the 3,600° K region—a fairly cool star (see Appendix IV).

Rigel, or β-Orionis, is Orion's left foot. This is a very hot blue-white star of spectral type B8; its surface temperature is in the region of 12,000° K. Rigel, believed to be about 800 light years from Earth, is the seventh brightest star in the sky.

γ-Orionis, or Bellatrix, is Orion's left shoulder. This is a star of approximately magnitude 2. ι-Orionis, in the sword of Orion, is a triple star. θ-Orionis, in the middle of the sword, is a quartet of stars in the shape of a trapesium situated in the famous Orion Nebula. σ-Orionis, "the Hilt of the Sword," is also a multiple star.

72

The Orion Nebula M42 (NGC 1976) lies around the middle star of the sword (θ-Orionis). With the naked eye this nebula looks like a faint misty patch, but when seen through a telescope it is a gem of an object. M42 lies at a distance of about 1,500 light years from Earth and measures some 15 light years in diameter. The cloud of gas fluoresces under the action of very hot stars embedded inside the cloud.

The Orionids meteor shower may be expected every year between 19–22 October. The radiant point of this shower is between Betelgeuse and Castor's toe.

Taurus
The Bull

Taurus, the Bull, lies west of Orion (Figure 30). This constellation represents the head, shoulders and front legs of a bull, and includes two beautiful and storied clusters of stars, the Hyades and the Pleiades.

Two stories from Roman mythology involving cattle are those of the bull and Europa and of the goddess Io, who was changed into a white heifer. Europa was the beautiful daughter of Agenor, King of Sidon. Jupiter fell in love with her and decided to abduct her. One sunny day Europa was playing with her friends on the beach close to her father's herd of bulls. She suddenly noticed a beautiful white bull among the herd and went up to him, stroked him and adorned him with the flowers she had gathered. Because the bull was of such a friendly disposition, she decided to climb on the bull's back to have a ride. As soon as she was seated, however, the bull—none other than Jupiter in disguise—ran off, straight into the sea, with his beautiful burden. Jupiter swam all the way to Crete. In Crete, Europa became the mother of Minos, who was destined to become King of Crete and, in turn, the father of Ariadne.

The other story tells us that Jupiter fell in love with Io, the beautiful daughter of the River God Inachos. It so happened that Io was a priestess in the temple of Juno, Jupiter's wife. When Juno found out about Jupiter's secret love affair with Io, she changed Io into a white heifer to stop the affair and ordered Argus, the giant with 100 eyes, to keep Io a prisoner. Jupiter decided that the least he could do to liberate poor Io was to attempt to kill Argus. This would be a dangerous exploit, however, because Argus never slept; he always had some of his eyes open. Nonetheless, Jupiter sent Mercury, the fast wing-footed god, to carry out the task. Mercury managed to decapitate Argus with the same sword which Perseus later used to kill Medusa. So, freed from her guard, Io fled to Egypt where Jupiter returned her to her human form. In Egypt, Io became the mother of Epaphus, who was destined to rule over the Nile Valley. As a monument to the slain Argus, Juno placed all of its eyes in Heaven. These eyes can now be seen as the eyes in the tail of the Peacock, a constellation visible in the Southern Hemisphere. The Peacock, from that time onwards, was Juno's personal bird.

The bull was also the animal devoted to Bacchus, the Wine God. The bull was decorated with flowers during wine orgies and other festivities. Ritual dances were provided by dancing girls, which are depicted by the Hyades, the group of stars in the Bull's face, and the Pleiades, the group in the Bull's neck.

The Pleiades

The Pleiades are sometimes seen as a bunch of grapes. When the Pleiades set in the west, Orion seems to be leaning forward dangerously in an attempt to pick them. Or is it that he has perhaps already had a little too much to drink?

When the Pleiades are seen as the Seven Little Sisters, they represent the seven daughters of Atlas and Pleione. Alcyone (η) is the most beautiful daughter and the brightest star in the group. The other sisters are Celaeno (16), Maja (20), Merope (23), Taygete (19), Sterope (21) and Electra (17) (Figure 30, inset). When Orion once attempted to burst into the private sanctuary of their home, Venus changed the seven frightened sisters into a flock of doves, so that they could flutter away to safety. Since that day the dove has been Venus' personal bird.

Aratus says in *Phaenomena*:

> These seven are called by name
> Alcyone, Merope, Celaeno, Electra, Sterope,
> Taygete and queenly Maia.
> Small and dim are they all alike
> But widely famed they wheel in heaven
> At morn and eventide, by the will of Zeus,
> Who bade them tell of the beginning of
> Summer and winter and of the beginning of
> Planting time.

In the 8th Century B.C. Hesiodus wrote that the Pleiades were stars to be observed as signs for reaping the harvest at the end of Summer, or sowing at the beginning of Spring.

> When, Atlas born, the Pleiades rise
> Before the sun in the dawning skies
> 'Tis time to reap; and when they set in the west
> When the sun rises in the east, 'tis time to sow.

The "lost" Pleiad refers sometimes to Electra and sometimes to Merope, because they are variable stars, but in mythology the stars become so dim because they cry and their tears blur the brilliance of their eyes. Remember that the Pleiades were placed in the sky by Zeus, who heard their cry for help when Orion tried to molest them. All of the Pleiades except one, either Electra or Merope, married gods. Sometimes this fact saddens the sisters and they start to cry.

Amongst the American Indians was the story that the Pleiades were seven children who longed to wander amidst the stars. They lost their way, however, and could not find their way home. Ever since, they huddled closely together to make sure they would not become separated.

One of the Pleiades is sometimes difficult to see; this is the youngest sister who sometimes becomes homesick and longs to go back to Earth. She cries so much that all the sparkle of her eyes is temporarily drowned in a flood of tears.

Modern photographs of the Pleiades reveal that the seven stars are immersed in a cloud of misty streamers. Tennyson described this so well in *Locksley Hall:*

> Many a night I saw the Pleiades, rising through
> the mellow shade,
> Glitter like a swarm of fire-flies tangled in a silver
> braid.

The Hyades

The half sisters of the Pleiades are the Hyades—the V of the Bull's face and the seven daughters of Atlas and Aethra. Together the Pleiades and the Hyades are known as the Atlantides. The names of the seven sisters were given by Pherecydes as Aesula, Ambrosia, Dione, Thyene, Koronis, Eudora and Polyxo. None of the stars in the Hyades, however, has been assigned a specific name from this list—the individual stars are not specifically named. Ovid called the Hyades Sidus Hyantis, "the Rain-Bringing Stars"—because the sisters were so grief-sticken after their terrestrial brother, Hyas, had drowned in a well that their tears caused heavy rainfall. The Hyades were trouble making stars for farmers and sailors alike, causing storms to rage on land and sea.

Points of Interest in Taurus

Aldebaran, α-Tauri, is the red eye of the Bull. Its distance from Earth is about 60 light years. The reddish colour suggests that it is a cool star; its spectral class is K5, with surface temperature at about 3,400° K. Aldebaran is the 14th brightest star in the sky.

The Hyades are an open cluster, the brightest stars of which form the characteristic V of the Bull's head. By sheer coincidence, Aldebaran represents the end of the left side of the V but does not actually belong to the Hyades group at all. The Hyades are about twice as far from Earth as Aldebaran. The cluster of the Hyades is moving in the direction of a point some 5° east of Betelgeuse, where it should arrive some 600,000 years from now.

The Pleiades are another cluster of stars moving through space like a flock of birds with a velocity of some 30 miles per second. In a million years the familiar little group will have moved so far away from Earth as to be only a faint, distant telescopic object.

Crab Nebula lies about 1° west of ζ-Tauri, the right horntip of the Bull. One cannot see this nebula with the naked eye, but with a telescope of about 6 inches aperture or more a misty patch can be seen. Messier numbered this nebula M1 in his famous catalog. Nowadays it is believed that this misty patch is the remains of a supernova which the Chinese recorded as having appeared in the year A.D. 1054. This does not mean that the explosion of this star occurred in A.D. 1054. It is generally believed that this nebula is at least 4,000 light years distant from Earth. So when the Chinese saw it suddenly appear, the explosion was already 4,000 years old. But even now, over 900 years after the date of the first appearance, this nebula is still visible and it is still expanding at the rate of some 70 million miles a day. When a supernova explodes, the original star blows itself to near destruction, throwing off shells of gas. It is these expanding gasses which we can still see. Supernovae also are sources of strong radio signals.

Taurus is one of the 12 zodiacal constellations. This means that the Sun passes through Taurus on its apparent journey through the ecliptic. In about 2450 B.C. Taurus was at the Vernal Equinox. Vergil (Roman; 70–19 B.C.) referred to this fact when he wrote:

The glistening Bull opens the year with golden horns
And the Dog sinks low, his star (Sirius) averted.

Today, due to precession, Taurus no longer opens the year. The Vernal Equinox is now in Pisces, the Fishes.

Auriga
The Charioteer

Auriga, the Charioteer, lies above the horns of the Bull. One of the stars of Taurus—Al Nath, the tip of the left horn of the Bull—is shared with Auriga.

Ancient charioteers or wagoners looked after the chariots and horses of their rulers or masters. Charioteers also watched over the livestock which was kept in the royal stalls to provide food for the dinner table. At regular intervals this livestock was replenished from the king's breeding farms in the country. The most common representation of Auriga shows him holding a kid in one arm and a bridle and whip in the other (Figure 39). Indeed Capella, the fifth brightest star in the sky, is a Goat; the Kids are depicted by the faint stars just below it.

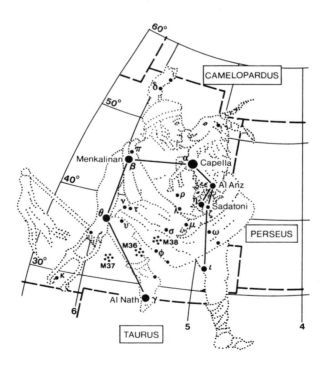

Figure 39. Auriga. The Charioteer as herdsman, holding a goat and two kids in his left arm and bridle bit and whip in his right hand. (A21; Bode, German, ca. A.D. 1800.)

78

There is one famous goat in ancient history, Amaltheia, the goat who, the legend says, fed Jupiter with her milk on the island of Crete, where his mother had taken him to safeguard him from his all-devouring father. Aratus says of Auriga and the goats (Figure 39) in *Phaenomena:*

> But if it be thy wish to mark the Charioteer
> And his stars, and if the fame has come to thee
> Of the Goat herself and the Kids, who often
> On the darkening deep have seen men storm-tossed,
> Thou wilt find him in all his might, leaning forward
> At the left hand of the Twins. Over and against him
> Wheels the top of Helice's head, but on his left shoulder
> Is set the holy Goat, that, as legend tells, gave the breast
> To Zeus. Her the interpreters of Zeus call Olenian Goat.
> Large she is and bright, but there at the wrist of the
> Charioteer faintly gleam the Kids.

One story that involves a charioteer and chariot is that of Myrtilos, the charioteer of the king of Elis. The king had a beautiful daughter, Hippodameia. Many men of the land sought the hand of Hippodameia, but the king did not want her to marry because an oracle had predicted that his son-in-law would cause his death. In order to make his refusal to give his daughter in marriage seem reasonable, the king did not refuse his daughter's suitors outright. Instead he required them to compete against him in a chariot race. The king owned beautiful horses and Myrtilos, his charioteer, kept them in first class condition. It was as good as certain that the king would always win these races. The loser of each was to be put to death.

One day, however, Pelops, a hero who claimed to be of divine parentage, visited the court. Hippodameia fell in love with him and she schemed, as only a woman in love can scheme, to save her lover from certain death. She knew that Myrtilos secretly loved her, but being only a charioteer, he had never dared to say so.

Needing Myrtilos' support, Hippodameia cleverly pretended that she might return Myrtilos's love. She made Myrtilos promise that he would remove the wheel-pegs from her father's chariot just before the race was to start. This he did. And so it happened that the king, when his chariot collapsed during the contest, was instantly killed. Hippodameia was now free to marry the man of her choice. Poor Myrtilos had served his purpose and, of course, Hippodameia could no longer make use of his love. When Myrtilos persisted in his efforts to love Hippodameia, Pelops pushed him from a rock into the sea. Pelops then became the master of Olympia and ruler of Arcadia, and he spread his power so widely over the peninsula that, after him, came to be called the Peloponnesus, which means the island of Pelops.

Another story that includes a chariot is that of Erichthonius. Erichthonius' father, Hephaestus, was lame. Hera, Hephaestus' mother, had thrown him off of Olympus because he was such a weakling child. On another occasion Hephaestus was thrown off Olympus by his father, Zeus, for siding with Hera in an argument. This second fall had caused Hephaestus' lameness. Erichthonius had inherited his father's lameness and, in order to get about his business with greater ease, he invented the chariot. Zeus, now appeased, placed the chariot in the stars of Auriga (Figure 40).

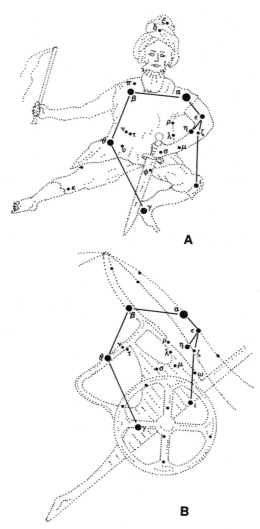

Figure 40. Auriga. A. The Charioteer. (A22; al-Sufi, Persian, 10th Century A.D.) **B.** The Chariot (A23).

Points of Interest in Auriga

Capella, α-Aurigae, is a bright yellow double star of spectral type G6, with a surface temperature of about 6,000° K. Capella, the fifth brightest star in the sky, is about 41 light years from Earth. β-Aurigae is a whitish-blue star with a surface temperature of about 14,000° K.

ε-Aurigae, at first sight a faint little star in the curious formation called the Kids, in the arms of the Charioteer, is in fact an eclipsing binary with a period of about 27 years. The star being eclipsed is a supergiant and would appear to be the largest known star with a diameter about 2,700 times that of the Sun. If the Sun were put in the centre of this star and the planets Mercury, Venus, Earth, Mars, Jupiter and Saturn positioned at their correct distances from the Sun, they would all be swallowed up in the gaseous envelope of the star with plenty of room to spare. This star is about 2,800 light years from Earth.

Slightly below the right knee of the Charioteer an open star cluster, known as M37 (NGC 2099), can be seen with a small telescope. It will revolve in small points of light.

The Aurigids meteor shower may be seen from mid-August to the beginning of October. The radiant point of this shower is a few degrees south of Capella.

Gemini
The Twins

The constellation of Gemini, the Twins, lies high above Orion. Gemini includes two bright stars, Castor and Pollux, the heads of the Twins. The outline of this constellation is nearly a perfect rectangle, each long side of the rectangle representing one of the Twins. The Twins were warlike heroes who were especially honoured by seafaring people (Figure 41). They were considered to be the protectors of sailors and were supposed to rid the high seas of buccaneers and pirates. Castor and Pollux were the protectors of the ship Argo during its journey to Colchis to recover the golden fleece. It was said that, when they got on board, two flames leapt up from the mast. (Sailors still see this as St. Elmo's fire.) In the sky, Castor and Pollux are always seen in a line directly above the constellations that form Argo Navis, the ship Argo.

According to the myth, Pollux was immortal but Castor was not. Castor was killed in a contest which arose in a quarrel over some cattle.

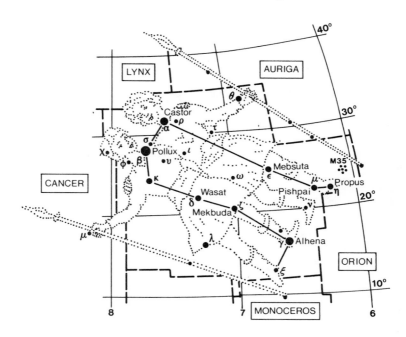

Figure 41. Gemini. Gemini, the Twins, each carrying a spear. (B47; Baeda, English, 7th–8th centuries A.D.)

Pollux beseeched Jupiter to let him die too; as the Twins were inseparable, the one could not live without the other. But an immortal cannot die so Jupiter allowed Pollux to spend one day among the gods and the other in Hades, the Underworld, with his beloved brother. This movement is reflected clearly in the daily rise and fall of Castor and Pollux. When Castor sets in the west, Pollux follows him immediately afterwards and, vice versa, when Castor rises in the east Pollux is immediately by his side.

The Chinese created no less than five asterisms within the boundaries of Gemini (Figure 42). These asterisms reveal a preoccupation among the Chinese with the use and control of water. Tsing-siou is the first house of the Red Bird of Summer, the House of the Well. Wells had to be cleaned after the long Winter, sites for new wells had to be selected, and new wells had to be dug. The location at which a new well would be dug was determined by placing buckets of water at various likely sites. When the surface of the water in the buckets had become perfectly still, the people would look in the water for reflections of the stars. Sites with buckets of water in which star reflections were seen were chosen as possible well sites.

Youe, the Axe, was a reminder that those people who squandered water indiscriminately would be severely punished and perhaps even beheaded. This illustrates how precious water was to the ancient Chinese. T'ien-tsoun is the Celestial Amphora, a reminder that the cooking pots and storage vessels should be scoured and made ready for the Great Summer Festival. Wou-tchou-hao are the five (actually seven) notables who were always at hand to assist the emperor. They consisted of a registrar, a wise man, four counselors, and a personal friend of the emperor.

Pe-ho and Nan-ho were the North and South rivers which, in times past, rose in the evening of the month of May. When these two asterisms were seen clearly, people knew that the Summer heat had made its entry. Since the ecliptic passes between these two constellations, the Chinese thought that they were the doorway of the skies, the doorway through which the Summer heat came in. Pe-ho presided over water, Nan-ho over fire, and the heat of Summer was hot and humid which, of course, was very favourable for the growing of crops. When both asterisms shone brightly people were happy. But when Mars happened to enter through this doorway as well, Chinese astrologers foretold that wars would break out and that the crops would not grow at all.

The constellations adjoining Gemini all have some connection with water: Tsi-choui is the Accumulated or Swollen Waters; Choui-wei is the Situation of the Water; Sse-tou is Four Channels, or Trenches; and Choui-fou is a Water Reservoir.

Points of Interest in Gemini

Castor, or α-Geminorum, consists of six stars which revolve around each other. Castor, at a distance of 49 light years from the Earth, is spectral type A1 with a surface temperature of about 11,000° K. Castor is the 22nd brightest star in the sky. Pollux, β-Geminorum, is a yellow star of spectral type KO with a surface temperature of about 5,000° K. Pollux is 40 light years from Earth.

The star cluster M35 (NGC 2168) can be seen with the naked eye if atmospheric conditions are perfect. Look near the left toe of Castor to find this patch. With a telescope you will see it resolve in wonderful streamers of stars with a reddish coloured star in the centre of the cluster.

The Geminids shower of meteors may be expected to appear every year between 4–16 December. The radiant point of this shower is above Castor and Pollux.

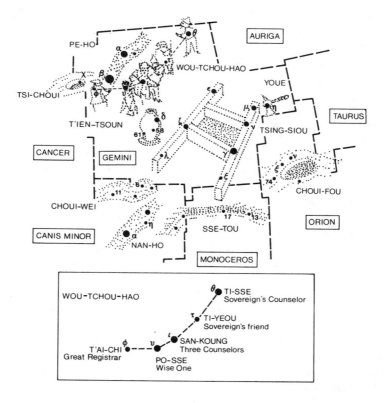

Figure 42. Gemini. Water is a unifying theme among the Chinese asterisms in and near Gemini, which include Tsing-siou, the House of the Well; T'ien-tsoun, the Celestial Amphora; Pe-ho and Nan-ho, the Northern and Southern rivers; Tsi-choui, the Swollen Waters; Choui-wei, the Situation of the Water; Sse-tou, the Four Trenches; and Choui-fou, the Water Reservoir. Also present are Youe, the Axe, and Wou-tchou-hao, the Five Notables. (Staal, British, A.D. 1986.)

Canis Major and Canis Minor
The Greater Dog and the Lesser Dog

Orion had two dogs, Canis Major and Canis Minor, the Greater Dog and the Lesser Dog. The Greater Dog, with the bright star Sirius, is located below Orion's feet whereas the Lesser Dog, with its bright star Procyon, stands behind Orion's shoulder (Figure 43). To find Procyon, draw a line through the two shoulder stars of Orion, Bellatrix and Betelgeuse; this line, continued to the east will lead you to Procyon.

The three stars Sirius, Procyon, and Betelgeuse should be remembered as the corners of a huge triangle called the Winter Triangle. This triangle can be seen in the middle latitudes of the Northern Hemisphere through the Winter until late February. Sirius is the first corner of this triangle to disappear in the west. When Betelgeuse begins to fade away in the west, Winter is over and Spring is returning. Procyon, however, can be seen until mid-April. And is not the influence of the Winter Triangle still noticeable even though Spring has started officially? How often do the middle northern latitudes still have nights of sudden frosts, cold winds, and even a last fall of snow or sleet in April or May?

Both dogs are Orion's faithful companions who help him track and fetch the game he is hunting. The Greater Dog is always seen as a dog sitting at the ready, alert to spring into action when called upon. He has his eye, Sirius, fixed on Orion and Lepus, the Hare, who sits crouching at the Hunter's feet.

The Lesser Dog has one bright star, Procyon, which means "The Dog Who Rises before Sirius." One can see this easily on a Winter night or on a planisphere. Procyon rises first; an hour later, Sirius comes up.

In the Northern Hemisphere, Sirius rises simultaneously with the Sun in September, when the Sun passes through Leo, the Lion. It is said that the heat of the Sun and that of Sirius (from Seirios, "the Scorcher") mix and give us very hot weather, hence the term "dog days."

In Egypt, Sirius was observed for its heliacal rising, which means its rising in the early morning a short time before the Sun appears. The rise of Sirius was associated with the overflowing of the Nile, an annual event of great importance to the Egyptians because it meant that the land would be made fertile again by the rich sediments deposited by the flood waters. In Egypt Sirius was depicted as a god with a dog's head, and was called Anubis.

Above Procyon are the stars of Castor and Pollux, the Twins—nearly a perfect rectangle. Sometimes this rectangle is seen as a table at which

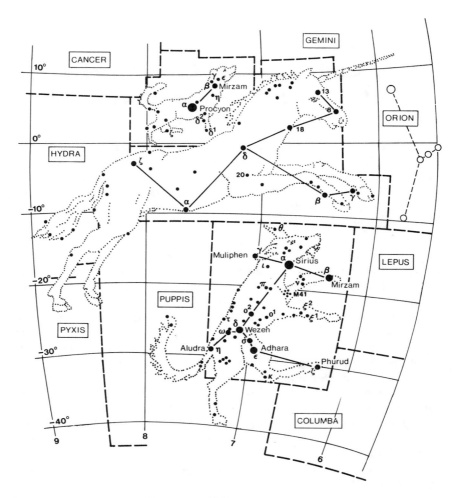

Figure 43. Canis Major, Canis Minor and Monoceros. The Greater Dog, sometimes called the Spotted Dog because of the large number of stars strewn across its body, is a strong and serious hunting animal. (A39; al-Sufi, Persian, 10th Century A.D.) The Lesser Dog is a more gentle and playful animal. Between the dogs is the mysterious unicorn, Monoceros (C31; Hevelius, Polish, ca. A.D. 1690.)

Castor and Pollux are eating; the two dogs are waiting patiently for the table crumbs. These crumbs can be seen as very faint stars of magnitudes 5 or 6, scattered between Gemini and Procyon.

The Chinese had several constellations in the region of Canis Major (Figure 44). These included Hou-chi, the Bow and Arrow; T'ien-kaou, the Celestial Dog, the 19th paranatellon of the first house of the Red Bird of Summer; and T'ien-lang, the Celestial Jackal, the 18th paranatellon of the first house of the Red Bird of Summer.

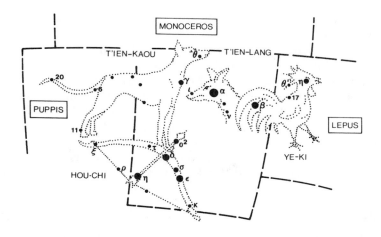

Figure 44. Canis Major. Chinese asterisms in and near Canis Major include Hou-chi, the Bow and Arrow; Ye-ki, the Wild Cockerel; T'ien-lang, the Celestial Jackal; and T'ien-kaou, the Celestial Dog. (Staal, British, A.D. 1986.)

T'ien-lang, the Celestial Jackal, was marked by a single star—Sirius. In the month of May the crops were standing high, level with the surrounding dikes. T'ien-lang, the Jackal or "Wolf of the East," loved to hide in the tall crops where he hunted unsuspecting birds, especially quails and pheasants. At night he went out prowling around the farmyards and worker's cottages to steal chickens. In May mother Jackal had her young which had to be fed, so father Jackal had to go out to find food for them. To safeguard the workers against the pilfering and devastation of their fields, the ancient kings of China used to organise hunting parties to get rid of these pests. To follow the spoor was an easy matter as the jackals had already flattened the crops, leaving trails which would lead the hunters to the lair. Once the lair had been located, the drivers would let loose the dogs, T'ien-kaou. The dogs would chase the jackals towards the hunting party, which was waiting for the pests with their bows and arrows, Hou-chi.

Another famous animal was Ye-ki, the Wild Cockerel, with a military record. Ye-ki is the seventh paranatellon of the first house of the Red Bird of Summer. It is represented by one star, 17-Leporis. Surrounding this star are the stars of Kiun-chi, the Military Market. Since Ye-ki was such a famous cockerel in Chinese military annals, he was placed inside the military market. (Some of the stars of the military market have been incorporated in Figure 44.) Ye-ki led a whole flock of chickens, tied together by ropes from which were suspended burning torches. A certain army commander, who was out-numbered, thought up this ruse. In the middle of the night he released this flying incendiary squad upon his unsuspecting adversary and thereby totally destroyed the opponent's camp with fire.

Yet another legend is that of Shen-i and his search for the Bird with the Golden Plumage. This bird would give Shen-i the exact times of rising, culmination, and setting of the Sun. This bird lived in a golden cage suspended in the Fu-sang tree, a tree several thousands of feet high and of tremendous circumference, that was located in the middle of the Eastern Sea. The bird lays eggs; the young chicks that hatch from these eggs have red combs on their heads. Every morning, all over the world these young answer the Golden Bird when he starts crowing. This Golden Bird is known as the "Cock of Heaven" and all the cockerels on Earth are his descendants. Shen-i had been given a charm which could open the cage.

Lastly, there is the story from the Song Dynasty (A.D. 960- 1279) of the Shooting of the Heavenly Dog. In this story, the Bow and Arrow represents Chang-hsien, the Patron of Child-Bearing Women. Chang-hsien is depicted as a white faced god with a long beard and a little boy by his side. He is worshipped by women. If the fate of a family was under the influence of the Heavenly Dog, the women would be either barren or, if they did produce sons, the sons would have short lives. So the women would send up prayers to Chang-hsien. If their prayers were answered, it meant that Chang-hsien had shot the Heavenly Dog with his bow and arrow and the spell over the unfortunate women had been lifted.

Points of Interest in Canis Major

Sirius, or α-Canis Majoris, is the most brilliant star of the sky. It is a double star with a period of about 50 years. For a long time the existence of a companion to Sirius was known, although it was not seen until 1862 when Alvin Clark, an American telescope builder, discovered it while testing an 18 inch telescope. Friedrich Bessel, in 1834, had pointed out that there should be a companion to Sirius on account of the irregular movement of Sirius in the sky. Sirius is of spectral type AO, which places the star in the surface temperature region of about 10,000° K. Sirius is about twice the mass and twice the diameter of the Sun, but is some 40 times more luminous that the Sun. Sirius lies at a distance of nine light years from Earth. If the Sun were located nine light years from Earth, it would appear only as a very faint star, hardly visible to the naked eye.

Sirius' companion star, called the Pup, is a very curious heavenly object famous for its great density, calculated to be some 40,000 times that of water. One gallon of water weighs ten pounds. One gallon of the material the Pup is made of would weigh about 200 tons. The distance between Sirius and the Pup is 20 times the distance between Earth and the Sun—20 × 93 million miles, or 1,860 million miles.

In the chest of the Greater Dog, about 4° below Sirius, is the open star cluster M41. M41 is hardly visible with the naked eye but is a fine subject for the telescope as it resolves in garlands of fine points of light with a slightly reddish star in its centre.

Points of Interest in Canis Minor

Procyon, α-Canis Minoris, is the only bright star in the constellation. It is the eighth brightest star in the sky. Procyon is of spectral class F5, which places its surface temperature at about 7,000° K. This is a double star with a period of approximately 40.65 years, and it is 11 light years distant from the Earth. The companion star is a white dwarf which, with a density of about two tons per cubic inch, is even more dense that the more famous companion of Sirius identified above.

Monoceros
The Unicorn

Behind Orion and between the stars of the Greater Dog and Lesser Dog lie the stars of Monoceros, the Unicorn, the fabulous mythical animal with the tail of a lion, the legs of a deer, and the head of a horse. One straight horn, growing from the forehead, was prized for its supposed mystical properties (Figure 43). The stars of this constellation are faint and difficult to distinguish, which is in keeping with the elusive nature of the animal they represent. In the animal world, it is said, the beasts of the forest like to drink from pools which have been frequented by the unicorn. Hunters would trade a lifetime of hunting just to catch a glimpse of a unicorn or, better still, to catch one and cut off its horn. The horn had magical powers and, if ground up and used in medicines, it would protect the user from evil. Needless to say there was a great deal of swindling in the courts of kings who pretended that they possessed such a horn.

The unicorn was believed to live in the most remote and loneliest place of the world. Some people say that place was Tibet, high in the Himalaya Mountains where the clouds covered the peaks. People in the Himalaya region said that the new crescent Moon was symbolic of the horn of the unicorn. The legend said that the Sun and the Moon symbolised the coming and going of the unicorn. In the morning, the Sun, or Lion, won the supremacy of the skies but in the evening he surrendered the sky to the Moon, or Unicorn.

In the Orion scene, the Unicorn is seen coming storming on behind the Hunter—yet Orion has never heard its approach. This symbolises the silent magical movements of the animal. The fact that its stars are embedded in the Milky Way sometimes make it the driving force of creation, as this misty band is, after all, the great disc of stars and gas where new stars are born.

Lepus
The Hare

Lepus lies directly below Orion's feet. The Hare is the symbol of speed and cunning. He may not have the power to fight his enemies, but he has been given other faculties with which to evade his foes. The Hare may be seen in a sleeping position, but he is not really asleep. He has already heard the crackle of the Hunter's footstep, and now he sits absolutely motionless . . . waiting (Figure 30). If the Hare's tactics work, the Hunter may pass him by. Should he be discovered by the Hunter, however, then he will have to resort to the elements of surprise. The Hare has very powerful hind legs and, if forced to flee, will suddenly bolt, momentarily startling the Hunter, and shoot off like a dart in the opposite direction.

Another myth says that the hare was at one time a bird who was changed into a hare by Ostara, the Goddess of Spring. Ostara allowed the hare to keep its power to run as fast as it could once fly. Once a year the hare is allowed to lay eggs, hence we have today Easter hares carrying eggs on their backs. (Easter is derived from Ostara—in German, Ostern).

Points of Interest in Lepus

γ-Leporis is a double star, the primary being yellow and its companion being greenish. This star can be found close to the rear legs of the Hare.

Eridanus
The River Eridanus

Eridanus starts near Rigel, in Orion's foot, and from there coils its way southward in great bends until it terminates close to the South Celestial Pole. The south end of Eridanus is marked by the star Achernar, which means "the End of the River." In Classical times, θ-Eridani was the most southerly bright star that could be seen from the latitude of Greece. This star, Acamar, marked the south end of Eridanus until travelers reaching more southerly locations described the river as extending to Achernar (Figure 45).

In the story of Helios and Phaethon we can read how Phaethon was catapulted out of the Sun Chariot and fell headlong into the river Eridanus, where he drowned. Phaethon's sisters cried bitterly and their tears fell into the Eridanus, where they were changed into amber. (In Italy, Eridanus is associated with the Po River, along which amber was traded in ancient times.) Ovid presents this story in Book II of *Metamorphoses:*

> But Phaethon, fire pouring through fiery hair,
> Sailed earthwards through clear skies as though he were
> A star that does not fall, yet seems to fall
> Through long horizons of the quiet air.
> Far from his home he fell, across the globe
> Where river Eridanus cooled his face.

Phaethon's sisters found the place where he had drowned. While they were weeping and lamenting his loss, they were slowly changed into trees. Ovid continues:

> As the bark begins to grow around their bodies, only their lips
> Were free to call their mother. And what could this mad woman
> Do but reach, to press each fading pair of lips against her own?
> Or more, if not enough, tear at the bark,
> Break twigs where drops of blood streamed from each wound.
> And each as she was torn cried, "Mother, save me, Mother it is
>   my body
> That you tear within the tree, O Mother, now farewell."
> As bark closed over lips their tears still ran,
> Tears that were drops of amber in the sun
> Fallen from green sides and branches of young trees,

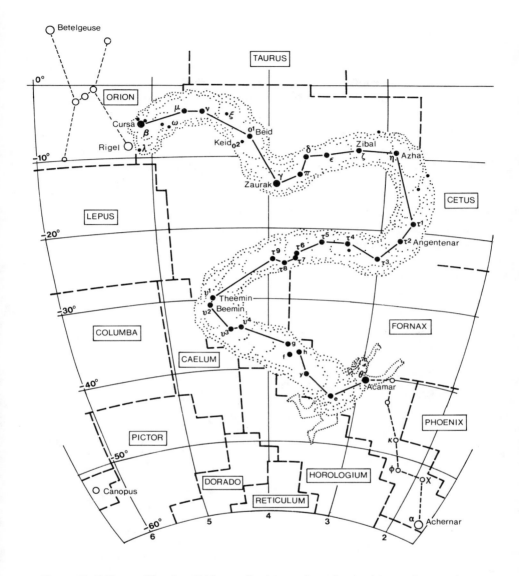

Figure 45. Eridanus. The river Eridanus, flowing southward toward its southern end at the star Achernar. (B40; Grienberger, German, ca. A.D. 1600.)

To flow in the clearest waters of the river
And later worn as jewels by Roman brides.

Under Hercules, below, is the story of how this hero summoned Eridanus and Aquarius to help him clean the stables of King Augeas.

Among the Egyptians, Eridanus represented their famous river, the Nile. The Egyptians always revered the Nile as a holy river because they depended upon its annual flooding to bring the fertile silt that was so necessary for the success of their agriculture. Other nations saw Eridanus as a representation of their own major rivers. The early Teutons, for example, saw it as the Rhine. The Franks thought it to be the Rhône, and the early Spaniards the Ebro. The Chinese saw Eridanus as the Huang He, or Yellow River.

In the literature about Eridanus there is much mention of stars which have connections with ostriches. Just as the Arabs and other nomads saw adult and juvenile camels in Draco, these same people saw in the stars of Eridanus two ostriches with two chicks in their nest, along with unhatched eggs and broken eggshells. In Figure 46, one ostrich is slaking its thirst in the river Eridanus. Theemin (v^1) and Beemin (v^2), stars in the head of one of these ostriches, are called "In the Water." Other prominent

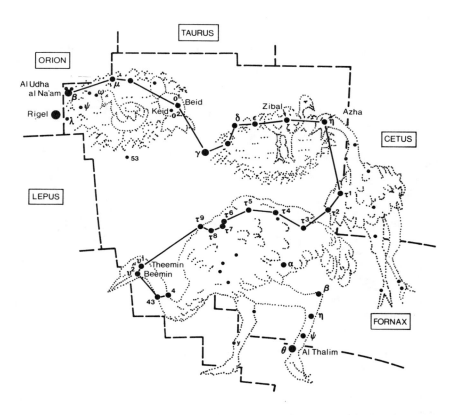

Figure 46. Eridanus. The Ostriches: Arab. (Staal, British, A.D. 1986.)

94

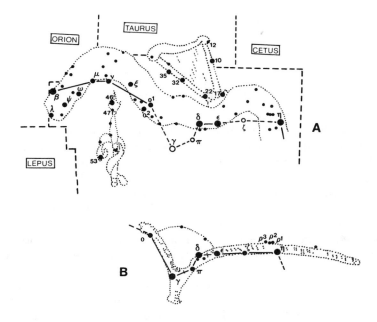

Figure 47. Eridanus. A. Psalterium Georgei and Sceptrum Brandenburgicum, two obsolete constellations in what is now Eridanus. (B41; Bode, German, ca. A.D. 1800.) **B.** A dancing accessory: Siusi; Brazil (B42).

stars in Eridanus related to the ostrich stories include Al Udha al Na'am (β), "the Ostrich's Nest;" Zibal (ζ), "the Ostrich's Chick;" Azha (η), "the Ostrich's Nest;" Al Thalim (θ), "the Ostrich;" Beid (o^1), "the Egg;" and Keid (o^2), "the Eggshell."

The Austrian astronomer the Abbé Maximilian Hell (A.D. 1720–1792) created the constellation Psalterium Georgei in honour of King George II of England. The German astronomer Johann Ehlert Bode (A.D. 1747–1826) included King George's harp on one of his figures of this constellation (Figure 47A). Gottfried Kirch (A.D. 1639–1710), the first astronomer of the Prussian Royal Society of Sciences, created the constellation Sceptrum Brandenburgicum (Figure 47A). This constellation was published subsequently by Bode.

The Siusi Indians of northwest Brazil saw in the stars o-, γ-, δ-, ε-, ζ-, η-Eridani a dancing implement (Figure 47B).

Points of Interest in Eridanus

Achernar, or α-Eridani, is a bluish star of spectral class B5, giving it a surface temperature on the order of 16,000° K. Achernar is the ninth brightest star, but it is not visible from the middle and higher latitudes of the Northern Hemisphere. β-Eridani—lying at the beginning of the river, near Rigel in Orion's foot—is a white star with a surface temperature of about 10,000° K.

Fornax
The Furnace

Cradled within the fourth bend of Eridanus is a multitude of stars of magnitude 5.5 that were not part of any ancient constellation. The Abbé Nicolas Louis de La Caille gathered these, along with two brighter stars α-, β-Fornacis (magnitudes 4 and 4.5, respectively), and created the constellation Fornax Chemica, the Chemical Furnace. Today, this constellation is known as simply Fornax. La Caille dedicated Fornax to the famous French chemist Antoine Laurant Lavoisier (A.D. 1743–1794), considered by many to be the father of modern chemistry. When France was swept by revolution, Lavoisier was executed at the guillotine by the revolutionaries.

A little to the west of Fornax is another collection of faint stars, belonging partly to Cetus and partly to Sculptor. The German astronomer Johann Ehlert Bode (A.D. 1714–1826) gathered these stars together to create Machina Electrica, the Electricity Generator, a forerunner of the van de Graff generator. Fornax is still in use today, but Machina Electrica is no longer recognised by astronomers (Figure 48).

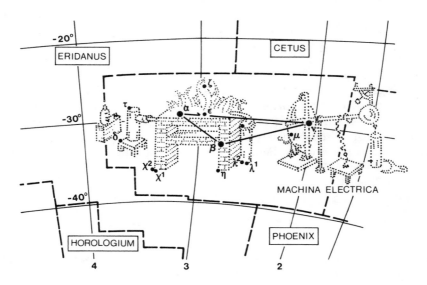

Figure 48. Fornax. Fornax, the Chemical Furnace, and the obsolete constellation Machina Electrica. (B43; Bode, German, ca. A.D. 1800.)

Horologium and Reticulum
The Pendulum Clock and the Net

The Abbé Nicolas Louis de La Caille gathered up the faint stars along the east bank of the river Eridanus and created the constellation Horologium Oscillatorium, the Pendulum Clock (Figure 49). Today this constellation is known simply as Horologium. All of its stars are faint ones of magnitudes 5 to 6, with the exception of its lucida α, which is of magnitude 4. This constellation is one of several that were created to commemorate important technological advances, in this case the pendulum that was designed to make the clock run more accurately. Other such constellations include Antlia, the Pneumatic Pump; Pyxis, the Compass; Fornax, the Chemical Furnace; Telescopium, the Telescope; and Microscopium, the Microscope. The clock face is to the east of Achernar, the star at the end of the river Eridanus. The pendulum weight is close to α-Horologii.

The Abbé Nicolas Louis de La Caille is also credited with creating Reticulum Rhomboidalis to memorialise his investigations of the skies of the Southern Hemisphere. The object selected by La Caille to commemorate these investigations was the reticle—a grid used to provide scale and location in the eyepiece of optical instruments. However, the German, Isaak Habrecht, is believed to have drawn a rhombus in the stars before La Caille did so (Figure 49). Today this constellation is known simply as Reticulum, the Net.

Horologium and Reticulum, Southern Hemisphere constellations, cannot be seen from most parts of the Northern Hemisphere.

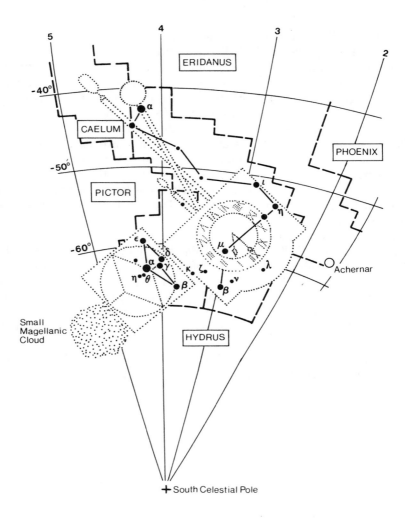

Figure 49. Horologium and Reticulum. The Pendulum Clock and the Rhomboidal Net. (C7; La Caille, French, 18th Century A.D.)

Caelum and Pictor
The Burin and the Painter's Easel

The Abbé Nicolas Louis de La Caille created Caelum from stars gathered up east of Horologium and Eridanus. Caelum is a rather inconspicuous constellation with only two bright stars, α-, γ-Caeli of magnitudes 4.5 and 4, respectively (Figure 50).

The burin is an engraver's tool. It consists of a hardened steel rod with a sharpened point for engraving or carving metal and stone. Although technically Caelum culminates some 10° above the southern horizon when seen from the latitude of Atlanta, Georgia (33° 45' N), actual visibility is influenced greatly by sky conditions. Clouds, pollution, mist, and city lights can make this collection of relatively faint stars a difficult constellation to see from some parts of the southern United States, and it cannot be seen at all from most of the Northern Hemisphere.

Pictor, too, was created by La Caille with the official name Equuleus Pictoris—the Painter's Easel (Figure 50). The formal name for the constellation has been reduced to Pictor, but the full original common name has been kept. The Abbé fashioned Pictor from stars lying south of Columba and Carina. Most stars of Pictor are faint. This constellation sets low in the southern sky and can be seen only from about the southern third of the Northern Hemisphere.

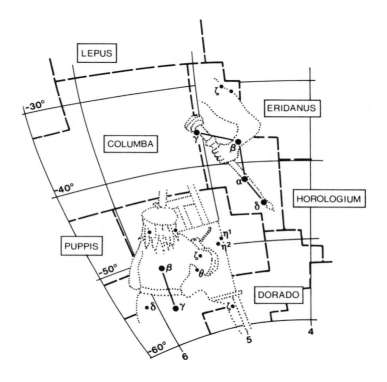

Figure 50. Caelum and Pictor. The Burin and the Painter's Easel. (JS66; Staal, British, A.D. 1986.)

Carina, Puppis and Vela of Argo Navis
The Keel, Stern and Sail of the Ship Argo

Argo Navis, the Ship Argo, is most commonly recognised as that vessel built by Argo for Jason and his fifty Argonauts for use in their expedition in search of the golden fleece. When placed in the sky as a constellation, this ship occupied a vast area in a region teeming with masses of stars. Consequently, astronomers today have divided Argo Navis into three smaller constellations—Puppis, the Stern; Carina, the Keel; and Vela, the Sail (Figure 51). Malus, the Mast, was a fourth constellation created out of Argo Navis, but this has fallen into disuse.

In the middle latitudes of the Northern Hemisphere only Puppis, the Stern or Poop, comes a little above the southern horizon. From the lower middle latitudes of the Northern Hemisphere, this constellation can be seen best during mid-January at midnight. To see Puppis and the rest of Argo Navis in its full beauty, one has to travel a good deal farther south to at least about 10°–12° North Latitude from where the sails and the complete hull of the ship can be traced in the sky. The Poop can be found behind the tail of Canis Major, the Greater Dog.

Under Aries, the Ram, was related the story of how a ram with golden fleece was sent by the goddess Nephele to rescue her two mortal children. While on Earth, Nephele had been married to the mortal Athamas, the King of Boeotia. After Athamas' death, his elder son Aeson became king. The younger son Pelias did not accept this and managed to drive his brother from the throne. Aeson, being a peace loving man, accepted this condition and thought he was well rid of the burden of being a king. Pelias had been told by an oracle that his death would be caused by one of his cousins and that he should look out in particular for a prince with only one shoe. Now Aeson had a son named Jason and immediately Pelias ordered his soldiers to seize this boy and have him put to death. Aeson, however, had expected this and had sent his son to the Centaur Chiron where he would be safe. When the soldiers came to take Jason, Aeson told them that the boy had died. The soldiers took this message back to Pelias, who seemed to accept the statement without suspicion.

Years later, when Jason had come of age, his old teacher Chiron told him what had happened in his youth. Jason prepared himself to put the injustice right, and returned home. Aeson, now an old man, was very glad to see his son again. After lengthy discussions with his father, Jason set out to find Pelias. Enroute to the village of Pelias, it happened that Jason had to swim across a river which was swollen with swirling flood waters. In the crossing, Jason lost one of his shoes. Later, as Jason strode

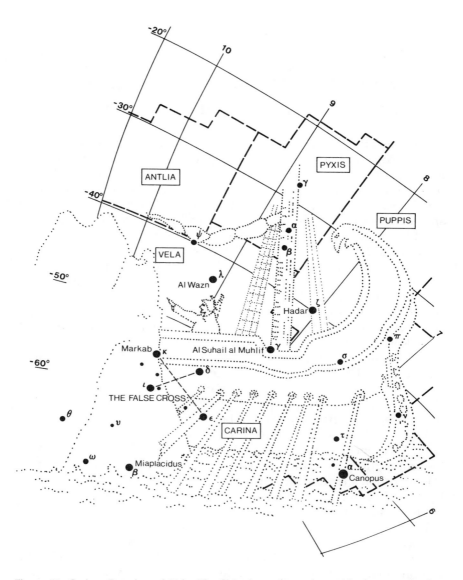

Figure 51. Carina, Puppis and Vela. The Ship Argo, formerly—with the now obsolete constellation Malus—the constellation Argo Navis. (A15; Bayer, German, ca. A.D. 1603.)

through the market place, Pelias noticed the princely boy and became terribly afraid when he discovered that the boy had only one shoe. Jason asked for an audience with Pelias and, after making himself known, demanded that Pelias abdicate in favour of his father, Aeson.

Pelias tried to postpone his decision and told Jason that he would abdicate if Jason could prove himself a hero first. Pelias told Jason that there was a curse on the nation because the golden fleece was held in a distant land. If Jason could return this fleece safely to his own country he, Pelias, would immediately abdicate in favour of Aeson, Jason's father.

Jason accepted this challenge and set about preparing for the search. A crew of many heroes now immortalised in the stars took part in this journey. Among the heroes were Hercules; Castor and Pollux—the Twins; Orpheus, the Singer-Hero; Zetes and Calais, sons of the North Wind; Theseus, the hero who slew the Minotaur; and many others, including one woman, Atalanta, an excellent archer. The helmsman was Glaucus, who is represented in Argo Navis by the star Canopus (α-Carinae), the rudder on the boat. The building of the ship was inaugurated; it was to be named Argo, the Swift One. On the advice of the Goddess Minerva, a beam made from Zeus' oak tree which grew in Dodona was placed in the bow of the ship; this oracular beam enabled the ship to speak.

When the ship was ready to be launched it was so heavy that it could not be moved at all. Orpheus, however, grasped his lyre and sang such a wonderful ode that the oak beam in the bow began to move, and so the whole ship set itself into motion and gently lowered itself into the water without the help of anybody. Such was the power of Orpheus that he could charm even the wild beasts of the forest and make the trees come down mountains to gather around him to listen in awe at his wonderful melodies. So, the journey started with Jason in command.

The Argonauts first passed Mount Pelion where Chiron, Jason's teacher, lived. After a night's rest the Argonauts moved on to Kemnos, where Hippolyte was queen of the Amazons. Then they reached Samothrace where Castor and Pollux were introduced to the mysteries of that place. Here, each of the Twins was given a star, which we can still see as the stars Castor and Pollux.

When the Argo sailed past the coast of Asia Minor, the supply of fresh water began to run low and the Argonauts decided to cast anchor, go ashore, and obtain a new supply. Hercules and Hylas volunteered to search for water, and they found a fine water well. But as they were pulling the pails up and down the well, Hylas was suddenly drawn down into the well by the water nymphs. Hercules decided not to continue with the other Argonauts but to remain behind and try to find his lost friend. So the Argo sailed without Hercules, a sad loss indeed, and set course to the place where Cybele lived. Cybele was a goddess who possessed a chariot which was not drawn by a horse but, rather, by a lion.

The next point the Argonauts had to pass was a dangerous one. It was somewhere along the northern coast of Asia Minor where the brutish giant Amycus lived. Amycus was a born fighter and he would not let anybody pass unless they were prepared to fight with him. Usually this meant the death of the challenged party. Castor and Pollux, however, between them managed to overpower this giant and tied him, with arms outspread, to a tree.

After dealing with Amycus, the Argonauts sailed on to the island Salmydessus, the home of King Phineus. This poor man was a seer who had been punished by the gods with blindness because, it was said, he had abused his divine seeing powers. Every time the wretched man tried to eat, great and dreadful birds, called Harpies, would fly in and steal his food. The Harpies had iron skins and were therefore quite safe from threats from mortals. When the Argonauts arrived, they found Phineus almost starved to death. The heroes offered their help, and sat as guests at Phineus' table waiting for the birds to come. When the birds arrived the heroes hacked at them with their swords but to no avail. Then Zetes and Calais, the sons of the North Wind, flew up into the air and pursued the Harpies. The birds flew so far from the palace that they became exhausted and fell into the sea where they drowned. So Phineus was freed from these monsters. He was so grateful for the Argonauts' help that he gave them much necessary advice for their journey.

The ship Argo turned to the high seas again and set course toward the huge rocks called the Symplegades. The Symplegades had a habit of rushing violently against each other, crushing everything in between, even fishes and birds. Whenever the Symplegades saw a ship which had to pass between them, they waited until the vessel was in the middle and then came rushing together, breaking up the ship and killing everybody on board. Afterwards they would recede and leave a wide and seemingly safe passage for the next victim.

But Phineus had given good counsel to the Argonauts. As the ship Argo approached the rocks they happened to be far apart, but seeing the ship coming nearer they at once started to move closer to each other. When very near to the entrance the Argonauts released a white dove, for they had been told that if ever any living thing did pass unscathed through the Symplegades, the rocks would never move again. The white dove, aided by Minerva, shot between the two rocks with such speed that they crashed against each other without killing the bird—only depriving it of a few feathers. This was a good sign. As the crags slid backwards the Argo plunged full sail between the murderous rocks. The rocks instantly started to move inwards again, but Orpheus began to play his lyre and slowed their movement with his soothing music while the Argo sailed safely through the Symplegades. The rocks discovered too late that they had been under the spell of Orpheus and crashed against each other for the last time. They have stood still ever since and are now known as the Dardanelles and the Bosporus, narrows guarding the ends of the passage between the Aegean Sea and the Black Sea. The heroic dove came back to the ship. Minerva later put her in the stars as the constellation Columba, visible only in the skies of the Southern Hemisphere.

The last adventure of the Argonauts before reaching Colchis was their slaying the wild boar in Calydon. Diana, the Goddess of the Hunt, had sent this boar to the Calydonians because they had failed to bring the necessary sacrifices to her. This was the feat where Atalanta, the only woman on board the Argo, came to the fore as she killed the boar with one of her arrows.

Finally, the Argonauts reached Colchis. King Aeëtes was very perturbed when he heard the reason for their visit. He was certainly not going to part with the golden fleece without resistance. But he hid his dismay and said to the Argonauts, "You can certainly have the fleece, but first you must yoke the brazen fire-breathing bulls and plough a field for me to sow some dragons' teeth."

Venus, however, made Medea, the daughter of King Aeëtes, fall in love with the princely Jason and promise to help him. Medea gave Jason a mighty potion of herbs which would render him fire and freeze proof if rubbed on hands, face and body. The day was fixed for this task, and early in the morning King Aeëtes went to the appointed field with his daughter and members of the royal retinue. Everybody tried to get a good vantage point as they made themselves comfortable for a day of good sport. Jason rubbed himself with the potion, entered the stable where the fire-bulls lived, untied the chains, and seized the bulls with one hand on each horn. The animals roared as they came out, and fire sprayed from their mouths and nostrils in all directions. Struggling and pulling, Jason forced the bulls under the yoke of the heavy iron plough, which Pollux had brought out to the starting point. All this time, Jason was forcing the bulls' heads down to the ground so that the fire could not shoot upwards, but now he grasped the handle of the plough and let the heads go. Immediately the bulls lifted their heads and, bellowing ferociously, tried to lunge forward. Jason strained at the harness, however, and they came to a dead stop. Thereafter, the oxen were obliged to plough quietly, and by midday Jason had finished ploughing the field. The ploughing done, the bulls were unyoked. Terrified by Jason's strong hand, the bulls fled into the mountains and never returned again.

Jason then went to King Aeëtes and asked for the dragons' teeth. The king gave him a helmet full of little teeth and Jason started to sow these in the furrows, closing the earth over them as he did so. No sooner had he finished this task than armed giants began to grow out of each furrow. Those whose feet were still in the ground brandished their spears and swords, while those already fully grown rushed madly at Jason. Now Jason did what Medea had told him to do. He threw a great stone in their midst and all the iron giants rushed to it, trying to possess it. A terrific battle ensued amongst the giants which ended in their killing each other. Meanwhile Jason went around the field cutting off the heads of those that had just started to grow.

Jason and Medea were glad that the ordeal was over but Aeëtes was furious. The next morning Jason demanded the fleece because he wanted to go home, but Aeëtes said, "Do stay for a while. It is not every day that we have such heroes in our midst." Jason agreed to stay, but in the night Medea woke him up and warned him to leave immediately with his men because her father had rallied his army and intended to kill them all.

So Jason and Medea fled quickly from the palace while the crew made the Argo ready for its homeward journey. Medea and Jason went to the tree where the fleece was nailed and guarded by a never-sleeping dragon who would devour anyone who dared to touch it.

As it was an immortal dragon, there was no sense in trying to kill it. But it had a great liking for sweets, and Medea had made it some honey cakes dipped in a certain juice that would put the dragon into a deep sleep. These she gave to Jason and he threw them to the dragon who soon ate them all and fell asleep. Jason pulled the fleece from the nails and sped back to the ship. Medea went with him, as did her little brother Apsyrtus, who was later killed by Medea to permit their escape.

When Aeëtes discovered that he had lost his fleece, and that the Argonauts were already under way, he decided to follow them with one of his swift warships. Aeëtes' ship soon began to catch up with the Argo. At this time Medea showed herself to be an awful, heartless woman. She killed her little brother, cut his limbs and body into pieces, and threw them one by one into the sea. In deep sorrow Aeëtes abandoned the chase and ordered his men to collect the remains of his son.

The Argonauts did not reach home again, however, until they had experienced other adventures. First, they had to sail past the Sirens, creatures that were half maidens and half fishes, who lived on rocks and sang beautiful songs in an attempt to lure sailors toward them. Sailors who became entranced by the music of the Sirens were doomed because their ships would wreck on the rocks. Orpheus, however, with his powerful lyre, could overpower the singing of the Sirens. In spite of this, one of the crew came so much under their influence that he fell overboard and, had it not been for Orpheus' lyre drowning the Sirens' singing and calming the waves, that sailor would have drowned. As it was, his fellow crewmen were able to haul him aboard again.

Another danger encountered by the Argonauts were Scylla and Charybdis, two monsters who lived in the Strait of Messina. Scylla had six long necks and six heads and it was her sport to attack each passing ship from which she would pluck six sailors. Charybdis had a different kind of attack. Three times a day she would drink the sea water in the Strait, devouring all the fishes for a meal, and spew out the water again. This caused heavy currents and, in the process of gathering her meals, she often collected an unfortunate ship or two. With the help of Thetis, the Goddess of the Sea, and the sea nymphs, the Nereids, the Argonauts were led to safety through this dangerous area. So the Argo reached the island where Circe the Enchantress lived. Circe sent bread and fruit to the ship and wished the crew a good journey.

Medea and Jason married when they arrived in the land of Phaea-cians. From there, the route went past the Peloponnesus. A storm caught the ship and drove it to the coast of Lybia. Here a golden steed rose from the sea with three goddesses seated on his back. These goddesses told the Argonauts that all would end well for them if the advice they were about to be given were followed. For twelve days, the goddesses said, the heroes should carry their ship through Lybia to escape the fury of the sea storm. This they did. During this gruelling trip one of the men was bitten and killed by a scorpion. Finally the Argonauts reached the sea, lowered the boat into the water again, and arrived home safely.

Then the Argonauts discovered that the treacherous King Pelias had put Jason's entire family to death, in the hope of forestalling the oracle's prediction that he would be killed by one of his cousins. Jason, Pelias thought, was as good as dead; he believed that Jason would never return from his mission to Colchis. Jason was desperate and Medea decided to seek revenge. She told the daughters of Pelias that she could rejuvenate their old father. To prove this claim, she cut up a goat in front of the sisters and then boiled it in a secret juice which brought the goat back to life as a young kid. This convinced the sisters of her powers and they killed their father. Then at the crucial moment Medea left them in the lurch and did not perform the critical part of the rejuvenation rite.

This was Medea's answer to the killing of Jason's family, and she did this in good faith because she believed in her husband. But Jason, upset by her witches' methods, turned away from Medea and finally married Creusa, the daughter of the King of Corinth, to whose kingdom Jason and Medea had had to flee after the murder of Pelias.

Medea could not understand her husband's infidelity, so she killed the bride and her father by sending the unsuspecting maiden a poisoned robe and tiara as wedding gifts. Then Medea murdered her own two children. After these awful deeds she returned, in a chariot drawn by snakes, to Colchis and her father Aeëtes.

Just as in the story of the labours of the hero Hercules, who had to perform twelve difficult tasks which are commemorated along the route of the Sun's passage through the zodiac, so has the journey of the Argonauts a connection with the Sun's trek through the zodiac. With a star chart or planisphere, the whole story can be followed quite clearly.

The start of the story is with the Sun somewhere between Scorpio and Sagittarius. Above Scorpio, we see Ophiuchus, the Healer of Anti-quity who, in this story, represents Jason, the Curer of Injustice. Hercules and Boötes are above Ophiuchus and symbolise members of the crew, whereas Virgo, the Virgin, depicts Atalanta, the only woman on board the Argo. When Ophiuchus, or Jason, rises in the east we can see the stars of Argo Navis, the Ship, lying ready in the west. The ship is launched when Vega, the bright star in Lyra, the Harp of Orpheus, appears in the east. Then Argo slides gently into the waters of the sea, which is depicted by the Milky Way.

The Journey of the Sun through Sagittarius recalls the Argonauts' visit with Chiron, Jason's old master and teacher. When the Sun sets in the evening, the Pleiades rise in the east, representing the visit to the Amazons. The next stop for the Sun is the constellation of Capricorn. Then, when the Sun sets in the evening, the Twins, Castor and Pollux, come up in the east denoting their visit to Samothrace where they were adorned with the two stars.

With the Sun passing through Aquarius, the Water Carrier, we can see Hercules, just before sunrise culminating high in the south. In the evening, when the Sun sets, we notice the Hyades coming up in the east. This points to the eternal search of Hercules for his friend Hylas, who was drawn into a water well by the water nymphs, the Hyades.

When the sun arrives in Pisces, the Fishes, we can see at sunset how Leo comes up, followed by Virgo, depicting the visit at Cybele, who has a lion in front of her chariot. Also, as the Fishes set, Orion stands high in the sky and depicts the giant Amycus, who always fought with strange intruders and passers-by, but was eventually slain by the Twins, Castor and Pollux, who stand above him.

When the Sun comes up in the Fishes, the three birds—Cygnus, the Swan; Aquila, the Eagle; and Vega, the Vulture—pale away in the light of early dawn, which points to the defeat of the Harpies at the palace of King Phineus.

When the sun passes through Aries, the Ram, we find the Argonauts in front of the Symplegades. The Ram represents the butting of the two rocks, whereas the Pleiades depict the white dove that was sent on a reconnaissance flight through the passage. When the Pleiades set in the west, the ship Argo culminates and Lyra, Orpheus' Harp, comes up in the northeast, which recalls the safe journey of Argo between the two deadly rocks.

When the Sun sets in the Ram, Virgo comes up in the east; this represents the slaying of the wild boar by Atalanta. With the Sun passing through Taurus, the Bull, the first part of the journey is over. The Argonauts are in Colchis.

Perseus stands above Taurus and depicts King Aeëtes. Algol, the demon star, is Aeëtes' daughter Medea, who knows witchcraft. The Ram represents the golden fleece which is guarded by the dragon, personified by Cetus, the Whale. The ploughing of the field is depicted in the presence of Taurus, here one of the brazen bulls.

Now the Sun arrives in Gemini, the Twins, the constellation diametrically opposite Sagittarius. The Twins represents the beginning of the homeward journey, when the Sun will travel through six other constellations, just as the ship Argo took a different route home.

Medea kills her brother, cuts up his body, and throws the limbs into the sea. This is depicted in Auriga, the Charioteer, who lies exactly in the Milky Way, the sea. The stars of Auriga represent the detached limbs. So the Sun arrives in Cancer, the Crab, when the Argo has to by-pass Scylla and Charybdis, which are depicted in Hydra, the Watersnake. One of the crew falls overboard, the story says. When the Crab rises in the east, Boötes tumbles down to the horizon in the west. When in the evening the Crab sets in the west, Boötes comes above the eastern horizon—having been rescued by the music from Orpheus' Lyre, which also rises in the east.

With the Sun passing through Leo, the Lion, the Argo passes safely through Scylla and Charybdis with the help of the Nereids, which we can see when the Sun in Leo rises in the morning. The Hyades, who now represent the Nereids, culminate.

Then the Sun treks through the constellation of Virgo, the Virgin, which represents the visit of the Argonauts to Circe, the Enchantress, who sent bread and fruit, represented by Spica, the Ear of Corn. The basket in which these goods were carried is depicted by the cup shape in some of the stars of Virgo and the Beaker, perched on top of the Hydra.

The Sun now enters the constellation of Libra, the Scales, and this points to the wedding of Jason and Medea on the island of the Phaeacians. The storms which the Ship Argo had to endure are depicted by the fact that the Hyades rise in the east when the Sun in the Scales sets in the west. The golden horse that rose from the sea carrying three goddesses is depicted by Pegasus, Andromeda and Cassiopeia.

The Sun arrives in the Scorpion and this depicts the Argonauts' trek through the Lybian desert, where one of the party was bitten by a scorpion. With Scorpio rising in the east we can see Orion set in the west, representing this sad event.

And so the Sun returns to its starting point, just as the Argo returned home after its heroic and successful journey to Colchis.

Columba
The Dove

When the ship Argo approached the clashing rocks of the Symplegades at the passage from the Aegean Sea to the Black Sea, Jason—who had been forewarned of this danger—sent out a dove to see how it would fare as it flew between these dangerous rocks. The dove escaped death, losing only a few tail feathers. The success of the dove was seen as a propitious omen, so the ship Argo was rowed into the dangerous area at top speed. The rocks did clash together, and some of the oars were destroyed and there was a little damage to the stern, but the ship completed the passage without being crushed by the clashing rocks. Ever since, the rocks have stood still. Columba was placed in the sky by Minerva as a memento of the bird's daring deed.

Sometimes this constellation is known as Columba Noae, Noah's Dove, which ties the bird closely to Argo, the Ark. After the flood, Noah sent the dove out to see if it could find dry land. When the dove returned carrying an olive branch in its beak, Noah knew that the waters were receding (Figure 52). When again Noah sent out the dove and it did not return, he understood that it must have found dry land.

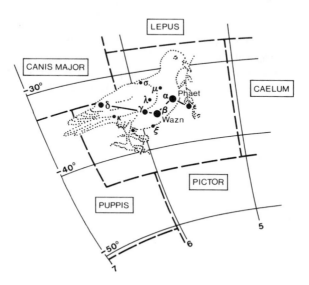

Figure 52. Columba. Columba, as the Dove of Noah, holding an olive branch in its beak. (JS25; Staal, British, A.D. 1986.)

The Stars of Spring

As Winter comes to an end and the Sun crosses ever higher in the sky, the days begin to lengthen and the nights to shorten. This is, of course, a pity from the point of view of any constellation hunter. But even during the nights of Spring, there is still a lot to be seen in the skies.

The dominant figure during the months of Spring is the enormous Lion, Leo, who seems to bound unimpeded across the sky. The Great Bear and the Little Bear run playfully around the North Pole Star, with Boötes and his Hunting Dogs, Canes Venatici, in pursuit. The faint streamers of stars in Coma Berenices provide tragic evidence of a classical love story which came to an untimely end. Crawling in all its coiling beauty is Hydra, slithering low over the southern horizon with the Crow and the Beaker on its back. Virgo, the Maiden, has also been recognised as the goddesses Isis, Astraea, Ceres, and Ceres' beautiful but unfortunate daughter, Proserpina.

Leo
The Lion

Pre-eminent in the Spring sky is Leo, the Lion. The outline of this constellation is so nearly like that of a lion that the star hunter will not have much difficulty finding it (Figure 53). The Lion faces west. The head of Leo is a reversed question mark. The dot of this question mark is the star α-Leonis, or Regulus or Cor Leonis, "the Heart of the Lion." Leo's neck joins his body at γ, γ and η represent the chest, and the rear quarters are formed by θ and δ. The end of the tail is marked by the star β-Leonis, or Denebola, from Deneb-el-Asad, "the Tail of the Lion."

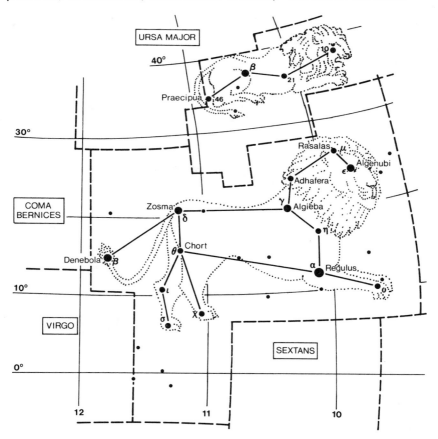

Figure 53. Leo and Leo Minor. Leo, the Lion, and Leo Minor, the Lesser Lion, in typical form (Leo Minor:C24).

Leo has not always been viewed as the small figure described above. At the time of Claudius Ptolemaeus, some 150 years after the birth of Christ, Leo was seen as an enormous animal which extended far to the west, incorporating stars of the constellation we now call Cancer, the Crab. A star cluster in the Crab, called the Beehive, formed the whiskers of the Lion and its nose. The question mark became the mane and hairy neck, the body remained the same as our present Lion, but Denebola formed the rear quarters and a wonderful curly tail stretched upwards to the stars of the constellation which we now know as Coma Berenices. In those far off days Coma Berenices formed the tuft of Leo's tail (Figure 54).

Some 4,000 years ago the Sun reached the Summer Solstice against the background stars of the Lion. This time of the year is the hottest as the regal Sun and the King of Animals unite their strengths. One Greek story says that the Lion lived on the Moon and one day descended to the Earth as a shooting star. The lion landed in Corinth and there ransacked the countryside until Hercules strangled it with his bare hands. This lion is known as the Nemean Lion, whom Jupiter put back in the sky from whence it originally came.

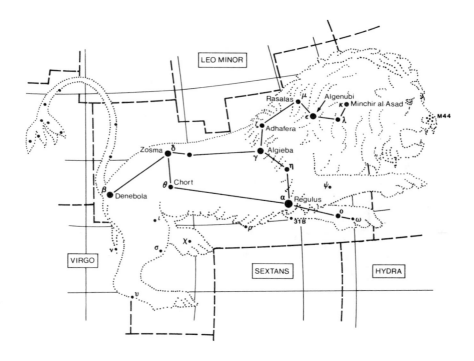

Figure 54. Leo. Leo, the Lion, in extended form (C17).

An old Babylonian story, related by Ovid, tells of two lovers, Pyramus and Thisbe, and the tragedy that befell them because of a lion. Pyramus, the boy, lived next door to Thisbe. They fell deeply in love, but their parents were against the match so they had to pursue their courtship in secret. They talked to each other through cracks in the wall that separated their house, and one evening they decided to meet at a spring near the edge of the forest. Thisbe, it so happened, arrived at the meeting site first. Then a lion appeared on the scene carrying its dead prey. The lion settled down to a hearty meal and did not take much notice of Thisbe. The girl, however, was so frightened that she ran off to see if she could get some help, and to warn Pyramus. As she ran off she lost her veil. The veil fluttered past the lion, who angrily snatched at it and stained it with blood. When the lion had satisfied his hunger, he took a hearty drink and then disappeared into the woods. Shortly thereafter Pyramus arrived and saw the veil, which he immediately recognised as Thisbe's. No other thought could have entered the poor boy's mind but to believe that a lion had killed and eaten Thisbe.

Pyramus blamed himself for the tragedy, because he had encouraged Thisbe to come to this tryst. He picked up the torn and blood-stained veil and kissed it for the last time. Then Pyramus drew his sword, plunged it deep into himself, and fell beneath a mulberry tree. A pool of blood formed, then soaked into the ground where the roots of the mulberry tree drank in the blood. The blood caused the colour of the mulberry fruits to change to a dark red. About this time Thisbe, who had failed to find help, returned. When she saw what had happened, she forgot everything in her despair and fell weeping onto the dead body of her lover. Grasping Pyramus' sword, Thisbe plunged it deep into her side. And so the two lovers were united in death.

Jupiter had pity on these young lovers. As a reminder to mankind of what could happen to true love if parents selfishly put their own feelings before those of their children's, Jupiter put Thisbe's veil among the stars. Thisbe's veil flutters today in the stars of Coma Berenices, wafted by an eternal cosmic breeze.

The Babylonians saw a great dog in the stars of Leo. To them, a ferocious guard dog to protect precious goods as well as men and beasts was of utmost importance. Every Babylonian caravan had its quota of these huge guard dogs (Figure 55A).

The Taulipang Indians of northern Brazil see in Leo's stars a mythological figure named Tauna, the God of Thunder and Lightning (Figure 56A). In equatorial regions Leo rises at nearly 90° to the horizon. When all the stars of Leo are above the horizon, Tauna stands upright in the sky. When the weather changes in Brazil and heavy thunderstorms occur, the Indians say that Tauna is bashing the clouds with his enormous cudgel—thus producing the lightning flashes and the rumble of the thunder.

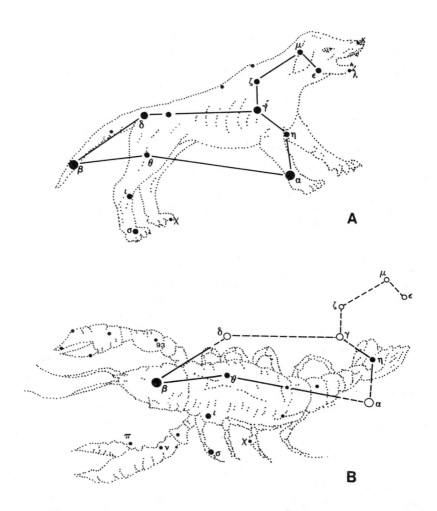

Figure 55. Leo. A. The Great Dog: Babylonian (C18). **B.** The Crayfish: Tukano, Kobeua and Siusi; Brazil (C22).

A crayfish was placed in the stars of Leo by the Tukano, Kobeua and Siusi Indians of northern Brazil. Most of the question mark, including even Regulus, was ignored in creating this constellation. Only η-Leonis played a role as the tail of the crayfish, whilst β-Leonis was the head of the crayfish. The southern claw reached into Virgo and the northern claw into Coma Berenices (Figure 55B).

From high in the Arctic region of Siberia the Chukchee saw a sleeping woman in the stars of Leo's forepart (Figure 56B). The head of this woman is in ε-Leonis and her feet rest in ρ-Leonis.

The Chinese saw several constellations in the area of Leo. One can easily detect the sense of concern for water supply and control among the Chinese from the variety of representations they saw in this area of the sky. The question mark, or sickle, was extended upwards and represented Hien-youen, the Rain Dragon (Figure 57). The dragon was seen as the symbol of the life-giving power of water. This same asterism was also seen as the meandering flow of water distributed over the fields by large water conveyors, sometimes called Water Chariots. On other occasions the sickle group of stars represented a funeral cart.

In the past when, during the months of May and June, the sky burned like a red glowing sphere of bronze and not a drop of rain fell, the greatest droughts occurred in China. When, in the middle of June, the stars of Hien-youen appeared in the night sky the time had come to start the ceremonies of the Rain Dragon. A great clay dragon was carried through the streets and through the fields while people prayed for rain. When finally the rains did come the people congratulated each other and said, "It is the joyous rain."

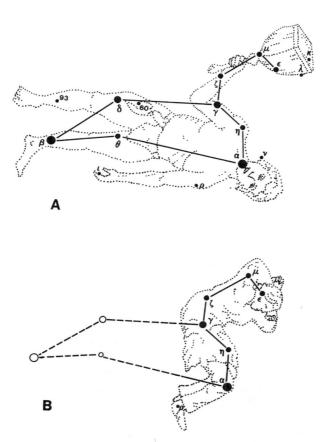

Figure 56. Leo. A. Tauna, the God of Thunder and Lightning: Taulipang; Brazil (C23). **B.** The Sleeping Woman: Chukchee; Siberia (C21).

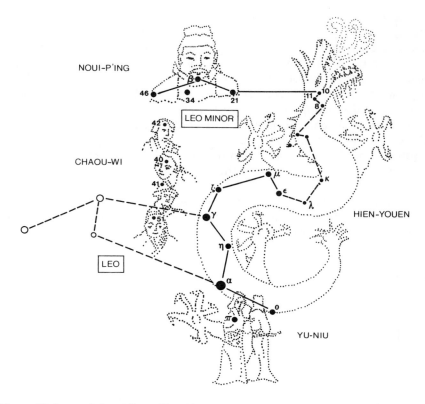

Figure 57. Leo and Leo Minor. The Chinese asterisms in Leo and Leo Minor include Hien-youen, the Rain Dragon; Noui-p'ing, the Administrator of the Interior; Chaou-wi, the Unknown of Low Rank; and Yu-niu, the Royal Daughters. (Staal, British, A.D. 1986.)

During the Song Dynasty a complicated rain ritual was held. First one searched for deep water, a pond or any other body of water in a dense forest. After a fast of several days and after having made offerings of wine and dried meat, two square altars, surrounded at a distance of twenty paces by an enclosure made of white ropes, were erected. On this altar a bamboo pole was planted from which was suspended a painting of a dragon. This dragon was surrounded by black snakes with their heads pointing to the left. The dragon was primarily white in colour with gold, silver and vermillion accents, and it was vomiting great black clouds. Below it were waves of water and tortoises, their heads also turned to the left, spitting blackish breath-like threads of silk. After a goose had been killed and offered on the altar, water was sprinkled on the dragon with a willow branch. When finally the rains came, the dragon was taken down from the pole and cast into the water.

While the people waited for the rain to come, however, something had to be done to keep the crops from shrivelling under the merciless heat of the Sun. For this, the Chinese used the Water Chariot (the other meaning of Hien-youen), actually an endless conveyor belt which scooped up small buckets of water from below and dumped it into irrigation ditches at a higher point. This belt was operated by two people working a treadmill. This belt was also called Choui-tche, Water Cart or Loung-kou-tche, Chariot of the Dragon's Skeleton. This last name refers to the conveyor belt which, to the Chinese, looked like the vertebrae of a dragon, a spine whose endless movement up and down the trough gave the impression of the undulating rhythm of the swimming dragon.

Summer was also the season for funerals and the decline of the Sun in the sky. Relative to these events, Hien-youen was also known as the funeral cart because such carts were often decorated with dragons.

Yu-niu, the Royal Daughters, were represented by the star π-Leonis (Figure 57). The star also represented the Great Mistress. According to another source, the Great Mistress was Tching-i, the star α-Leonis, or Regulus. The next star above Regulus, η-Leonis, represented the Ladies of the Bedchamber; γ-Leonis was the Concubines; and all the other stars farther to the north represented the Girls or Daughters of the Palace.

Points of Interest in Leo

Regulus, white in colour, is a star of magnitude 1.35 and it is the 20th brightest star in the sky. The distance of this star from Earth is estimated to be about 69 light years.

Denebola, in the tail, is a bluish-coloured star. With a powerful telescope, or even field glasses, many of Denebola's companion stars can be seen. γ-Leonis, in the chest, is a double star—the primary being orange and the companion green.

A very famous meteor shower—the Leonids—is expected every year during the middle of November. This shower peaks in the early hours of the morning and comes from the head of the Lion. Regularly returning meteor showers are generally believed to be remains of comets which have broken apart and left their particles in the path they originally traveled around the Sun. Every time the Earth approaches the point of intersection between its own orbit and that of the former comets, we may expect a display of shooting stars or meteors.

The Leonids are believed to be the remains of Comet Tuttle. Every 33 years the Leonid shower should be more spectacular than during the intervening years. Splendid meteor showers occurred in 1799, 1833, and 1866, but displays in this century have been disappointing. Perhaps the debris has diminished or perhaps its orbit has been changed gradually by the gravitational influence of the colossal planet Jupiter.

Leo Minor

The Lesser Lion

There is no known Classical mythology about Leo Minor. The Polish astronomer Johannes Hevelius (A.D. 1611–1687) created this constellation from 18 left-over stars, or supernumeri, located between Leo and the rear legs of Ursa Major (Figure 53). Hevelius named star 46 Praecipua, "the Excellent One."

The Chinese placed Noui-p'ing, the Administrator of the Interior, in Leo Minor. By some accounts, Noui-p'ing was the magistrate who equalised punishments, and by others he was the officer in charge of the imperial harem (Figure 57).

Chaou-wi represented the Unknown of as Yet Low Ranks. The hidden small ones were those in inferior positions, not yet discovered, but who deserved to be promoted to higher ranks. Star 51 (in Leo) was Hou-sse, the Tiger or Military Chief. Stars 40, 41 and 42 were Po-sse, the Wise Ones, I-sse, the Counselors, and Ta-fou, the Eminents, respectively. Chaou-wi represented the place where the virtuous—the ones who would be rewarded for their merits—were seated. Astrologers maintained that the clarity of these stars foretold the election of meritorious men (Figure 57).

Ursa Major
The Great Bear

High above the Lion lie the stars of the Great Bear, one of the oldest of the constellations. Originally restricted to the seven stars α-, β-, γ-, δ-, ε-, ζ-, η-Ursae Majoris, this constellation has been enlarged to include, according to the German astronomer Eduard Heis, some 227 stars visible to the naked eye. The seven familiar stars—which at a glance remind us of a saucepan with a long handle—are called the Big Dipper by Americans, but are well known as the Plough to the British and the Great Wagon and Three Horses by many other Teutonic peoples. The stars of the Big Dipper include Dubhe (α), Merak (β), Phecda (γ), Megrez (δ), Alioth (ε), Mizar (ζ), and Benatnasch (η). The Wagon, or Cart, is formed by the stars α-, β-,δ-, γ- Ursae Majoris, and the Three Horses by the stars ε-, ζ-, and η-Ursae Majoris. Close to Mizar (ζ) is another little star known as Alcor, "the Faint One." In England Mizar and Alcor are also known as Jack on the Middle Horse, Jack (Alcor) being the rider on Mizar.

To see the constellation of the Great Bear one must not only look at the seven familiar stars of the Big Dipper, but add many fainter stars situated to the west and south. On a moonless night one can then distinctly see three legs and three pairs of toes, and a chubby head with a pointed snout (Figure 58).

Merak and Dubhe are called the pointer stars; a line drawn through these stars and continued to the north will lead to Polaris, the North Star. A line drawn through the same two stars and continued to the south will lead to Leo, the Lion. Polaris is the tail of the Little Bear, or the Little Dipper, which also consists of seven stars arranged in a pattern similar to those of the Big Dipper.

The best known story of the Bears comes from ancient Greece. King Lycaon of Arcadia possessed a beautiful daughter named Callisto. Callisto was very fond of hunting and worshipped Artemis, the Goddess of the Hunt. One day Callisto promised Artemis that she would devote her entire life to the goddess, which meant among other things that Callisto had to remain a virgin. All this happened not very long after the fatal ride of Phaethon. The Earth had been scorched and everything was badly damaged. Jupiter descended from Olympus to see for himself what he could do to restore the Earth to its former condition. Seeing that every living thing had been scorched and that the rivers and the lakes were dry, Jupiter applied his godly power to restore the Earth to a productive condition. Gradually, the rivers began to fill with water

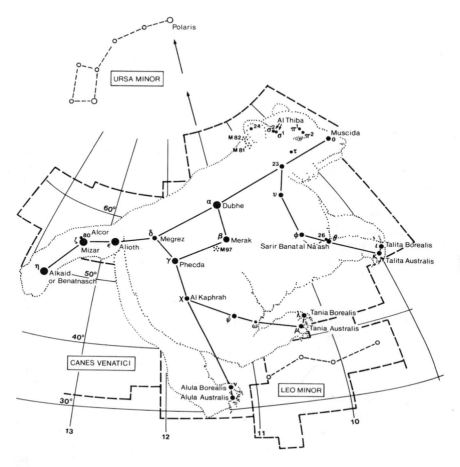

Figure 58. Ursa Major. The Great Bear, after an illustration by Claudius Ptolemaeus made during the 2nd Century A.D. (E5; Bode, German, ca. A.D. 1800.)

again, the grass stood green once more, and the forest came back to life. Once again, the Earth could pride herself on all her finery and foliage.

Jupiter rambled around the woods of Arcadia at that time and, while looking approvingly at all that he had done, he suddenly discovered a beautiful young Arcadian girl resting in the afternoon warmth in a shady part of the forest. Instantly, Jupiter was inflamed with great passion for the girl who was none other than Callisto. She had removed her bow and quiver and, slumbering amidst the heavy scent of the herbs of the forest, did not notice Jupiter's presence. Jupiter, seeing a good opportunity for another of his many secret love affairs, said to himself, "This secret love my spouse will not know about, and even if she should find out it would be worth her quarrelling." With that he changed himself into the guise of Artemis and spoke to Callisto. "Well, beautiful young woman of my hunting retinue, in what mountains have you been hunting?" Dumbfounded, Callisto jumped up and greeted the goddess. "Greetings, O goddess, whom I put higher in esteem than Jupiter." Jupiter was amused to hear himself being put above himself by the girl. However, unable to restrain himself any longer, he embraced and kissed her, but not in a moderate way as a goddess should kiss a member of her own sex. And so Jupiter gave away his real identity. Callisto resisted him with all her might, but who could resist Jupiter, the highest of all the gods? And so it happened that he lay with Callisto. After he had enjoyed the delights of love, Jupiter returned to Olympus and left Callisto behind in the forest, the only witness of her disgrace.

Callisto was sad because she had broken her vow to Artemis. As Callisto was pondering her sin, Artemis and some of her followers happened to pass where Callisto was sitting. Hearing her name being called, Callisto took fright lest it was Jupiter again. First of all she tried to flee but, seeing that they were really her hunting companions, she joined them. Callisto, however, was no longer the same girl. Usually she was cheerful and sprightly, always had a lot to say, and was ever first in the group. Now she was quiet and distraught, and she could hardly hide the shame in her eyes.

Then came the time, after the Moon had been full nine times, that all the nymphs gathered by a spring to refresh themselves with a bath. Callisto tried to stay behind, but the nymphs pulled her playfully with them, undid her garments and, of course, thereby discovered her sin. The nymphs were horrified and spoke to her, "Go far from here and do not pollute the waters of this spring." And so Callisto was driven from the retinue of Artemis. This punishment, however, was not enough. Juno, the quarrelsome spouse of Jupiter, found out that deep in the forest of Arcadia a little boy had been born, named Arcas after his birthplace. Juno reproached Callisto in no uncertain manner and uttered an awful threat which she carried out instantly as she said, "Not without punishment will you pay for this disgrace, because I shall take away your beautiful figure with which you managed to allure my husband."

With these words, Juno grasped the poor girl by her locks and threw her face downwards. Suddenly her arms became shaggy with hair, her pleading voice faltered and changed into an awful roaring sound, while her erect gait became a prone walk on four legs. So the beautiful Callisto was changed into a bear, and she fled into the woods to look for refuge from the hunters to whom she had once belonged.

For many, many years Callisto lived in the forest, frightened by the bark of the hunting dogs who once were her companions. Meanwhile, Arcas had grown into manhood and also had taken up hunting. One day Arcas encountered a bear which was, in fact, his mother. Forgetting that she looked like a bear, Callisto rushed forward as soon as she recognised her son whom, of course, she wished to embrace. Arcas, however, thought that he was being attacked and ordered out his dogs while he drew his bow and levelled an arrow. He would have shot with a deadly result had not Jupiter intervened, driven by pity for Callisto. With a vigorous sweep he grasped mother and son and, changing Arcas into a bear too, he swung them both into the heavens where they landed amongst the stars. The ferocious tug at their tails, as they were slung skyward, caused their normally bushy, stumpy tails to stretch (Figures 58, 59). Today we know Callisto and Arcas as the Great Bear and the Little Bear, and in such a way did Jupiter compensate Callisto and Arcas for all the agony he had caused them on Earth.

Jupiter had not reckoned with Juno, however, who was not so easily reconciled. She swore at him. "Sure enough! I prevented Callisto from being a human being, but you of course have to make a goddess of her. So this then is the strength of my divine power. Why don't you take Callisto as your wife. Now I have to live with an adultress in the same Heaven."

Deeply hurt, Juno thought of revenge and carried it out without delay. Ovid described Juno's actions beautifully in Book II of the *Metamorphoses*:

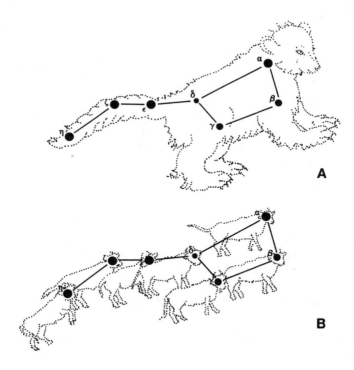

Figure 59. Ursa Major. A. A preclassical Greek concept of the Great Bear. (E6; Apianus, German, ca. A.D. 1535.) **B.** The Seven Ploughing Oxen: Rome (E8).

When she beheld Jove's mistress in the skies
Glittering against the night, pale Juno's rage
Swelled hot and like a meteor in flight
She dropped to Tethys and to ancient
Oceanus, two elders of the sea
To whom the Gods gave reverence and awe.
They asked her why she came and she replied,
"Why do you question me, the Queen of Heaven,
When yet another queen shines in the sky."
Say I am a liar, if tonight you do not see
New constellations rising in the dark . . .
That brilliance who usurps my place in heaven
Of the high north, the farthest shortest circle
That turns above the pole. With this in sight
Who cares to worship Juno or hold me in awe?
Or who should fear my rage? I seem to glory those
Whom I destroyed; what great things rise from
Deeds that I have done. And she whom I shipped and
Banned out of human shape is now Goddess!
Such is the punishment I give to enemies,
Such the great power for which my name is known.
And in the case of Io, Jove has only
To give the girl freedom of bestial state,
Restore her shapeliness . . . since I am fallen
What shall prevent him now from leading her
Into my bed, and Jove himself being
Her husband and Lycaon's son-in-law?
If this dishonour to your adopted child
Stirs in your hearts, forbid these bearlike
Creatures in the stars to wade your waters;
Shut out the creatures who at cost of sin
Shine down from heaven, nor allow that whore
To taint the waters of your sacred streams."

And so it is that of all the constellations, only the Bears never bathe in
the ocean—never cool their tired paws in the soothing waters of the sea.

Homer, in Book V of the *Odyssey*, described the departure of Odysseus from the island of Ogygia, where he had sojourned for a year with the beautiful enchantress Calypso, and the role played by the Great Bear on the ensuing voyage.

It was with happy heart that the good Odysseus
Spread his sails to catch the wind and used
His seamanship to keep his boat straight
With its steering oar.

There he sat and never closed his eyes in sleep
But fixed them on the Pleiades, or watched Boötes
Slowly set; or the Great Bear, nicknamed the Wain
Which always wheels around in the same place
And looks across at Orion the Hunter, with wary eye.
It was that constellation, the only one
Which never bathes in Oceanus' stream
That the wise Goddess Calypso had told
To keep on his left hand as he crossed the sea.

Under Hercules is the story that the three stars in the tail of the Great Bear represent the three golden apples which Hercules had to fetch from the garden of the Hesperides. When these three stars culminate in the spring, Hercules is just rising in the east, meaning that he is just beginning his adventure.

The Babylonians saw a wagon in Ursa Major, the sort of wagon used to carry supplies for soldiers on the march (Figure 60A). Egyptians placed a bull's hind leg in these stars. In the Book of the Dead, this is alluded to as the constellation of the Thigh in the Northern Sky (Figure 61A).

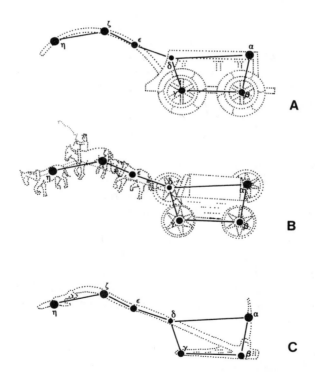

Figure 60. Ursa Major. A. The Wagon: Babylonian (E11). B. The Wagon with Horse Team: northwest Europe (E13). C. The Plough: northwest Europe (E14).

126

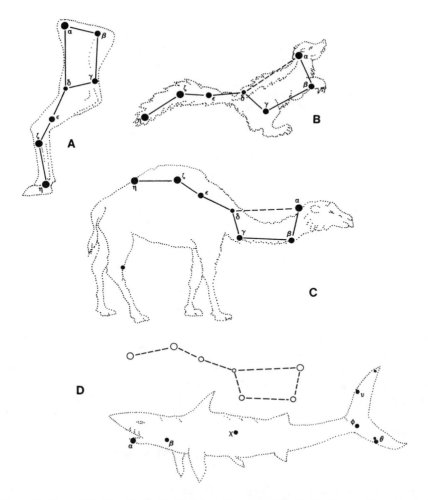

Figure 61. Ursa Major. A. The Bull's Hind Leg: Egyptian (E9). **B.** The Skunk: Sioux; central North America (E21). **C.** The Camel: North Africa (E22). **D.** The Shark: East Indies (E26).

The Romans saw seven oxen in these stars (Figure 59B). The proximity of these stars to the North Celestial Pole gave the impression that they were wheeling around this point, pulling perhaps a plough behind them to till the heavenly fields. Another version of this story has it that the oxen were tied to the polar axis and were driven on by Arcturus, assisted by his two dogs Canes Venatici, in order that the rotations of the heavens should never cease.

The natives of the Mentawai Islands and the Dayak in Borneo see a hog's jaw in the stars γ-, δ-, ε-, ζ-, η-Ursae Majoris (Figure 62A). (When I lived in the Dutch East Indies—now Indonesia—I often saw how

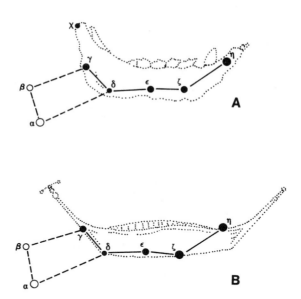

Figure 62. Ursa Major. A. The Hog's Jaw: East Indies (E25). **B.** The Prahoe, or Canoe: East Indies (E24).

important the pig was at various religious and other festivals, both as ceremonial offerings and as food. Often a stew was made of pigs' jaws cooked in a large pot from which the stew was ladled into bowls. It was customary to spit out any teeth that might have gotten into one's bowl, very much similar to the way that Americans spit out the seeds of watermelons.)

The Great Bear among the Chinese

When, due to precession, the Bushel in Sagittarius—the first house of the Black Tortoise—no longer fulfilled its purpose, another bushel was found in the stars that we call the Big Dipper. This asterism represented the Winnowing Shovel, or possibly a bushel to measure out rations to the people in times of food shortage during severe Winters or following a poor harvest, or shortages caused by plundering by the Barbarians from the north. In more recent times this same bushel represented the seat of the emperor and his government officials. The Hebrews also saw a bushel in these stars (Figure 63A).

The Chinese of the third millenium B.C. and after saw in the stars of Ursa Major the God of Literature, Wen-chang, sitting on his emperor's throne, giving audience to K'uei, Minister of Literary Affairs of the World. Behind K'uei was Chu-i, Mr. Red Coat, Minister Who Looks After the Welfare of Students. Next was Chin-chia, Mr. Gold Armour, a minister who searches for talent among young people who could later serve

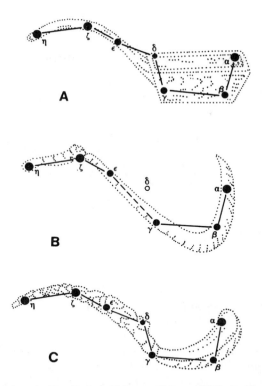

Figure 63. Ursa Major. A. The Bushel: Hebrew, Chinese (E10). **B.** The Sickle: Abchase; Caucasia (E15). **C.** The Big Dipper: Tlingit; northwest North America (E16).

the state well. Lastly, there was Kuan-ti, God of War—actually a god who prevented wars. Also present at Wen-chang's audience were such retainers as the emperor's groom, his horse, a court jester, and some of the emperor's favourite pets—a dog, a couple of multi-coloured birds and a bird of paradise (Figure 64).

The story of K'uei is rather an interesting one. K'uei was very gifted and talented and passed his literary examinations with flying colours. The winner of this examination competition was to be presented to the emperor, to receive the coveted reward of the Golden Rose. The emperor, on this occasion, had not been forewarned of the fact that K'uei had a deformed face. When the time came to hand over the rose, the emperor was so shocked by what he saw that the rose slipped from his fingers, fell onto the floor, and shattered into a thousand pieces. K'uei felt so disgraced by all this that he threw himself from a cliff into the sea. No sooner did he feel the water close over his head than he became aware that he was being lifted slowly upwards again. Soon he found himself astride a sea-monster named Ao, who carried him all the way up to the Jade Palace where the emperor received him kindly and gave him the

KUAN-TI   CHU-I   γ WEN-CHANG
CHIN-CHIA   K'UEI

Figure 64. Ursa Major. The Emperor Wen-chang giving audience to K'uei, Minister of Literary Affairs of the World; Chu-i, Mr. Red Coat; Chin-chia, Mr. Gold Armour; and Kuan-ti, God of War.

post of looking after the literary affairs of mankind. From this story came the expression *Tu-chun-Ao-t'ou*, "to stand on Ao's head"—in other words, to pass a test with flying colours.

Chu-i, Mr. Red Coat, also is an interesting personality. He was the sort of god who tried to help students who had to struggle hard to pass their examinations. There was a saying among students that anyone with a poor chance of passing might get a nod from Mr. Red Coat. This came about one day when an examiner, after having corrected a student's essay, put it aside as unsatisfactory. Suddenly, the paper was replaced by another in front of the examiner's very eyes. He examined the paper again and, at the same time, a reverend old gentleman dressed in red entered the room, nodded his head to the examiner as if he wished to indicate that the student should be passed. Then the old man vanished. The examiner, realising that this gentleman in the red coat was one of the supernaturals, could of course do nothing but bestow the literary degree upon the student.

Chin-chia, Mr. Gold Armour, armed with a flag and sword, was the god who went about in search of sons who would win literary honours and later would be promoted to high public office. When he saw a likely candidate, Mr. Gold Armour would wave his flag in front of the house of the candidate, thus marking the family for future honours. Mr. Gold Armour's flag was acknowledged as a fortuitous sign, but his sword could strike terror into the hearts of wicked students.

Kuan, the God of War, became—after a wild and boisterous career—China's renowned military hero. Kuan was made a duke, then a prince. Finally Emperor Luan-ti of the Ming Dynasty conferred on him the title Ti, Supporter of Heaven and Protector of the Kingdom. Kuan-ti has ever since been worshipped as the God of War.

The Great Bear among the American Indians

Several bear stories are known from among the American Indians. One of these takes place in a forest of oak trees. The trees in this forest were not fixed to their places. Every night, after midnight, the trees would move about and visit each other. One day, a bear lost its way in the forest and that night, at the stroke of midnight, the trees started to wander. The bear could not find its way out of the forest and, not used to the wandering trees, he could not avoid colliding with them. One of these proud oaks took umbrage when the bear did not apologise for colliding with the tree.

Indignant at this impoliteness, the oak began to chase the bear. Seeing that matters were not quite in his favour, the bear started to run as fast as he could. In the deep of the night a fantastic marathon took place, but the tree was not quite quick enough to catch the bear. This chase went on until dawn was near, at which time the tree was supposed to go back to its own place lest the Sun God should notice its absence. Furious that it had not been able to catch the bear, the tree made a last effort and reached for the bear with all its might. By stretching its longest branches it just managed to grab hold of the bear's tail. With a ferocious swing the tree tossed the bear into the skies. The bear soared all the way to the dome of Heaven, where it can now be seen as the Great Bear.

Among the American Indians, the body of the Bear is formed by the stars α-, β-, γ-, δ-Ursae Majoris, just like the Bear of the preclassical Greeks (Figure 59A). The only difference is that, usually, the Bear of the Indian's does not have a long tail. Instead, the three stars of the handle of the Big Dipper—ε-, ζ-, η-Ursae Majoris—are frequently viewed as three hunters who are pursuing the Bear. When they catch the bear they plan to cook him in the cooking pot, Alcor, Mizar's little companion star.

In the eyes of the Cherokee Indians of the southern Appalachian Mountains, the three hunters are chasing the bear from the Spring, when at midnight he stands high in the sky, until Autumn, when at midnight he is low on the northern horizon. Between these seasons the hunting scene moves progressively, day by day, across the sky towards the northern horizon where, each day, the whole spectacle of the celestial bear vanishes in the atmospheric haze of the horizon as the stars set (Figure 65). Only the stars of the three hunters are sufficiently bright to remain visible through the haze. This phenomenon gave rise to the notion that the three hunters move helplessly around after the bear has been killed.

The Kootenay Indians of the Columbia River drainage saw in the stars of Ursa Major a grizzly she-bear, the metamorphosis of a young Indian woman. This myth parallels the Greek myth of Callisto.

One of the most splendid of North American Indian fantasies involving the Great Bear, however, comes from the Iroquois Indians of the St. Lawrence River region and the Micmac Indians of Nova Scotia. To these

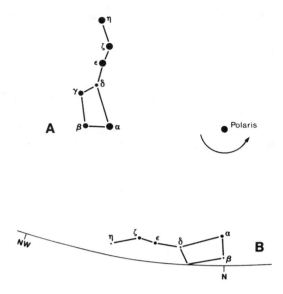

Figure 65. Ursa Major. The Bear Hunt of the Cherokee Indians of southeastern North America. **A.** The Bear and three hunters are fully visible when the constellation is high in the sky in Spring. **B.** In Autumn, when the constellation is near the horizon, the stars are dimmed so that only the three hunters ϵ-, ζ-, η-Ursae Majoris remain visible.

Indians, the quadrangle (α-, β-, γ-, δ-Ursae Majoris) represents a bear which, in this story, is hunted by seven Indians (Figure 66). These hunters all have bird names: Robin (ϵ-Ursae Majoris), Chickadee (ζ-Ursae Majoris), Moose Bird (η-Ursae Majoris), Pigeon (γ-Boötis), Blue Jay (ϵ-Boötis), Owl (α-Boötis), and Saw-Whet (η-Boötis). The hunter called Chickadee carries the pot, represented by Alcor, in which the bear will be cooked when it is finally killed.

In the Spring the bear leaves his den (represented by Corona Borealis, the Northern Crown) and the hunt begins. As Autumn approaches, the four Indians farthest from the bear abandon the hunt, their stars setting one after the other. When Autumn arrives, the hunters are no longer to be found after midnight at the lower transit of the bear (Figure 66). This leaves the three foremost hunters (Robin, Chickadee and Moose Bird) to continue the hunt. The hunter called Robin finally hits the bear with an arrow as, in Autumn, the bear attempts to stand on his hind legs. According to the Micmacs, the fatally wounded bear sprays blood onto Robin. Robin then shakes himself and thereby colours the leaves of trees blood-red. Just one red mark remains on Robin's breast, which explains how the Robin got its name *Redbreast*. The Iroquois say that it is the bear who shakes himself and colours the leaves of the forest. Finally, the hunt completed, the bear is prepared and eaten.

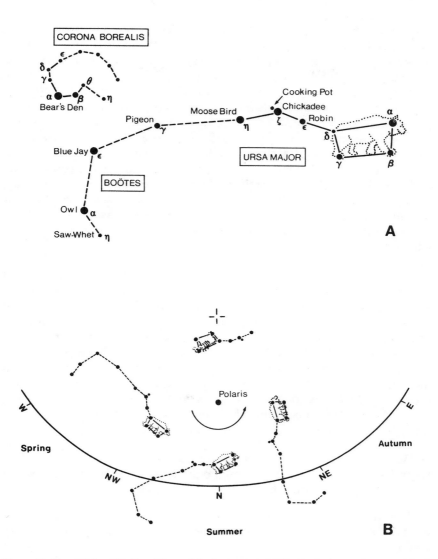

Figure 66. Ursa Major. The Bear Hunt of the Iroquois and Micmac Indians of eastern North America. **A.** Upon leaving his den (Corona Borealis) in the Spring, the Bear is pursued by seven hunters. **B.** The progressive circular movement of Ursa Major around the sky moves this constellation from the beginning of the hunt in Spring, through Summer and Fall when some of the hunters become lost, to the death of the bear in Autumn and subsequent movement of its skeleton, back side down, across the Winter sky toward rebirth and renewal of the hunt in Spring.

After the hunt, only the bear's skeleton remains in the sky, lying on its back as the quadrangle makes its upper transit (Figure 66). The bear spends the Winter in this position with its back (α-, δ-Ursae Majoris) turned toward the horizon. Another bear leaves the den the following Spring and the hunting scene is reenacted. In this way, the Indians have linked together, in a splendid myth, observed celestial phenomena and ordinary events of nature around them.

The Aztecs saw the stars of Ursa Major as their god Tezcatlipoca, who the Mayas called Hunracan—from which comes the modern word hurricane. Tezcatlipoca, "He Who Can Go into All Places," was an evil god who was always stirring up strife and war amongst men. He was a sorcerer too and could assume any form he wished. His favourite disguise was that of a jaguar, as which he roared through the countryside and the underworld with hurricane force. On one such occasion, when he wanted to rush into the underworld, his enemies slammed the door on him and he lost his lower left leg. That is the reason why he now hops around on an artificial leg. Tezcatlipoca also possessed a mirror with which he was able to spy upon mortals and see what they were doing.

On the other hand, Tezcatlipoca's brother, Quetzalcoatl, was a kind god who taught people many useful skills, such as how to smelt silver and set precious stones in jewelry, how to make statues, how to write signs in books and keep count of the Suns and Moons, how to build houses, and how to till the fields. One day Tezcatlipoca attempted, with near success, to destroy all Quetzalcoatl's good work. However, Quetzalcoatl changed Tezcatlipoca first into a jaguar, then a puppet. Quetzalcoatl then placed his brother in the sky where he must dance forever, sometimes upright on his pegleg and sometimes on his hands, depending upon whether the constellation happens to be over the eastern horizon (upright) or the western horizon (upside down) (Figure 67).

Figures 68 through 70 present yet other asterisms in the stars of Ursa Major, drawn from cultures throughout the world and attesting to the universal appeal of this constellation.

The interpretation of the 14 stars of the Great Bear and Little Bear has become a famous Dutch nursery rhyme, of which I give a free translation, as follows:

> At night when I lay myself to rest
> Fourteen angels for me do their best
> Two by my right hand
> Two by my left hand
> Two at my head-end
> Two at my feet-end
> Two who will cover me
> Two who will awaken me
> Two who will show me
> To Heaven's Paradise.

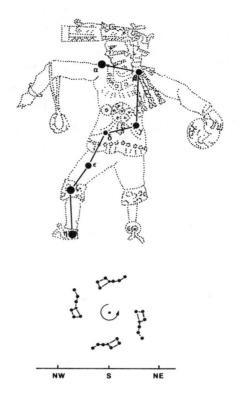

Figure 67. Ursa Major. The troublesome Aztec god Tezcatlipoca and his pattern of endless dance around Polaris (E23).

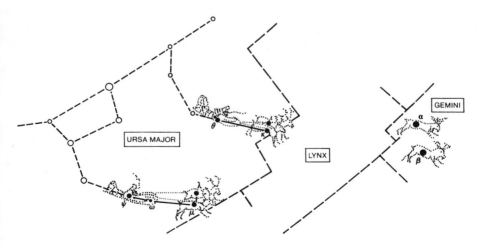

Figure 68. Ursa Major. Two hunters on reindeer sleds hunting moose: Chukchee; Siberia (E18).

Since the stars of the Bears never set over most of the Northern Hemisphere, perhaps they can be seen as guardian angels who keep a sharp eye on all the people below, and in particular on children who, as they lie in bed, can perhaps see those easily recognised stars before they go to sleep.

The Theme of the Great Bear

Why has Ursa Major so often been seen as a Bear? According to the late Dr. Helmet Werner of the Carl Zeiss optical firm in Oberkochen, West Germany, the widespread popularity of the constellation as a bear may be attributed to two simple facts of nature. First, the bear is a quadruped but is able to stand upright on two legs and move about like a human being. Much mythological significance has been ascribed to this similarity between the posture and movement of humans and bears. Second, the daily circumpolar movement of Ursa Major is simple, easy

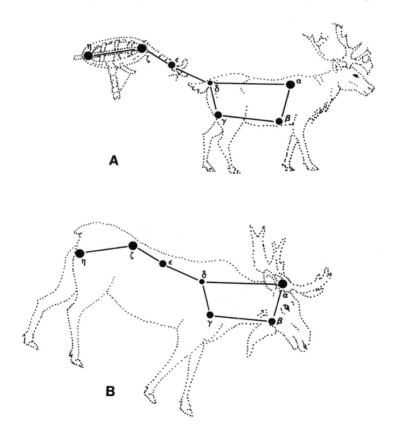

Figure 69. Ursa Major. A. The Kayak Stool and Reindeer: Eskimo; Greenland (E17). B. The Moose: Ostyak; Siberia (E19).

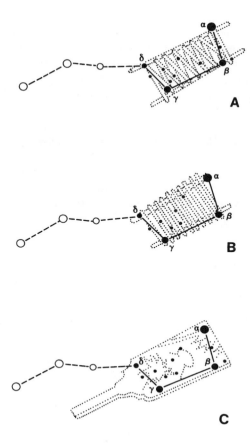

Figure 70. Ursa Major. A. A stretcher or litter: Arabs, Hindus, Omaha and Pawnee Amerindians, Minangkaban; North Africa, India, central North America, Sumatra (F65). **B.** A barbecue grill: Taulipang; Brazil (F66). **C.** The Battledore, or bat for hitting shuttlecocks: Japan (F67).

to observe, and can be imagined readily as similar to the shifting movement of a bear changing regularly from quadrupedal to bipedal to quadrupedal posture. As Ursa Major makes its daily transit around the Pole Star, it gives the appearance of a bear running on all fours when it is near the lower culmination of its transit. However, a few hours after lowest culmination the quadrangle gradually rises into an upright position, just as a real bear would do as it stands up in its cumbersome way (Figure 66B).

Points of Interest in the Great Bear

Simple field glasses will reveal a wealth of faint stars in and around the area of the Big Dipper. On a star map many nebulae are denoted, but many of these are too faint to be observed by ordinary telescopes.

Two well known nebulae in the Great Bear are M97 and M81. M97, the Owl Nebula, is a faint spot that can be found a little to the left of the star β-Ursae Majoris, or Merak. This is called the Owl Nebula because Sir John Herschel likened it to two great eyes staring at him from the depth of space. In the head of the Great Bear, near one of his ears, is M81—the famous spiral nebula of Ursa Major. Half a degree away is another nebula called M82.

The stars Mizar and Alcor, in the middle of the tail of the Bear, are seen easily with the naked eye as an optical double star. In a small telescope, however, it can be seen that Mizar is itself a double star. Reputedly, Mizar and Alcor were used in ancient times to test the eyesight of new recruits destined for military service. This is always a good pair of stars with which to test one's own eyesight.

Ursa Minor
The Little Bear

Ursa Minor represents Arcas, Callisto's son by Jupiter, as is described under Ursa Major. When Jupiter decided to place Callisto in the stars he also changed Arcas into a bear and placed him near his mother so that the two would never be separated again. Thus they wheel together around the North Celestial Pole.

Two different orientations of the Little Bear are known. In one, the line of the back—β-, ζ-Ursae Minoris, is toward Ursa Major. In the other, the feet point towards Ursa Major (Figure 71).

The Egyptians saw a hippopotamus in the stars of Ursa Minor (Figure 72A). The stars appear on the planisphere of Denderah as an enormous

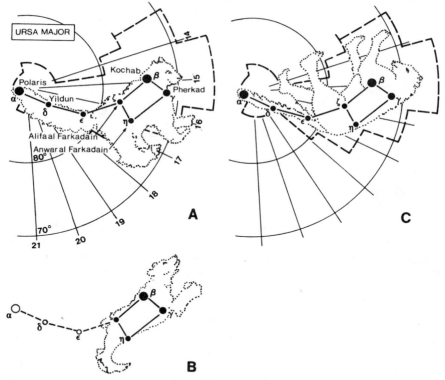

Figure 71. Ursa Minor. A. The Little Bear in typical long-tailed form, with back toward the Great Bear. (F68; Apianus, German, ca. A.D. 1535.) **B.** The Little Bear, with short tail, and back toward the Great Bear. (F70; Hipparchus, Greek, 2nd Century B.C.) **C.** The Little Bear, with long tail and feet toward the Great Bear. (F69; al-Sufi, 10th Century A.D.)

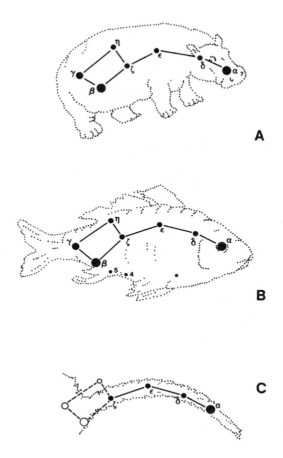

Figure 72. Ursa Minor. A. The Hippopotamus: Egyptian (F73). **B.** A fish: Arab (F72; al-Kazwini, Persian, 13th Century A.D.) **C.** Cynosura, the Dog's Tail: Greek (F71).

hippopotamus, or sometimes as a crocodile, who devoured the dead who had lived a life of dreadful sin. Some of these stars have also been identified as the goddess Hesmut, or Shesemtet, the Raging Mother. Sometimes Hesmet is shown holding in her hand an object that resembles a ploughshare which has been identified as some stars of the Big Dipper in Ursa Major. The hieroglyph of this hippopotamus stood for the heavens in general, the Cosmic Mother who possessed great powers of nature. The Cosmic Mother is supposed to have been Ta-Urt, wife of Set and mother of Isis. Since these northerly stars never set, they were sometimes considered to be evil. The hippopotamus was strong and therefore moved around to keep a constant vigil on these circumpolar stars, lest they might cause some harm.

Ursa Minor has been recognised as a constellation since at least about 600 B.C., when Thales of Miletus recognised it as formed by the group β-, γ-, η-, ζ-, ε-, δ-, α-Ursae Minoris. The three stars ε-, δ-, α-Ursae Minoris form the tail, which — as in the case of Ursa Major — is unnaturally long, and for the same reason.

Aratus (ca. 270 B.C.) described the relationship between the two bears in his *Phaenomena:*

Encompassing (the Pole) two Bears wheel together
Wherefore they are also called the Wains.
Now they ever hold their heads each toward the flank of the other
And are borne along, always shoulder wise,
Turned alternate on their shoulders . . .
Now the one, men call Cynosure (Ursa Minor)
And the other Helice (Ursa Major)
It is by Helice that the Acheans (Greeks) on the sea
Devine which way to steer their ship, but in the other
The Phoenicians put their trust when they cross the sea.
But Helice appearing large at earliest night
Is bright and easy to mark; but the other is small
Yet better for sailors: for in a smaller orbit wheel all its stars.
By her guidance then, the men of Sidon (Phoenicians)
Steer the straightest course.

From the foregoing passage we can see that the constellations were in use as navigational aids by the time of Aratus.

Hipparchus (ca. 160–120 B.C.) clearly recognised a bear in Ursa Minor. The head was in β-Ursae Minoris and the forelegs were at γ-Ursae Minoris. Eratosthenes (ca. 230 B.C.) and Ptolemaeus (ca. A.D. 150) both referred to the stars ζ-, η-, γ-, β-Ursae Minoris as a Brick, Πλινθιον. Ptolemaeus also sometimes simply called this constellation the Quadrangle.

The German cosmographer Petrus Apianus (A.D. 1495–1522) created in this polar region the three Hesperides, the daughters of Atlas and Hesperus (Figure 73A). Mythology tells us that the Hesperides had their abode at the western end of the world where they guarded the golden apples which Gaia, Goddess of the Earth, had given to Hera when she married Zeus. Ladon, the dragon who never slept, guarded these apples. One of Hercules' twelve tasks was to steal these apples, which he succeeded in doing. The apples were given to King Eurystheus, who dedicated them to Athena, who in turn restored them to their rightful owner, Hera.

As with Ursa Major, numerous other constellations have been created in Ursa Minor by various cultures. Several of these constellations are represented in Figures 72 and 73.

Points of Interest in Ursa Minor

The Ursids meteor shower can be expected each year on 20–21 December. This shower comes from the neighbourhood of β-Ursae Minoris, the brightest star in the Little Bear.

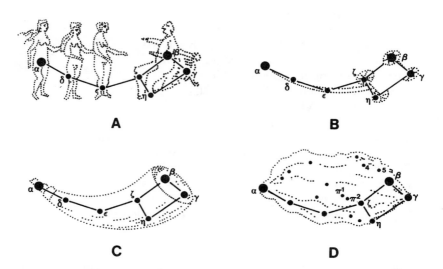

Figure 73. Ursa Minor. A. The Hesperides. (E27; Apianus, German, ca. A.D. 1535.) **B.** The Lesser Wagon: Babylonian (F74). **C.** The Bocina, or Hunting Horn: Spanish, Portuguese (F75). **D.** Myrobalanum, the edible fruit of the Indian almond and cherry plum trees: Arab, Perisan (F77).

Lynx
The Lynx

In Book V of the *Metamorphoses*, Ovid described how Pluto abducted Proserpina, daughter of Ceres, Goddess of Agriculture. Ceres searched far and wide but could not find a trace of her daughter. In her sorrow Ceres smashed all the ploughs and caused the crops to die of blight, and vowed that she would not let anything grow until Proserpina was restored to her. The Earth lay barren, and this brought ruin to mankind.

The story of Ceres' search for her daughter is a very long one but, finally, it was revealed to Ceres that Proserpina was residing in Hades as the wife of Pluto and Queen of the Underworld. Out of sympathy for Ceres, Zeus decreed that Proserpina would spend six months in the Underworld with her husband Pluto and the other six months in the Upperworld with her mother Ceres. This arrangement, of course, symbolises the seasons of Winter, when nothing grows, and Summer, when crops grow and mature. Ceres was pacified with this arrangement and she instructed Triptolemus to take her dragon-pulled chariot and rain the seeds of harvest upon the raw earth and fallow soil.

Triptolemus steered his chariot to Scythia where King Lyncus lived. The king asked the purpose of Triptolemus' visit. "Ceres has commanded me to bring these gifts. They are seeds and they should be scattered across your lands. If you do this it will bring you a harvest free of all weeds and thorns."

The savage and jealous king received this news with envy, because he felt that he should be the one to take the credit for this gift from Heaven. So Lyncus made his guest welcome, entertained him royally, and lulled him to sleep. When Lyncus was about to run his sword through Triptolemus, however, Ceres suddenly changed Lyncus into a Lynx. As punishment, Ceres put the former king in a part of the sky where the stars were so dim that nobody could see him in his new guise, unless—so people said—one had the eyes of a lynx. Thus savagery and arrogance were rewarded by relegation to insignificance.

There is a rather obscure reference to stars near Lynx in the *Phaenomena* of Aratus:

> For dread is the Bear and dread stars are near her.
> Such stars are borne along, beautiful and great, one
> In front of her fore paws, one on her flank and one
> Beneath her hind knees. But all singly, one here,
> One there, are wheeled along without a name.

143

Whether Aratus was referring to the stars that we call Lynx today is not at all certain. Officially, the constellation Lynx was a creation of the Polish astronomer Johannes Hevelius (A.D. 1611–1687) (Figure 74).

Most of the stars of Lynx are of magnitude 6. Even α-Lyncis, in the tip of the tail, is only magnitude 3.5 and the eye, star 15, is magnitude 4.5. Although the sixth magnitude stars nicely outline the hind quarters and body lines of Lynx, very few people have a sky that is sufficiently dark and free of pollution to pick out these faint stars with the naked eye.

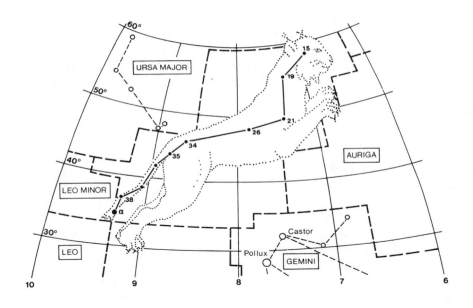

Figure 74. Lynx. The Lynx, after an illustration in Thomas Heath's *Popular Astronomy*, A.D. 1908. (JS52; Staal, British, A.D. 1986.)

Cancer
The Crab

The Crab is a constellation with very few bright stars. The most conspicuous pattern is, perhaps, a small square of stars, γ-, δ-, η-, θ-Cancri, which is fairly easily located between the constellations of Gemini and Leo, the north of the head of Hydra (Figures 75, 76).

Under Hercules and Hydra is the story of how Juno sent a crab to prevent Hercules from killing the Hydra and how Hercules trampled the crab under foot and succeeded in killing the Hydra. The celestial Crab of the later Classical period is that of the Hercules story.

Earlier, the Egyptians had seen their sacred beetle, Scarabaeus, in the stars of Cancer (Figure 77A). The serrations on the front of the beetle were symbolic of the rays of the Sun. These beetles make dung pellets and roll them into their underground living quarters. Eggs are laid in these pellets. Consequently, the Egyptians regarded the pellets as symbols of birth, resurrection, and immortality. Replicas of Scarabaeus were

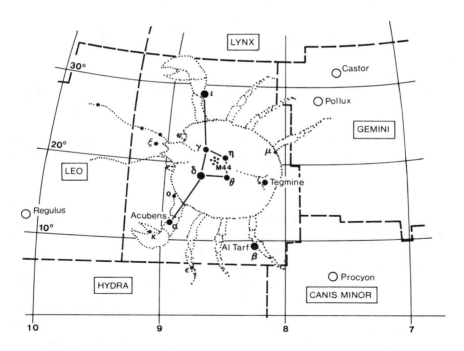

Figure 75. Cancer. The Crab. (A33; al-Sufi, Persian, 10th Century A.D.)

145

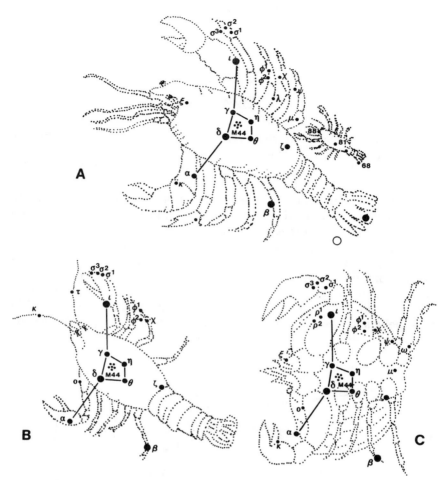

Figure 76. Cancer. A. The Greater and Lesser Lobsters (A32; Cellarius, German, ca. A.D. 1661.) **B.** The Crayfish. (A31; Dürer, German, ca. A.D. 1515.) **C.** The Crab crawling across the outer side of the celestial sphere, as viewed from within the sphere. (A35; Flamsteed, English, ca. A.D. 1729.)

carved out of stone or metal to be used as charms. Another practice was that the Egyptians used to remove the heart of a deceased person and replace it with a large carving of Scarabaeus, often richly decorated with jewels, before the body was embalmed.

In the time of Hipparchus, about 150 B.C., the Sun in its annual track through the zodiac would reach the Summer solstice in Cancer, thus giving the Crab the longest day of Summer. For quite a while the Sun seemed to hesitate at its solstice height before descending again to its lower Autumn and Winter heights. This hesitancy can be seen in the peculiar movements of the living crab. Anyone who has watched a crab on the beach

146

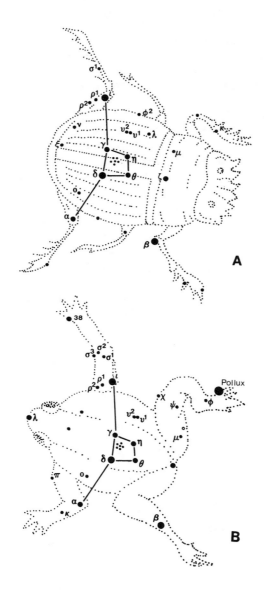

Figure 77. Cancer. A. Scarabaeus, sacred beetle of the ancient Egyptians (A36). **B.** The Frog: Tibet (A37).

must have noticed its peculiar sideways walk, its sudden forward movements, and its occasional circles—as though it cannot make up its mind where to go.

Praesepe, the Beehive

In the middle of the faint square of stars is a fuzzy patch, M44, commonly known as Praesepe, the Beehive. If one observes this patch on a clear night late in January or early in Spring through field glasses or a small telescope, one can easily imagine a hive of busy bees in the profusion of silvery stars of this cluster.

Sometimes Praesepe is also seen as a manger, or as a pile of hay from which some of the four nearby stars, or donkeys, are eating (Figure 78). The four stars are sometimes called Aselli, Latin for donkeys.

Another story involving the Praesepe relates to King Midas who once wished that everything he touched should turn to gold. His wish was fulfilled, but he soon realised that he would starve to death because even the food he touched turned to gold. As punishment for his greed, the gods gave Midas donkey's ears. These ears were very long and Midas tried to hide them under a cap, but his barber found out and told the reeds about them. The reeds whispered the secret in the wind, and soon everybody knew about the ears. As a warning to others, Midas was later placed in the stars of Praesepe. The faintness of the patch depicts Midas' attempts to hide his long ears, but they keep falling out of his cap as is attested by the four stars around the patch.

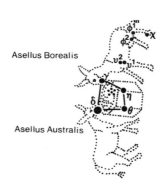

Figure 78. Cancer. Two donkeys feeding from the manger in which Jesus once laid. (A38; 15th Century.)

Coma Berenices
The Hair of Berenice

Under Leo the story is told of Pyramus and Thisbe, the unfortunate lovers who were driven needlessly to their death by confusion arising from the coincidental appearance of a lion. Pyramus, after finding Thisbe's blood-stained veil, killed himself because he thought a lion had devoured Thisbe. He did not realise that Thisbe had lost her veil as she ran for help. Jupiter placed the veil in Heaven as an eternal reminder to young lovers to express their emotions with caution. This veil is also sometimes seen as the tuft of hair at the tip of Leo's tail (Figures 54, 79).

This same constellation appears as Coma Berenices in the story of King Ptolemy Soter and his beautiful wife, Berenice. It happened that Ptolemy had to fight against the Assyrians. Berenice feared for his life and went to the temple to pray that her husband would emerge victorious from the fray. In her anxiety she promised to sacrifice her hair to Venus, the Goddess of Love, if Ptolemy were to return safely.

After weeks of tension and waiting Ptolemy returned safe and sound. The nation rejoiced but when Berenice told Ptolemy about her promise to sacrifice her hair, Ptolemy was very upset because it was the crowning glory of his queen; it was looked after with loving care by Berenice's ladies-in-waiting, it had the admiration of the nation, and it gave inspiration to the poets. Nothing, however, would change Berenice's mind.

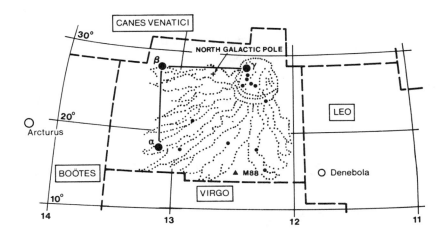

Figure 79. Coma Berenices. The Hair of Berenices. (JS26; Staal, British, A.D. 1986.)

She went to the temple where her beautiful locks were cut off and laid on the altar by the priests.

The next day when the king went to the temple to have a look at his wife's hair, he was furious to find the hair had been stolen. He summoned the priests and would have put them to death, then and there, had not the court astronomer intervened in the nick of time. "No, no, your majesty. Do not blame the priests. It is not their fault. Wait until it is dark and I will show you where your wife's hair is."

So when day turned into night the astronomer took the king to look at the night sky. "Look! Dost thou not see the clustered curls of thy queen, too beautiful for a single temple to possess, placed there by the gods for all the world to see? Look! They glitter like a woven net, as golden as they were on Berenice's head." And there, between Canes Venatici, Boötes, Leo and Virgo, twinkled a mass of very faint stars. The astronomer declared that Jupiter had descended from Heaven the night before to take the golden locks up to the heavens where they it could be admired by the whole world, not only by one nation. The king was satisfied with this explanation and Berenice was delighted that Venus had so honoured her.

There was no such romantic story as the beautiful hair of Queen Berenice in the skies above China. Instead, the whole region in and around Coma Berenices represented to the Chinese a scene at the Royal Court (Figure 80). In the centre of this Court was the Royal Prince, T'ai-tsze, surrounded by all his dignitaries—counselors, generals, other military officers, judges, a body guard, an escort, etc. All of these asterisms belong to the sixth house of the Red Bird, which contains no less than 26 paranatellons. Close inspection of the Royal Court reveals that there is a right hand side and a left hand side to this assembly of dignitaries. On the right hand side are a pair of counselors, called Chang-siang and Tsse-siang; a pair of generals called Chang-tsiang and Tsse-tsiang; a right judge, called Yeou-tchi-fa; a body guard, Hou-fun—the "Fast Tigers," soldiers and officers who accompany the prince, always marching at the double; and an officer in charge of the retinue, Tsoung-koan. On the left hand side are a pair of counselors and generals, named as on the right side; a left hand judge, called Tso-tchi-fa; three aulique counselors represented by one person called San-koung; nine noblemen, represented by one person called Kiou-k'ing; five officers for special duties, called Wou-tchou-hao; a guard commander, Lang-tsiang; the officers' mess, Lang-wei (our Coma Berenices); officers of honour, represented by one person, called Hing-tchin; and the permanent escort, Tchang-tchin.

The naked eye can really see a wealth of glitter in the area of Coma Berenices, but a small telescope reveals an even more glorious display of astral abundance.

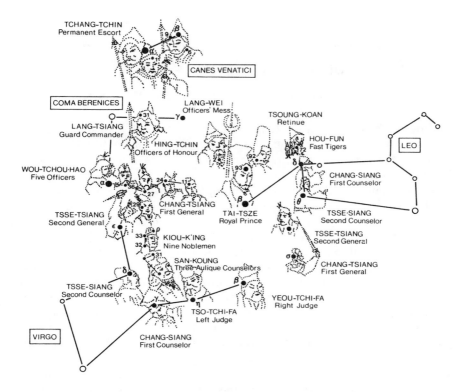

TCHANG-TCHIN
Permanent Escort

CANES VENATICI

COMA BERENICES

LANG-WEI
Officers' Mess

TSOUNG-KOAN
Retinue

LANG-TSIANG
Guard Commander

31

γ

HOU-FUN
Fast Tigers

LEO

HING-TCHIN
Officers of Honour

WOU-TCHOU-HAO
Five Officers

CHANG-SIANG
First Counselor

TSSE-TSIANG
Second General

CHANG-TSIANG
First General

T'AI-TSZE
Royal Prince

TSSE-SIANG
Second Counselor

KIOU-K'ING
Nine Noblemen

TSSE-TSIANG
Second General

SAN-KOUNG
Three Aulique Counselors

CHANG-TSIANG
First General

TSSE-SIANG
Second Counselor

YEOU-TCHI-FA
Right Judge

TSO-TCHI-FA
Left Judge

VIRGO

CHANG-SIANG
First Counselor

Figure 80. Coma Berenices. A scene at the Court of the Royal Prince, T'ai-tsze. (Staal, British, A.D. 1986.)

Points of Interest in Coma Bernices

One glance at a star map will show the amateur astronomer that the Hair of Berenice does not consist only of a multitude of stars, but that it is also the home of several clusters, nebulae and galaxies. The best known and most famous galaxy here is M88 (Figure 79).

Coma Berenices is the constellation in which the North Galactic Pole is situated. Just the same as an imaginary axis through the Earth cuts the sky at a point where we place the North Celestial Pole near the star Polaris, so can we imagine an axis running through the centre of the gigantic disc-like city of stars, or galaxy, known as the Milky Way. This axis would pass through a point in the sky in the constellation of Coma Berenices; this point is referred to as the North Galactic Pole. The South Galactic Pole lies diametrically opposite the North Galactic Pole in the Southern Hemisphere, in the constellation Sculptor. The South Celestial Pole lies in Octans near the star σ-Octantis.

Boötes and Canes Venatici
The Bear Driver and his Hunting Dogs

Sliding one's eyes down the tail of the Great Bear will lead the observer to the star Arcturus, or α-Boötis. Boötes can best be found by first locating Arcturus and then by tracing the outlines of a boy's great kite, by drawing lines along the stars ε, δ, β, γ and back to α. In the *Almagest* of Ptolemaeus, the star α-Boötis, although the brightest star in that part of the sky, is not incorporated in the actual main list of Boötes' stars. However, in the *Informatae*, the additional information, we find *Quae est inter crura et vocatur Arcturus, Subrufa*, "the star between the legs and the one which is called Arcturus, slightly red in colour."

Boötes actually means Ox Driver (Figure 81), but in connection with the two Bears he is often seen as a Bear Driver who chases the Bears around Polaris (Figure 82A). Other views represent Boötes as a Herdsman (Figure 82B) or Ploughman. The Plough is, of course, the bucket shaped figure outlined by the stars Merak, Dubhe, Phecda and Megrez of the Great Bear. The Three Horses are Alioth, Mizar and Benatnasch. It is said that Boötes invented the plough to enable mankind to till the ground better. This pleased Ceres, the Goddess of Agriculture, so much that she asked Jupiter to place Boötes amongst the stars as a token of gratitude.

In yet another story, Boötes is seen as Icarius, a grape grower in Attica. Icarius was a very friendly man and unwittingly gave Bacchus, who happened to be incognito, the freedom to inspect his vineyards. Bacchus was so impressed with these vineyards that he decided to tell Icarius how to make wine from grapes. Icarius did so, and was delighted with his results. Icarius invited all the other shepherds and friends of the neighbourhood to a festival to taste the heavenly liquor for themselves. The party was a great success but they all drank too much and, under the influence of the wine, fell asleep. When they awakened, they discussed what had happened and decided that Icarius must have planned to poison them all. They agreed that Icarius should pay for this with his life. They overpowered the innocent man in his sleep, killed him, and threw his body in a ditch.

The Dogs, Canes Venatici or Asterion and Chara, missed Icarius, their master, and began to whine. Erigone, Icarius' daughter, heard the dogs and let them off their leashes. Immediately, the dogs started to sniff and search for Icarius until they found his dead body in the ditch. In despair, Erigone committed suicide and the dogs leapt in the deep ditch to die with their master.

The whole tragic story of Icarius, Erigone, and the Dogs can be seen unfolding in the sky. When Boötes (Icarius) culminates high in the south, Taurus, the Bull, the sacred animal of Bacchus, has just set, which means that Bacchus has left Icarius after his visit, leaving the wine recipe with Icarius. At the same time Orion also sets which means that the shepherds fall asleep under the influence of the wine. Next morning when Orion comes up he appears as an enormous giant, just awakening from his sleep and brandishing his club, the signal that the shepherds have decided to kill Icarius. This can be seen in the west where Boötes sinks below the horizon. Then, as the shepherds sneak off, notice how Orion sinks down to the west. In the east rises the constellation of Virgo, the Virgin, who represents Erigone. The Hunting Dogs also rise and the search begins. When Boötes culminates again it means that the dogs have found Icarius. Next we see the trio sink towards the west which indicates the end of the story when they all die.

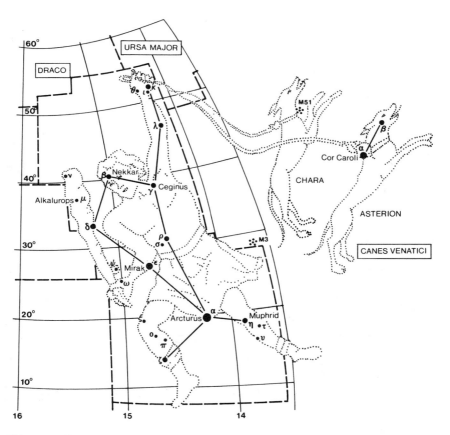

Figure 81. Boötes and Canes Venatici. The Bear Driver and his Hunting Dogs. (A28; Flamsteed, English, ca. A.D. 1729.)

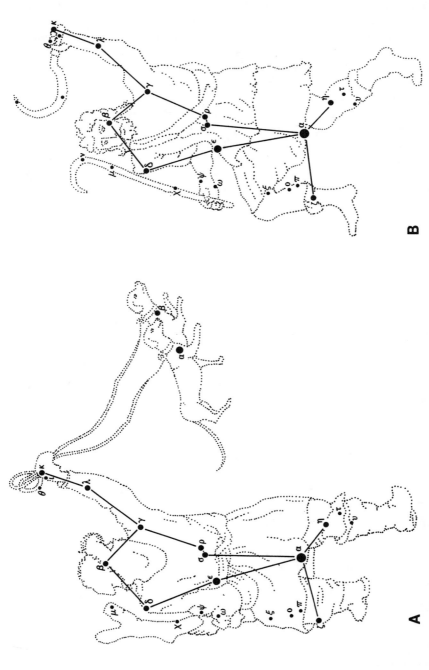

Figure 82. Boötes and Canes Venatici. A. Boötes as Bear Driver with his Hunting Dogs. (A27; Boötes: Ptolemaeus, Greek, 2nd Century A.D.; Dogs: Hevelius, Polish, ca. A.D. 1690.) **B.** Boötes as Herdsman, holding sickle and shepherd's crook. (A24; Bayer, German, ca. A.D. 1603.)

154

The Kobeua Indians of northern Brazil saw a Piranha in the stars of Boötes (Figure 83). In the tropics, this constellation rises more or less horizontally above the eastern horizon, belly upwards, and sets below the western horizon, belly downwards.

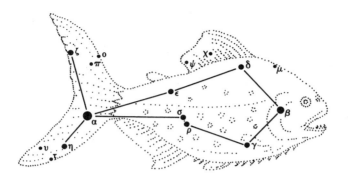

Figure 83. Boötes. The Piranha: Kobeua; Brazil (A29).

Points of Interest in Boötes

Arcturus, α-Boötis, is a reddish-orange coloured star located at a distance of approximately 34 light years from Earth. The surface temperature of Arcturus is in the region of 5000° K. Arcturus is a famous star in modern history, because it was used in 1933 to open the World Fair in Chicago. Forty years prior to that date there was another World Fair in Chicago and it was thought appropriate that the light of Arcturus, which left the star in 1893, should be used to open the World Fair forty years later in 1933, when the light rays had crossed the empty void of space and reached our Earth. The rays from Arcturus were caught in a telescope which focussed these beams on a photoelectric cell, thus generating a small electric current which, after amplification, was employed to turn on the lights of the fair.

The star ε, or Mirak or Pulcherrima, "the Most Beautiful One," is a double star. These stars can be seen as separates with the use of a small telescope. The two components are orange and green.

Cor Caroli, or α-Canum Venaticorum, is a double star—the components being orange and blue. Halley named this star Cor Caroli, "the Heart of Charles II," because the personal physician of the king had noticed that this star became exceptionally bright on the return of Charles to London. The story goes that α-Canum Venaticorum shone with a much greater brightness on the night of 29 May 1660, when King Charles II returned to London after his defeat by the army of Richard Cromwell. Hence the Royal Crown on top of a heart shaped figure around the star Cor Caroli.

In Canes Venatici are many nebulae but, unfortunately, these are only visible through the largest of telescopes. Among these nebulae, however, we must mention the famous Whirlpool Nebula, M51. This nebula, seen in plan view from the Earth, reveals a central core from which distinct spiral arms rotate outwards. The nebula lies just below Benatnasch, the star in the end of the tail of the Great Bear.

A globular cluster, M3, lies halfway along the line between Cor Caroli and Arcturus. M3 is a fine object for viewing through a telescope of 8 inches or larger aperture. Photographs reveal that this cluster contains some 30,000 stars.

Between 10–12 March the meteor shower named the Boötids may be expected from a point near the star ζ-Boötis, slightly below and to the east of Arcturus.

Virgo
The Maiden

To find the constellation Virgo, start from the handle of the Plough, slide the eyes down this handle, follow its slight curvature, and one will arrive at Arcturus, the brightest star of the constellation Boötes. Continuing south from Arcturus one will find another conspicuous star named Spica. This is the brightest star in Virgo and represents an ear of grain (Figure 84).

Virgo is sometimes identified as Ceres, the Goddess of the Fields and Growing Crops and, in general, of all agricultural activities. Sometimes, however, Ceres is personified as Proserpina, Ceres' beautiful daughter. It was this beauty which brought trouble to Proserpina. One day the God of the Underworld, Pluto, was having a ride in his black chariot, pulled by black horses, to have a look at the fields of Springtime as they

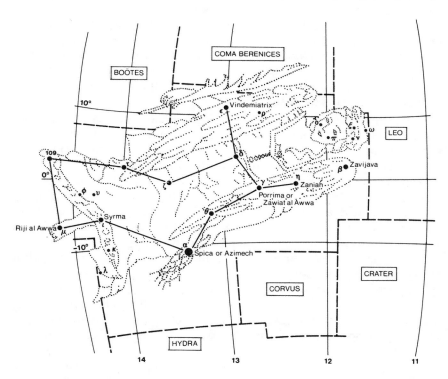

Figure 84. Virgo. Virgo, the Maiden. (E28; Flamsteed, English, ca. A.D. 1729.)

gradually started to come into bud. It so happened that Proserpina was playing with some friends in the fields, and when Pluto noticed her he was so impressed by her tender beauty that he swiftly abducted her in his chariot and hurried back to the dark place of the world of the wraiths and the dead.

Ceres was in utter despair, and she decided to have nothing further to do with the crops until she found Proserpina. So it happened that everything died, nothing would grow, and the Earth was threatened with a worldwide famine. This Jupiter could not tolerate. He ordained that Pluto should allow Proserpina to be with Ceres for six months of each year in the Upperworld and that she could spend the other six months with Pluto in the Underworld. This is why we can see the constellation of Virgo from March until August, during the months when the grain and other crops grow, ripen and are harvested. From August to the following March, Virgo is invisible; at that time the fields lie barren because Ceres weeps when separated from her daughter Proserpina.

Virgo is usually depicted with an ear of corn in her hand and wearing flowing robes, but on old star maps she is sometimes depicted as Astrea, Goddess of Justice, holding scales in one hand and a sword in the other. Very close to Virgo are the stars of the constellation Libra, the Scales. Astrea used these scales to weigh the good and bad of men. Long ago Astrea mixed with mortals; she was their Goddess of Justice and administered just law. This unspoiled golden race of men did not know feuds or wars. They obtained all their needs from the soil which they tilled themselves with the oxen and the plough, and no foreign ships brought goods from far away. All was peaceful and everything was shared equally according to the needs of the people.

Then the silver race of men gradually appeared on Earth. Although this race was slightly inferior to the golden race Astrea still visited them, but more rarely, and usually to tell them about their crimes. Her voice was stern and she had no gentle word for any of them.

When the silver race died out there was created a brazen race, men who fashioned swords and weapons to conduct wars on each other. Astrea loathed this race; she decided to leave the Earth and flew off to take her place in Heaven where we can still see her nowadays. This is why we can sometimes see her depicted with wings like an angel.

Other nations have known Spica and Virgo in different ways, but always involved with some form of justice or with something to do with agriculture. In Egypt she was known as Isis. It is said that Isis once was frightened by the monster Typhon and fled quickly. In the process, she dropped a sheaf of grain which scattered all along the path she took. This path is now known to the Chinese as the Yellow Road—another name for the zodiac.

The ancient Chaldeans saw the Goddess Ishtar in Virgo. Ishtar's husband, Tammuz, was once overpowered by King Winter and dragged off to the Underworld. Ishtar neglected the fields and the Winter, with its ice and snow, took possession of them and nothing would grow. Ishtar searched the Underworld and found Tammuz, but she also became imprisoned in the Underworld. When the gods in Heaven saw the deplorable state of the Earth, they sent a message to the Underworld keeper to release Ishtar and Tammuz. This legend is obviously similar to that of Proserpina and Ceres.

Points of Interest in Virgo

Spica, a star of magnitude 1.21, is the 16th brightest star in Heaven and is located at a distance of about 220 light years from Earth. Spica is one of 9 stars often used in navigation. The others are Hamal, Aldebaran, Pollux, Regulus, Antares, Altair, Fomalhaut and Markab. Spica is a very hot star with a temperature of about 25,000° K.

γ-Virginis is a double star easily visible with a small telescope. These stars have a period of about 170 years. γ sits as a central star in a cup-shaped configuration formed by the stars β and η on the right, and δ and ε on the left. ε is also known as Vindemiatrix, the Grape Gatherer, the one who collects the liquor in the bowl.

The diamond of Virgo is formed by drawing lines from Spica, to Denebola, to Cor Caroli, to Arcturus in Boötes.

Spica is about 2° below the ecliptic. Regulus, "the Heart of the Lion," is about 1° above the ecliptic while μ-Geminorum, one of the feet of the Twins, is about 2° below it. A line drawn through these three stars will indicate approximately the path of the ecliptic—a handy guide to use for this purpose early in Spring if no planets are visible.

Hydra, Corvus, and Crater
The Female Watersnake, the Crow, and the Beaker

During the later part of March and the beginning of April, round about midnight, it is of the greatest interest to try and find the winding, grotesque outline of the Watersnake slithering low over the horizon below Libra, Virgo, Leo and Cancer. The head of Hydra lies under Cancer and is rather pointed. The heart of the Snake is in the star α-Hydrae, or Cor Hydrae or Alphard. The remainder of the Snake's body is composed of very faint stars which, once located, form a fine winding line reminiscent of the slithering movement of a snake (Figure 85).

Hydra was perhaps the snake which Hercules had to combat. The snake encountered by Hercules had nine heads. Every time one head was cut off it was replaced by two new ones. Eventually, Hercules burned the stump of each decapitated head and so prevented the two new heads from growing. Juno made Hercules' task more difficult by sending a crab after him, which—as Cancer—can be seen in the sky above the Snake's head. Hercules, however, crushed the crab under his feet.

When, in the Northern Hemisphere Summer, the Sun rises in the Crab, the head of Hydra also comes up—meaning that Hercules has managed to cut off the first head, because the stars of Hydra begin to fade in the morning light. This goes on until the end of October, by which time the Sun has traveled through the zodiac constellations Leo and Virgo, which lie parallel to the stars of Hydra. This lengthy transit is symbolic of the long battle of Hercules as he overpowered the snake bit by bit. Every time Hercules cuts off another head, a little bit more of Hydra disappears in the morning sunlight.

Halfway down the Snake's body we find the two small constellations of Corvus, the Crow, and Crater, the Beaker. One story maintains that the Crow was the bird of Apollo. Once Corvus had white feathers and a beautiful singing voice, but he lost these as punishment for not carrying out the orders of Apollo, who had sent him to fetch a beaker of water. Corvus left immediately to carry out Apollo's order. On his way, however, he passed a fig tree upon which were some lovely juicy figs. However, these figs were not quite ripe. Corvus, who thought it a pity to leave these figs behind, decided to wait until they ripened. This he did and, finally, he enjoyed a tasty meal.

When Corvus had eaten all of the figs he suddenly remembered his task of fetching water for Apollo. Corvus quickly filled the beaker and raced back to Apollo, offering some weak excuse that the Watersnake had hindered his efforts to scoop up the water. Apollo, however, was

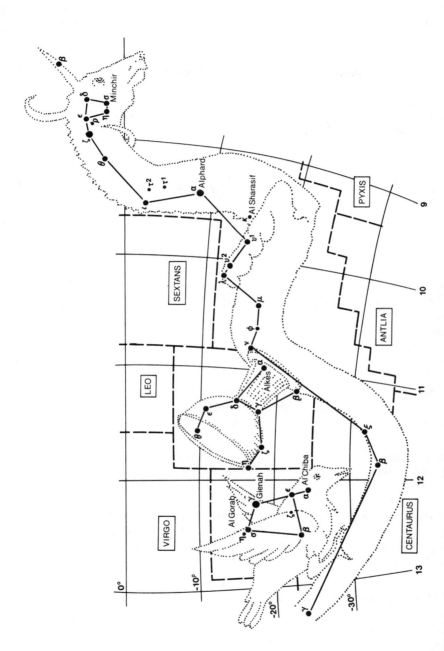

Figure 85. Hydra, Corvus and Crater. The Female Watersnake and its eternal passengers, the Raven and the Beaker. (Hydra: C8; Corvus: B22; al-Sufi, Persian, 10th Century A.D.; Crater: J50; Staal, British, A.D. 1986.)

161

not so easily fooled; he punished Corvus by changing his shiny white feathers into dirty black ones and by altering the birds beautiful voice into a dull screech. The worst punishment of all was that Apollo placed Corvus and the Beaker in the sky on the Waternake's back. Hydra was instructed to make sure that Corvus never came within reach of the beaker to quench his thirst. This arrangement can be seen clearly in the Spring as the Snake glides across the horizon. Corvus, a small but very clear constellation, is rather forlornly perched on Hydra's back. As Hydra slithers forward with great coils of its elastic body, the Beaker always remains well in front of Corvus.

Corvus is shaped in a sort of trapesium cornered by the stars α-, β-, δ-, γ- Corvi. Crater is made up by the stars α-, β-, γ-, δ-Crateris, which represent the stem of the Beaker. On either side of γ and δ are very faint stars shaped like the bowl of an ancient silver drinking vessel.

Under Hercules one can read that the Beaker is the Sun's boat in which Hercules crossed over the Straits of Gibraltar. The Sun uses this boat to travel from west to east during the night so that it can refresh itself and be ready to begin its journey across the sky next morning.

The Roman poet-astronomer Gaius Julius Hyginus (ca. A.D. 1) placed a mulberry tree in front of Hydra (Figure 86A). Some say this was the tree of the Golden Apples of the Hesperides which were guarded by Ladon, a dragon or snake. Hercules overpowered Ladon and triumphantly carried off the branch with the golden apples.

Two other stories relate to the mulberry tree. In the first, Hydra must be used as a "locator constellation." The stars of the tree will then be found in Canis Minor. The star α-Canis Minoris, our Procyon, should be near the centre of the branches and foliage. The setting for this scene is near the end of the story of Pyramus and Thisbe, as described above under Leo. As Pyramus lies dead, Thisbe uses his sword to take her own life so that the two will be together in death. Before she dies, Thisbe addresses the tree growing at the place of their secret meeting. "And you, o tree, whose branches weave their shadows dark over the pityful body of one lover shall soon bear shade for two. O fateful tree, be the memorial of our twin death and your dark fruits the colour of our mourning." Then Thisbe placed the sword beneath her breast and leaned upon it till she sank to the ground. The ripe fruit of the tree, originally white, turned first rose-coloured and, later, black—the colour by which we know ripe mulberries today.

The other story that connects Hydra with a mulberry tree goes back to Polyidus of Argos. Polyidus, a soothsayer, was summoned with others to the court of King Minos of Crete, whose son Glaucus had mysteriously disappeared. Minos had been advised that the person who could give an appropriate comparison between a cow which assumed three different colours and any other object would hold the secret to lead him to his missing son. Polyidus likened the cow to a mulberry tree, whose

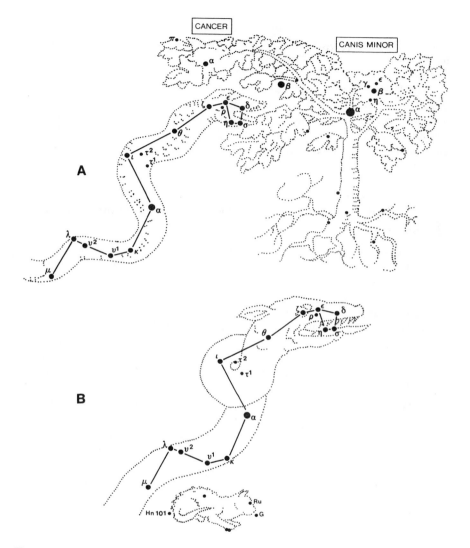

Figure 86. Hydra. A. The Female Watersnake and the Mulberry Tree. (C11; Hyginus, Roman, ca. A.D. 1.) **B.** Hydra and Felis, the Cat. (C10; Bode, German, ca. A.D. 1800.)

fruit was at first white, then red and finally black. And so Polyidus was charged with finding Glaucus.

By his prophetic powers and the guidance of an owl and some bees, Polyidus found Glaucus—drowned in a vat of honey. Minos then ordered Polyidus to restore the boy to life. Polyidus was unable to perform this miracle, so Minos entombed Polyidus with the dead boy. In the tomb Polyidus saw a snake crawl towards the boy. He killed the snake but, lo . . . another snake appeared and put a leaf on the dead snake, which was immediately restored to life. Polyidus broke off a piece of the leaf and placed it on the body of Glaucus, who miraculously came to life. When news of this reached Minos, Polyidus was released and presented with a great sum of money for his services.

The French astronomer Joseph Jerome le Francais de La Lande (A.D. 1732–1807) used the stars of Hydra as "locator stars" to facilitate locating a small constellation he created and published in his *Bibliographie Astronomique* in 1805. La Lande called the new constellation Felis, the Cat. Allen, in his book *Star Names*, provided the following anecdote (p. 221):

> I (La Lande) am very fond of cats. I will let this figure scratch on the chart. The starry sky has worried me quite enough in my life, so now I can have my joke with it.

The German astronomer Ehlert Bode (A.D. 1747–1826) included the constellation Felis in *Die Gestirne* where it appeared as Katze, while the Italian Father Angelo Secchi (A.D. 1818–1878) called it Gatto. Today the constellation is no longer used.

The Chinese saw a willow branch in the stars we associate with Hydra's head (Figure 87A). The third house of the Red Bird was called Lieou-siou, the House of the Willow. The Red Bird was the emblem of Summer, the season for making sacrifices to the ancestors. A feast, or sacramental reunion, known as Hia accompanied the common celebration of this responsibility. A willow branch, a symbol of immortality and eternity, was planted beside the doors of the temple of the ancestors as part of this Summer activity. The people would observe in which direction the branch leaned and then prepare the feast in that direction.

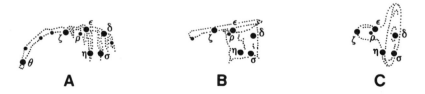

Figure 87. Hydra. A. The Willow Branch: Chinese (F45). **B.** A flag: Jaina; India (F46). **C.** A potter's wheel: Hindu; India (F47).

The Chinese saw a cart in the stars of Corvus (Figure 88E). This cart represented the seventh house of the Red Bird, and is the 28th lunar station. The Chinese called this constellation T'ien-tche, the Celestial Cart, which symbolised the carts and chariots that brought the feudal princes to the Great Feast of Pleasure in the last month of Summer. Chinese astrologers said that Tso-hia, the left wheel of the chariot or cart (δ-, η-Corvi) represented the feudal subjects of the same name as the emperor's, while Yeou-hia, the right hand wheel (α-Corvi) represented the subjects of different family names. These carts were laden with contributions consisting of the offerings of the feudal subjects. T'ien-tche presided over luggage and transportation, and—because of the great speed with which these carts could move about—it also presided over the wind.

Numerous other mythological renditions of the stars in Hydra, Corvus and Crater are known. Several of these are represented in Figures 87–89.

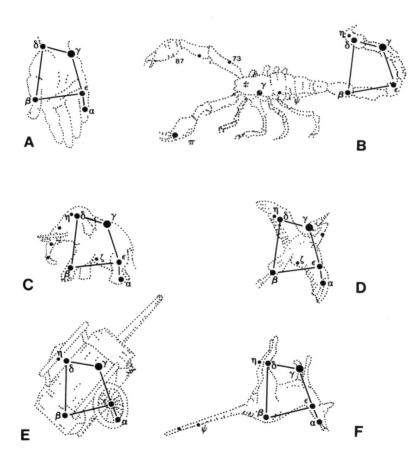

Figure 88. Corvus. A. A hand: Hindu; India (F16). **B.** A scorpion: Aztec; Mexico (B23). **C.** An elephant: Khmer; Kampuchea (F17). **D.** A heron: Kobeua, Tukano; Brazil (F20). **E.** A cart: Chinese (F18). **F.** A kangaroo: Wailwum; Australia (F21).

165

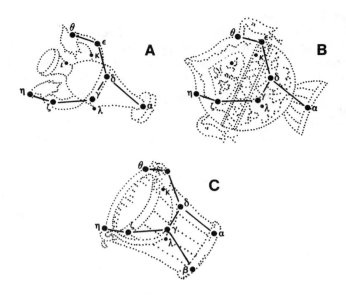

Figure 89. Crater. A. An amphora: Spanish (F22). **B.** A wine cup: Persian (F23). **C.** A bucket: German (F24).

Antlia
The Air Pump

The Abbé Nicholas Louis de La Caille invented the constellation Antlia presumably to eternalize the age of inventions of instruments used in science. This constellation is strewn with extremely faint stars; α-, ι-, ε-Antliae are of magnitude 4.5 and others are of magnitudes 5 and 6. Consequently, Antlia has not been frequently represented pictorially. Figure 90 shows an old fashioned laboratory air pump consisting of a cylinder and operating handle.

Allen noted that this constellation is of special interest because it contains the variable star S-Antliae. Discovered in 1888, this star has the unusually short period of 7 hours, 46 minutes, 48 seconds. For a while, this was the shortest period known for a variable star.

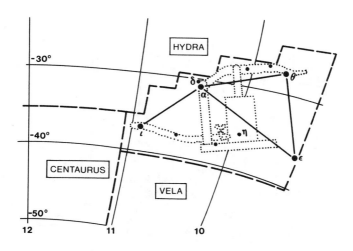

Figure 90. Antlia. The Air Pump. (JS2; Staal, British, A.D. 1986.)

Pyxis
The Mariner's Compass

Claudius Ptolemaeus (ca. A.D. 150) mentioned the stars of Pyxis which he placed in Malus, the Mast of the Ship Argo (Figure 51). The placement of a compass so close to the ship Argo is of course very fitting, although it is doubtful that Jason had a compass when he made his hazardous journey to Colchis to retrieve the golden fleece. Ptolemaeus' compass could have been only a very primitive one, like the ones the Chinese used. It probably consisted of a steel needle which had been wiped with a lodestone to give it its magnetic properties. The needle would have been fastened to a small piece of wood and made to float in a bowl of water. The north-seeking pole of the needle would indicate north.

The constellation Malus has fallen into disuse. La Caille gathered up the stars of Malus and formed them into a ship's compass. This constellation is officially named Pyxis Nautica, but astronomers today refer to it as just Pyxis. A modern compass, employing the principles of the primitive compass described above, is illustrated in Figure 91.

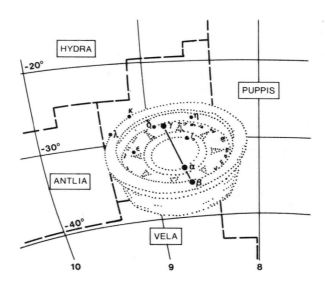

Figure 91. Pyxis. The Mariner's Compass. (JS70; Staal, British, A.D. 1986.)

Sextans

The Sextant

The Polish astronomer Johannes Hevelius had a beautiful observatory at his house in Danzig. Hevelius was also a man of law and, at one time, was the mayor of Danzig. In his observatory, Hevelius had a collection of beautifully decorated instruments, including a huge sextant which he used for measuring star positions, in which he was ably assisted by his wife. Unfortunately, Hevelius' observatory burned down in September, 1679, with the loss of all of his instruments. As Hevelius put it—"Vulcans overcame Urania;" Vulcans was the God of Fire and Urania the Muse of Astronomy.

To commemorate his sextant, Hevelius created the constellation Sextans Uraniae. Unfortunately, Hevelius placed this constellation in a rather unrewarding area of the sky between Leo's fore paw and the first coil of Hydra, a region not befitting his famous sextant at all. The stars here are very dim. The brightest star, α-Sextantis, is only magnitude 4.5 and the remainder are of magnitudes 4.9 to 6. Although the constellation is officially known as Sextans Uraniae, astronomers today refer to it as Sextans (Figure 92).

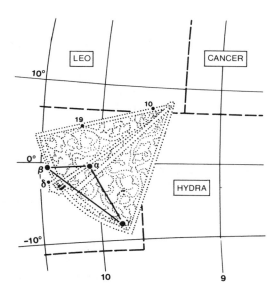

Figure 92. Sextans. The Sextant (D50).

Centaurus and Lupus
The Centaur and the Wolf

Centaurs—four-legged creatures that were half horse, half man—were a savage lot. One legend explaining their origin holds that Ixion, the scorching midday sun, was in love with Juno, Jupiter's wife, and desired to have her. To protect his wife, Jupiter created a cloud in the image of Juno. Ixion had intercourse with this cloud and thereby became the father of the Centaurs.

Another legend explaining the origin of the Centaurs is that the god Cronos slept with Phylira, a sea nymph. In order that his wife Rhea should not recognise him while he was with Phylira, Cronos changed himself into a horse. Consequently, the offspring of Cronos and Phylira were half horse, half man.

Chiron, the only gentle and intellectual Centaur, was an educator; he knew music, poetry, mathematics and medicine. Many heroes such as Achilles, Aesculapius, Hercules and Jason were educated by Chiron. After Chiron's death, Jupiter placed the old master amidst the stars where he now shines as the constellation Centaurus (Figure 93).

Another type of Centaur were the Sileni. These creatures were also half ungulate and half man, but they walked on two legs instead of four. The Minotaur, a creature half bull and half man, walked on four legs as did the true Centaurs. The Minotaur was kept in the labyrinth on the Isle of Crete. Both Centaur and Minotaur have been represented in the constellation Centaurus, often being shown presenting some kind of large animal as an offering (Figures 93, 94).

In figures of the Centaur in which an offering is being made, the offering incorporates stars of the constellations Scorpius, Norma, and especially Lupus, the Wolf. Lupus is a very old constellation, but does not contain many bright stars and is, therefore, relatively inconspicuous. The Classical Greek and Roman view of Lupus saw a nondescript wild animal—a beast—in these stars. When pictured, however, this beast usually was shown as a recognisable animal. Some Arab groups pictured Lupus as a leopard or lion. West Europeans have considered Lupus to be a wolf.

During the time of Ptolemaeus, the Southern Cross—Crux Australis—was not known as a distinct constellation. Ptolemaeus considered the stars of the Southern Cross to be part of the rear legs of the Centaur. Much later these stars were separated from the Centaur and given the name Crux Australis.

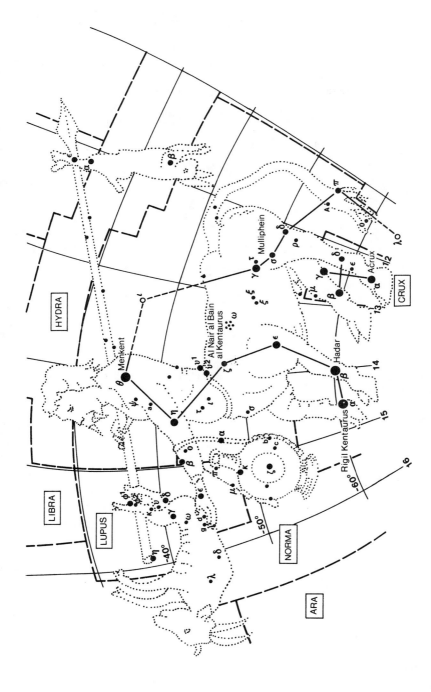

Figure 93. Centaurus and Lupus. Centaurus as a Minotaur, offering a goat to be placed on Ara, the Altar. (B9; Hyginus, Roman, ca. A.D. 1.)

171

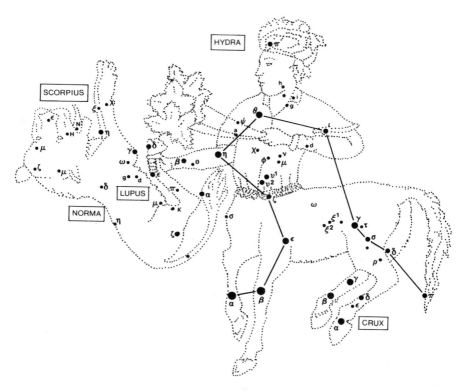

Figure 94. Centaurus and Lupus. Centaurus as a Centaur, offering a lioness. (B10; al-Sufi, Persian, 10th Century A.D.)

The Stars of Summer

Summer is probably the worst season of the year for star spotting. The nights are never very dark and are rather short, and it is vacation time and the mind is perhaps not so easily focused on the majesty of the heavens. But the Summer months do have certain advantages for star hunting. The nights are rarely cold and one can enjoy outdoor observation, in comfort, for a much greater length of time than in the Winter. There is, too, something very wonderful about the calmness of a Summer's night when all is at peace. Whether you are on vacation, perhaps at the seaside, or at home, what greater relaxation is there than to cast an eye at your starry friends who cannot disappoint you with their ever unfolding stories.

Paramount in the Summer sky is Hercules, the great strong man of antiquity who performed such heroic deeds and who was finally lifted to the sky to be eternalised in the stars. There is Ophiuchus, the Medicine Man of ancient times, who carries the wriggling Serpent in his mighty hands. In the stream of the Milky Way we can spot the outlines of the graceful Swan. The Swan is the best friend of Phaethon, the son of Helios, who tried to steer the Sun Chariot one day and came to bitter grief while doing so. The Milky Way is the scorched path of the hazardous ride of Phaethon. The Eagle flies along the eastern bank of the Milky Way while the Lyre, or Vulture, lies on the western bank. High in the zenith stands the threatening Dragon, whereas low over the horizon creeps the Scorpion—followed by his arch enemy Sagittarius, the Archer. Libra, the Scales, reminds the sky watcher of celestial justice.

Cygnus
The Swan

During the Summer months and early in Autumn, Cygnus, the Swan—also known as the Northern Cross—can be seen fairly high overhead in the Northern Hemisphere. Cygnus, looking like a giant cross lying against the background of the silvery light of the Milky Way, is easy to recognise. To see a swan in this cross does not demand a great deal of imagination. The upright of the cross is the long stretched body of the Swan in flight, with α-Cygni (Deneb) in its tail. γ-Cygni is the Swan's heart and β-Cygni, or Albireo, is the head. The cross bar, made up by the stars ζ-, ϵ-, δ-, ι-, κ-Cygni, forms the outspread wings of this swan in flight (Figure 95).

There are various stories about the Swan. One legend says that Cycnus was the friend of Phaethon, the mortal son of Helios, who tried to drive the Sun Chariot for one day. Phaethon could not manage the fiery steeds and became a menace along the celestial highway, endangering the heavenly vault and the palaces of the gods as well as the Earth and its inhabitants. Finally, Phaethon was catapulted out of the Sun Chariot by Jupiter himself, and he fell to Earth like a shooting star where he landed in the river Eridanus.

Cycnus could not believe that his faithful friend was dead and did all he could to collect the charred bones from the river bed, so that he could give Phaethon a proper burial. In those days it was believed that, unless the human remains were given a proper resting place, the soul would not have peace in the Underworld but, instead, would roam as a ghost in the Upperworld. So again and again Cycnus dived into the waters of Eridanus until he had collected all the remains of his friend's body. Jupiter and his heavenly host were very moved by the devotion Cycnus showed for his dead friend Phaethon. So, eventually, when Cycnus had given his friend a proper resting place, Jupiter performed a miracle. Cycnus' voice grew thin and reedy; white feathers began to sprout all over his body and webbed membranes started to grow between his toes. Wings came forth from his arms and, where his lips once were, a long beak now protruded. His name was changed from Cycnus to Cygnus, and so the Swan was created. This particular swan was placed in the stars by Jupiter amidst the Milky Way, the scorched path of Phaethon's disastrous ride. The offspring of this swan, however, shunned fire and always stayed in tranquil pools and lakes.

Another story involving the swan is that of the love scene between Jupiter and Leda, the wife of Tyndareus, King of Sparta. One evening,

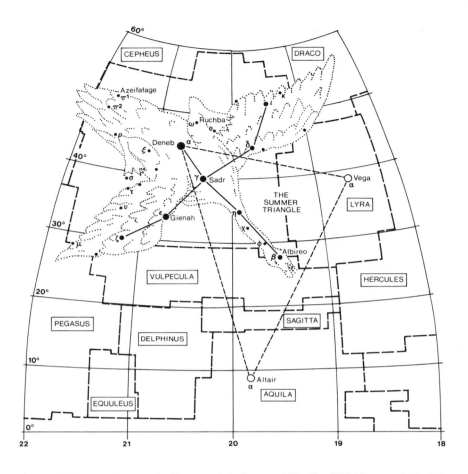

Figure 95. Cygnus. Cygnus, the Swan, and the Summer Triangle. (B28; Flamsteed, English, ca. A.D. 1729.)

as Leda took a bath in a pool, Jupiter—watching from on high—fell desperately in love with her. He could not wait a moment longer, so he changed himself into a swan and sailed gracefully from Olympus down to the lake and swam up to Leda. He looked to be a magnificent swan of irridescent whiteness. Leda stroked the friendly creature. After a while, Jupiter discarded his disguise and lay with Leda, from which union were born Pollux and Helen. The same night, however, Leda also lay with her own husband, Tyndareus, by whom she became the mother of Castor and Klytamnestra. So Castor and Pollux were brothers, but Pollux was immortal whereas Castor was mortal; the difficulties this caused were described under the legend of Castor and Pollux.

In ancient Greece the constellation we now know as Cygnus was known as the Bird ('Ορνις). The Romans gave it the more specific title of the Swan. There are other variants of the name of this constellation,

176

such as the Duck and the Hen. The Swan was Venus' personal bird. In this sense, the Swan could represent the disguised Jupiter who made love to Leda or the boy Cycnus who was transformed into a swan by Jupiter. Early Christians saw in the stars of Cygnus the Cross of Calvary, now known to astronomers as the Northern Cross.

How the Swan provided the down and feathers for Antenteh's tub was described in the story of the Fishes. In the Oriental stories of the Swan described under Lyra, the first stars of Aquila and Lyra, called Altair and Vega, were considered two gods in love. These gods were separated by the Milky Way because they thought more about their own love-making than taking care of their divine duties. Only once a year were they allowed to meet each other, this when the Swan—who in the Far East is called the Magpie—formed a bridge by which the lovers could cross the stream of the Milky Way.

Points of Interest in Cygnus

α-Cygni is a double star with a very high surface temperature, estimated to be approximately 10,000° K. This is a fine white coloured star, called Deneb by the Arabians, but also sometimes called Arided. The distance between this star and Earth is not known for certain, but is estimated to be about 1500 light years. β-Cygni is also a double star, and is called Albireo.

Near the tail of the Swan, in the Milky Way, is a bright cloud of ionised hydrogen with obscured regions, shaped somewhat like the continent of North America. Consequently, this area is referred to as the North American Nebula.

The stars α-, γ-, ϵ-Cygni form three corners of a parallelogram. The fourth corner is the star 61-Cygni. 61-Cygni became famous after 1837 when the Prussian astronomer Friedrich Wilhelm Bessel of Königsbergen, for the first time in history, measured the distance of a star from Earth. Bessel reasoned that if you look at, say, a tree, you will see this tree against the background of, perhaps, a distant church. If you now walk to another point a few hundred yards away from your first observation point and look again at the same tree, you will find that the tree is not seen any more against the background of the church but has shifted to, let us say, the background of a distant hilltop. This *apparent* change in the position of an object is called parallax. Bessel attempted to use the parallax of several stars to determine their distance from Earth. The distance of most stars from Earth is so great, however, that a difference of only a few hundred yards between observation points on Earth will produce no apparent shift in the position of the distant stars. Nor will there be any visible shift even if one were to observe a star first from one side of the Earth and then from a point diametrically opposite it on the other side of the Earth. Even the diameter of the Earth's orbit—186,000,000 miles—will not produce an apparent shift in the position of some stars. Bessel did, however, detect a very small apparent shift in the placement of 61-Cygni. This shift was only 1/2660th part of the width of the full Moon, but from this parallax the distance of 61-Cygni from Earth was calculated at about 11 light years.

Meteor showers may be seen coming from κ-Cygni between 9–25 August. There is also another stream in July and August coming from α-Cygni. These streams are named the Cygnids.

Aquila
The Eagle

South of the Swan on the eastern bank of the Milky Way lie the stars of the Eagle. The Eagle has always been a bird of kings, and is found frequently on heraldic signs, shields of warriors, banners, and flags. Aquila was Jupiter's bird, the one that can rise highest of all. Aquila's brightest star is α-Aquilae, or Altair, "the Rising One" (Figure 96).

Aquila has carried out many a difficult task for Jupiter. For example, it was the Eagle who swooped down upon Ophiuchus and killed him with one of Jupiter's arrows. On another occasion, when one day Hebe twisted her ankle and could not be hostess at the table of the gods, Jupiter ordered Aquila to fly down to Earth and select the most handsome youth he could find to serve as cup bearer and wine pourer. Aquila

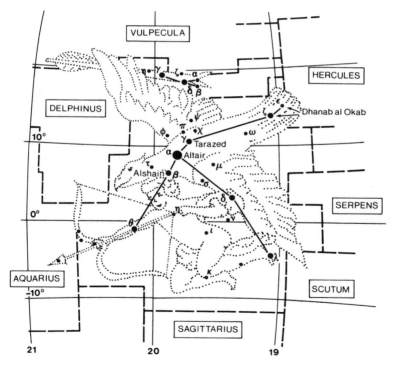

Figure 96. Aquila and Sagitta. Aquila, the Eagle, abducting Ganymede, and Sagitta, the Arrow. (Aquila: A10; Hevelius, Polish, ca. A.D. 1690; Sagitta: A8; Dürer, German, ca. A.D. 1515.)

sailed down from the Olympus and noticed Ganymede, the son of the King of Troy, who was peacefully tending his father's herds. Aquila hovered overhead and then with great skill dived down, lifted Ganymede in his talons, and flew back to Olympus. So Ganymede was promoted from a royal shepherd to a celestial waiter of the gods of Olympus, where he was accepted as their equal and pleased the eye of all by his manly beauty. Under Aquarius, the Water Carrier, was the story of how Jupiter eternalised Ganymede in the stars of Aquarius, which are located just below the stars of the Eagle. So, the rape of Ganymede is symbolised by these two constellations in the sky.

Aquila also was ordered to carry out the terrible punishment inflicted on Prometheus, one of the Titans, who had managed to conceal secretly a ray of sunlight in the hollow of a reed and take it to mankind. This act gave mortals fire and, of course, meant that mortals could now cook their food, warm their houses, and work iron into weapons. This act and its consequences displeased Jupiter very much. As punishment, poor Prometheus was chained to the Caucasus Mountains, where the Eagle came to eat his liver every day. Prometheus' liver would grow back but, each day, Aquila came again. This went on until one day Hercules set Prometheus free by killing the Eagle with a poisoned arrow. Jupiter placed the Eagle among the stars in commemoration of his devoted service.

Aquila, the Eagle of Jupiter, frequently is depicted with either both wings closed or one wing stretched out, symbolising the fact that he is falling, mortally wounded.

In Hindu religion Brahma was the creator of the world, Shiva was the destroyer of the world, and Vishnu was the preserver of the world. Vishnu sent his messages to the world through mighty hero-teachers of which Rama, Krishna and Buddha were the greatest. In the stars of Aquila the Hindus saw the footprints of Vishnu, made as he strode through the heavens going about his business (Figure 97A). This asterism also represents Sravana, the Fig Tree, the 23rd Hindu lunar station.

The Jaina of India pictured within part of Aquila a pikolan, or shoulder yoke (β-, α-, γ-Aquilae) with two baskets (σ-, μ-Aquilae). This type of yoke and basket assembly (Figure 97B) was used to transport agricultural

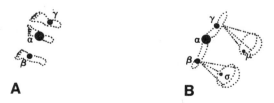

A **B**

Figure 97. Aquila. A. The Three Footsteps of Vishnu (F1). B. The Pikolan, or Shoulder Yoke and Baskets (F2).

goods and other merchandise to and from market. This asterism also represents the second Jaina lunar station.

Points of Interest in Aquila

α-Aquilae, or Altair, is a brilliant star of approximately the first magnitude located at a distance of about 16 light years from Earth. β-Aquilae lies below, and γ-Aquilae lies above, Altair. This trio sometimes reminds the observer of the belt stars in Orion. η-Aquilae is a variable star with a period of about seven days.

A line drawn from Deneb in the Swan, to Altair in the Eagle, to Vega in the Lyre forms a distinct triangle called the Summer Triangle (Figure 95). This triangle can be seen until late in the Autumn, over the western horizon, until it finally disappears below the horizon towards the end of November.

Sagitta
The Arrow

The Arrow which killed Aquila is also to be found in the stars, slightly above the Eagle. Some see the Arrow pointing to the east, others to the west. In conjunction with the story of Aquila it should be seen pointing to the west, aimed at the Eagle. The stars α-, β-Sagittae form the two-pointed arrow which was used in the Roman army (Figure 96).

In conjunction with Hercules, who lies west of Aquila, the Arrow is seen to point eastward. The stars α-, β-Sagittae then become the feathers of the shaft.

In his *Phaenomena*, Aratus finished describing Sagittarius, the Archer, when he continued:

> Further up there is another arrow shot . . . alone without
> A bow. By it is the Bird (Cygnus) outspread nearer the
> North, but hard at hand, another bird (Aquila) tosses in
> Storm, of smaller size but cruel in its rising from the
> Sea, when the night is waning and men call it the Eagle
> Or storm-bird.

The three birds Cygnus, Aquila and the Vulture (Lyra) are sometimes seen as the Stymphalian birds which Hercules shot with the arrow Sagitta. Then again Sagitta is seen as the arrow which Hercules used to kill the Eagle of Jupiter who daily pecked out Prometheus' liver.

Lyra
The Lyre or the Vulture

On the western edge of the Milky Way we find a small compact constellation called Lyra—the Lyre, the Harp, or the Vulture (Figure 98). This constellation includes Vega—a star of great beauty. Blue in colour, Vega is the fourth brightest star in the heavens.

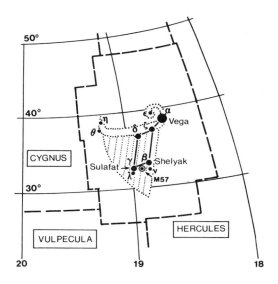

Figure 98. Lyra. The Lyre. (F49; al-Sufi, Persian, 10th Century A.D.)

Mythology tells us that one day Mercury rested by the banks of the Nile when he happened to see an empty tortoise shell. He picked up the shell and toyed with it for a while. Suddenly he noticed hollow echoes coming from the shell while he tapped it. These echoes gave him an idea. Mercury fastened several strings to the shell and, with his magic touch, produced the most exquisite sounds—sounds audible only to the ears of the immortals. Mercury took this lyre with him to Olympus where Apollo became very interested in the instrument. Apollo possessed a staff, called the caduceus, made from three shoots—one shaped into a handle, the other two twisted and intertwined at the top. This staff was an emblem of life and death; it also was supposed to bring wealth and prosperity to the owner and give the owner the power to fly. Mercury exchanged the lyre for the caduceus. Ever since, with winged sandals and the caduceus in his hand, Mercury has been the swiftest messenger of the immortal gods.

Mercury taught Apollo to play the lyre. Later, Apollo passed the lyre on to his son, Orpheus, and it is always Orpheus with whom we associate the lyre.

On the day that Orpheus married Eurydice, a fatal accident happened. Eurydice stepped on a viper which bit her heel. She died instantly. Orpheus was inconsolable and decided to go to the Underworld and see Pluto, King of the Realm of the Dead, to see if he could retrieve his wife. Orpheus charmed Pluto with his lyre. Also Proserpina and all the spirits of the dead were unable to resist the wonderful music which expressed the sorrow of the bereaved husband. Eventually, they all agreed that Eurydice should be allowed to go to the Upperworld again with Orpheus. Pluto, however, imposed one condition. Orpheus was not to look back until they had left the dim realm of the dead. Agreeing to this condition, Orpheus and Eurydice set out on the journey back to the light of the Earth. But, when they had nearly reached the gate that would lead them to freedom, Orpheus panicked and glanced back for only a fraction of a minute to see if Eurydice was really following. It was too late. He just saw her slide back again into the doom and gloom of Hades, this time forever. No wooing with his lyre could now redeem Eurydice.

The story says that Orpheus roamed the hills and the woods playing his lyre, sweet but sad melodies flowing from the magic tortoise shell. Even the trees and the wild animals came to listen and gathered around him while he played. Many beautiful girls, brought under the spell of his music, tried unsuccessfully to enamour him with their charms. Finally, the rejected girls, furious at this denial of their beauty, swore that they would seek revenge by killing Orpheus. At first they did not succeed because every weapon they used against him, be it knife, arrow, or stone, stopped in midair on hearing the enchanting melodies of Orpheus' lyre. Only when the infuriated girls shrieked so awfully in their madness were the lyre's sweet tones overpowered. The girls then fell upon Orpheus and stabbed him to death. Thereafter they cast the lyre into the river, at which time it gave a discord.

Jupiter, having seen all of this, sent a vulture to scoop the lyre out of the river. The lyre was then placed in the heavens, where it can still be seen today.

The Arabs called part of this constellation Al Naar al Waki, the swooping "Stone Eagle of the Desert." The word Vega, the name of the brightest star in Lyra, derives from this Arab name and means the "Plunging One."

This little constellation is easily seen as a Harp, the four faintest stars just by Vega forming a nice parallelogram depicting the tortoise-shell instrument. Lyra has also been seen as such diverse objects as a tortoise, clay tablet, vase, etc. (Figure 99).

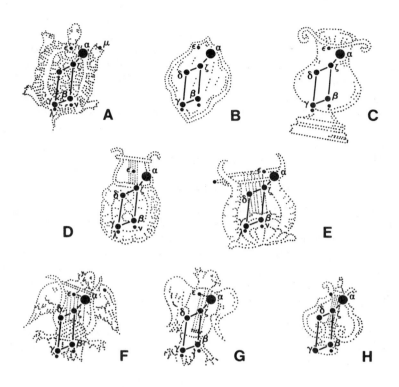

Figure 99. Lyra. A. The Tortoise (F51; al-Sufi, Persian, 10th Century A.D.) **B.** The Clay Tablet. (F52; al-Kazwini, Persian, 13th Century A.D.) **C.** The Vase. (F53; Avenares, Roman.) **D.** A tortoise-shell lyre (F48). **E.** A lyre with bull's horns. (F50; Hyginus, Roman, ca. A.D. 1.) **F.** A lyre with vulture. (F55; Bayer, German, ca. A.D. 1603.) **G.** A bass viol with vulture. (F54; Dürer, German, ca. A.D. 1515.) **H.** A lyre. (F56; Flamsteed, English, ca. A.D. 1729.)

In Chinese mythology, Lyra and Aquila are represented by the famous stars of Tchi-niu, the Weaving Princess, and her cowherd lover, Kien-niou. Tchi-niu was the daughter of the Sun God and she was very deft at spinning and weaving. One day she happened to look out through one of the windows of the palace and see her father's herdsman Kien-niou driving the king's flock along the banks of the Milky Way. Their eyes met and, as is fabled to happen so often, they fell in love at first sight.

After a short courtship the king consented to their marriage. Tchi-niu and Kien-niou were very happy together. In fact, they were so happy that they neglected their duties. She forgot all about her loom and he did not bother to care for the royal herd, which—as a result—strayed all over the heavens. After repeated warnings the king finally decided to banish Kien-niou to the other side of the Milky Way. Tchi-niu pleaded with her father to change his mind, but to no avail. The heavenly gods, however, took pity on the couple. It was decided that once a year, on the seventh day of the seventh month, all the magpies in China should fly to the Milky Way and make a bridge across it with their outspread wings. The lovers could then rush over this bridge, fall into each other's arms, and spend the remainder of the day together. On that day a soft rain—tears of happiness—would fall in the morning. But in the evening the soft rain would turn into a downpour caused by the couple's tears of sadness over having to part for another year. In Figure 100 the princess is seen on one side of the Milky Way and the Cowherd on the other, while the magpies are arriving to begin building the bridge.

Points of Interest in Lyra

α-Lyrae is a beautiful blue star located 25 light years from Earth. Slightly to the left of Vega is ε-Lyrae, which can be seen in a pair of binoculars to be a double star, but keen unaided eyesight will also reveal this! A more powerful telescope will show that each of the pair is also a double star; so, ε-Lyrae is really a foursome. ζ- and δ-Lyrae are also double stars.

β-Lyrae is a double star and, like Algol in Perseus, it has a companion which causes fluctuations in the light of the star. These stars fluctuate with a period of about 13 days.

Between γ-, β-Lyrae one can see a wonderful ring nebula, M57, which looks like a misty haze when observed with a small telescope. Very powerful telescopes have discovered a central star within this nebula. On account of their round appearance these ring nebulae are also called planetary nebulae. Study of many hundreds of these planetary nebulae has revealed that they are very large, sometimes a thousand times larger than our solar system. The central star usually is a very hot star (18,000° K or more) and seems to be responsible for the luminescence of the nebulae.

Between 20–22 April, in the early hours of the morning, the annual meteor showers called the Lyrids may be seen.

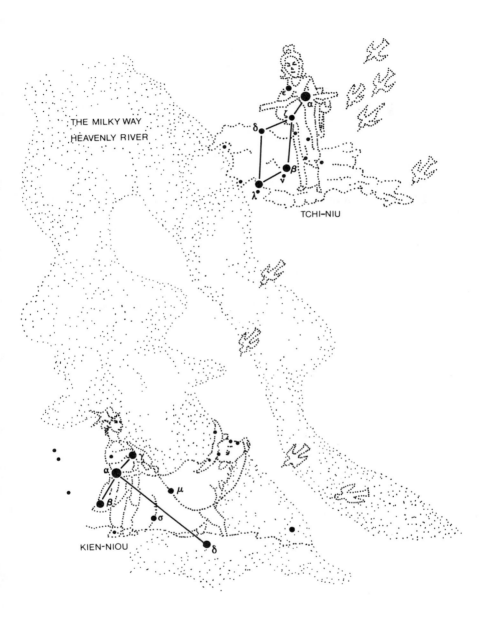

Figure 100. Aquila and Lyra. Tchi-niu, the Weaving Princess, and Kien-niou, the Cowherd, awaiting the annual return of the magpies (C30). Each year, the magpies build a bridge over the Milky Way with their wings so that Tchi-niu and Kien-niou may cross and spend one day together.

187

Scutum
The Shield

The constellation Scutum commemorates John Sobieski III, a king of Poland during part of the 17th Century. John performed valiantly as a soldier in the defense of his country. When the Turks marched on Vienna in September, 1683, John's army met and defeated them in battle at Kalenberg.

Johannes Hevelius wished to commemorate his king and therefore placed John's shield in the stars. This shield was adorned with the cross for which John Sobieski had fought so valiantly. Although the complete title of this constellation is Scutum Sobiescianum, sometimes given as Scutum Sobieskianii, astronomers today refer to it as Scutum.

Scutum Sobiescianum lies wedged between Aquila to the north, Sagittarius to the south, and Ophiuchus and Serpens to the west (Figure 101). Scutum lies embedded in the Milky Way and is therefore not an easy constellation to locate. This constellation contains two stars of magnitude 4 and two of magnitude 4.5. The remainder of the stars are of magnitudes 5 or 6.

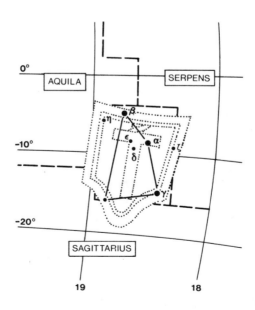

Figure 101. Scutum. Sobieski's Shield. (D48; Flamsteed, English, ca. A.D. 1729.)

Delphinus
The Dolphin

Halfway between Pegasus and Aquila lie the stars of the prettiest little constellation in the skies—Delphinus, the Dolphin (Figure 102). The four brightest stars of this constellation are not very brilliant but they are of equal luminosity, and are arranged in the shape of a diamond or parallelogram. A fifth star is situated a little below the brightest four. Little imagination is required to see a tiny dolphin in this figure. The diamond represents the body and a line to the fifth star forms the tail. The Arabs saw this constellation as a Camel, with the hump represented by the diamond shape of the constellation. In England, these stars form what is known as Job's Coffin.

The best known story of the Dolphin is that about Poseidon's attempt to win Amphitrite as his wife. Amphitrite was the daughter of Oceanus, and consequently, was quite at home in water. At first Amphitrite would

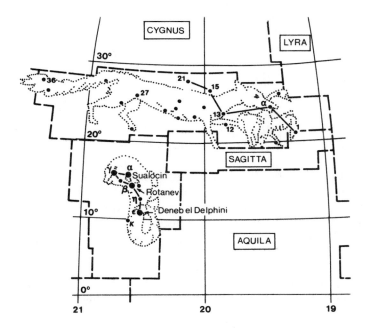

Figure 102. Delphinus and Vulpecula. Delphinus, the Dolphin, and Vulpecula, the Little Fox with the Goose. (Delphinus: F37; Flamsteed, English, ca. A.D. 1729; Vulpecula: E33; Flamsteed, English, ca. A.D. 1729.)

have nothing to do with Poseidon. To escape Poseidon she tried to hide, sometimes in deep water, sometimes on land. Poseidon asked the Dolphin to trace her, which the playful little Dolphin always was able to do. The Dolphin also spoke about the Lord of the Sea in glowing terms. Finally, Amphitrite agreed to become Poseidon's wife. To express his gratitude, Poseidon placed the little Dolphin in the stars to be remembered forever.

Not only have dolphins helped immortals but they have also helped humans. Once upon a time there was a harp player called Arion who, in or about the year 600 B.C., was court musician at Periander's palace in Corinth. Arion was such a good musician that he soon became renowned and gradually accumulated a great deal of wealth. After some time Arion began to yearn for his homeland and asked Periander for leave to visit his family and relations. This request was granted, and a ship was equipped for Arion's journey there and back. The sailors, however, knew Arion was rich. The sailors planned to get rid of Arion once they were on the high seas, and pretend that he had met with an accident when questioned about his disappearance. Then, they could divide Arion's belongings among themselves.

As soon as the ship was far beyond the coast, Arion learned what the crew had planned for him. Quite unperturbed, he said, "I shall jump overboard, but may I, as a last request, play my harp once more?" The sailors had no objection. Arion started to sing the most wonderful song of praise to Apollo, the God of Music and the Arts. Apollo listened and was well pleased. As soon as Arion finished his hymn, however, the sailors grabbed him and flung him overboard. They then sailed away as rapidly as they could.

Apollo, however, had seen all of this and he summoned a dolphin to come to Arion's rescue. The gentle dolphin raced to the place where Arion had plunged into the sea, dived carefully under Arion, and lifted him above the water so that he would not sink again. The dolphin then swam with his unusual cargo to the coast of Greece, where he let Arion safely dismount from his back, and then swam away. Arion went overland to Corinth and told King Periander what had happened. One can imagine the surprised faces of the crew when they arrived and tried to explain that Arion had met with an accident, only to find him safe and sound back at the palace of Periander. Periander, of course, had the untrustworthy sailors put in prison and made them return all of the goods they had stolen from Arion. Arion thanked Apollo for his safe return. In Apollo's honour, Arion had a little statue of the dolphin made and placed in the temple as a memento of the experience. Apollo later placed this statue of the dolphin among the stars so that all mankind could see the brave and friendly little dolphin forever.

The Chinese saw two calabashes, or gourds, in the stars of Delphinus (Figure 103G). These gourds are the fifth and sixth paranatellons of the

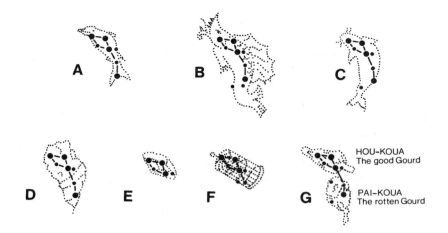

Figure 103. Delphinus. A. The Dolphin (F33). **B.** A predatory fish (F35). **C.** The Seal: Chukchee; Siberia (F38). **D.** The Trumpet Shell: Torres Strait, Australia (F39). **E.** A wooden bowl: Marshall Islands (F40). **F.** The Bird Cage: Jaina; India (F41). **G.** Hou-koua, the Good Gourd, and Pai-koua, the Rotten Gourd: Chinese. (Staal, British, A.D. 1986.)

third house of the Black Tortoise of Winter, called, respectively, Hou-koua, the Good Gourd, and Pai-koua, the Rotten or Frozen Gourd.

Hou-koua was made up of the stars α-, β-, γ-, δ-, ζ-Delphini and Pai-koua of η-, ε-, κ-, ι-, θ-Delphini. The Winter gourds could be eaten in the eighth month of the Chinese year (our September) when they were fresh and green. After they had been frozen, the shell was removed with a bamboo knife and the flesh was then left to soak in a pint of alcohol and a pint of rice water. This would make a sweet refreshing alcoholic beverage. Utensils such as drinking cups, rice bowls and spoons were made from the shells. Such utensils would not be too durable, so an adequate supply was needed to replace the broken objects. Consequently, before the invention of pottery, a good gourd crop was eagerly anticipated. The emperor, who needed great numbers of drinking cups and wine to entertain his guests, had his own gourd plantation—"the Fruit Garden of the Emperor."

The farmers had to be very careful not to over freeze the gourds because that made them soft and useless for cup making. The Good Gourd and the Rotten Gourd were placed in the stars as a reminder to the people to avoid allowing their gourd crop to become frostbitten.

The gourds were also called Toung-koua, the Iced Melons. At weddings, which would take place in the 11th month of the Chinese year (our December), slices of iced melon preserved in sugar were eaten and gourd wine was served for toasting the newlyweds.

Points of Interest in Delphinus

α-Delphini is a double star; one is yellow and the other is green. γ-Delphini is also a double star, the primary being orange and the companion green.

There is an interesting story attached to the stars α- and β-Delphini. α- Delphini is called Sualocin and β-Delphini is known as Rotanev. These two curious names baffled astronomers for a long time. Then, the Reverend Thomas William Webb (A.D. 1807–1885) happened to stumble on the solution of these cryptic names. When read backwards, the names Rotanev Sualocin become Nicolaus Venator—the Latinised form of Niccolo Cacciatore, assistant to and successor of Giuseppi Piazzi (A.D. 1746–1826), director of the Palermo Observatory in Sicily.

Vulpecula
The Little Fox with the Goose

Vulpecula is the name of the combined constellations Vulpes and Anser, the Little Fox and the Goose, two small and inconspicuous constellations located between Cygnus, the Swan, and Sagitta, the Arrow (Figure 102). Vulpecula is of interest only to those who find excitement in trying to test their eyes with very faint and elusive stars. There is no known story about Vulpes, and the only story involving the Goose is that of the Fishes, where Antenteh fills his tub with feathers and down from the Swan and the Goose.

Johannes Hevelius created Vulpecula. In Allen's book *Star Names* is a quotation (p. 473) attributed to Hevelius which reads:

> I (Hevelius) wished to place a fox and a goose in the space of the sky well fitted to it; because such an animal is very cunning, voracious and fierce. Aquila and Vultur (Lyra) are of the same nature, rapacious and greedy.

Equuleus
The Little Horse

Equuleus lies tucked between the nose of Pegasus and the little dolphin Delphinus (Figure 104). Allen, in his book *Star Names*, quotes Thomas Hood (ca. A.D. 1590), an English writer on astronomical subjects, as saying (p. 213):

> This constellation was named of almost no writer, saving Ptolemee and Alfonsus who followeth Ptolemee, and therefore no certain tail or historie is delivered thereof, by what means it came into heaven.

Some people think it was Hipparchus, the Greek astronomer, who lived about 160–120 B.C., who created Equuleus. There is no actual mythology of this little flying horse. Some see it as an offspring of Pegasus, hence the flying foal is sometimes shown upside down like his mother. Others say it is Equus Primus, because it rises before Pegasus. The Arabs preserved this latter notion in one of their names for the constellation—Al Faras al Awal, "the First Horse."

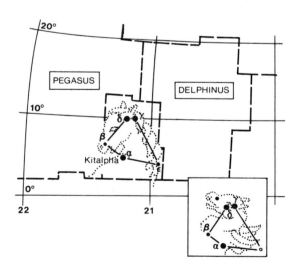

Figure 104. Equuleus. The Little Horse. (F43; al-Sufi, Persian, 10th Century A.D.) **Inset:** The Flying Foal. (F44; Vitruvius Pollio, Roman, 1st Century B.C.)

Ophiuchus and Serpens
The Serpent Bearer and the Serpent

Although this constellation is called Ophiuchus, which is derived from the Greek words *ophis* (serpent) and *cheiro-o* (to handle)—hence Snake Bearer—a person of this name does not seem to have existed. Ophiuchus is always associated with Aesculapius, the son of the god Apollo and a mortal woman called Coronis, daughter of Phlegyas, King of the Lapiths in Thessaly. When Coronis was about to give birth to her son, she married an Arcadian, called Ischys. The crow which Apollo had put as guard over Coronis flew hurriedly to Apollo and told him about this marriage. Apollo was furious and cursed the crow, whose feathers turned black as a result.

Apollo put the two lovers to death on a pyre, and when Coronis' body was already burning Apollo snatched away his nearly born child. He put Aesculapius under the care of the Centaur Chiron, who taught the boy the arts of medicine and healing.

Not only did Aesculapius (Ophiuchus) cure illness, but he also mastered the art of restoring life to the dead. It was said that he once killed a snake. As soon as he had strangled this snake another came sliding on, carrying an herb in its mouth. The live snake gave the dead one the herb, which revived the dead serpent. Ophiuchus snatched a little of the herb from the snake and ever since had the power to restore life.

This, however, was not to the liking of Pluto, the King of the Underworld and the Realm of the Dead. His empire was threatened with a depletion of dead on a grand scale, due to Ophiuchus' art. He complained to Jupiter about it. Jupiter called a stop to this by sending Aquila the Eagle after Ophiuchus with one of his thunderbolts. The Eagle hit Ophiuchus with this weapon and the great doctor sank dead to the Earth. As Jupiter did not wish to let the knowledge of Ophiuchus disappear into oblivion, he placed the famous medicine man of antiquity among the stars, carrying the snake who gave him the secrets of life's elixir (Figure 105). (By studying the movements of the constellations with a planisphere one can see how the Eagle stands threatening over Ophiuchus, as he slowly sinks below the horizon in the west on an Autumn night.)

The Scorpion's body is situated below Ophiuchus' left foot. It is a reminder of the Orion-Scorpius legend. Briefly, when Orion swore he would kill all the animals on Earth, Gaia, the Earth Goddess, sent the Scorpion after him. Scorpius stung Orion and he fell mortally wounded. This act is represented in the sky movement of these two constellations.

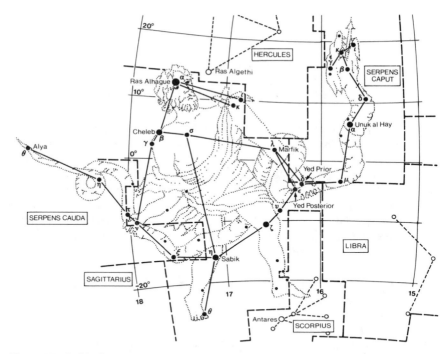

Figure 105. Ophiuchus and Serpens. The Serpent Bearer and the Serpent. (C34; Flamsteed, English, ca. A.D. 1729.)

When Orion, mortally wounded, sets in the west, the Scorpion is just rising in the east, gloating over the success of his mission. Scorpius' triumph does not last long, however, for the next evening—as Scorpius sets in the west—Ophiuchus stands above Scorpius and tramples him to death. Ophiuchus then gives Orion a sip of his elixir and restores Orion to life. Thus Orion is seen to rise in the east again as both Ophiuchus and Scorpius descend in the west.

In an older Babylonian view, this constellation represented the monster Tiamat, the Bitter Ocean (Figure 106). Tiamat personified Chaos from which all other things came forth. Tiamat took Apsu, God of the Fresh Waters, as her husband. Out of this union were born many evil deities whose main purpose was to create conflict, confusion, friction and strife. Tiamat, however, was not satisfied with her brood and decided to destroy it. In the war that ensued, Apsu was killed by his son Ea who, fearing his mother's wrath, subsequently fled to the farthest corner of Fresh Waters. Tiamat remarried her son Kingu, by whom she also had offspring. Still, Tiamat was not satisfied with her progeny and did battle with them—during which time she was killed by her grandson, the Sun God Marduk. The entire story reflects, of course, the eternal battle

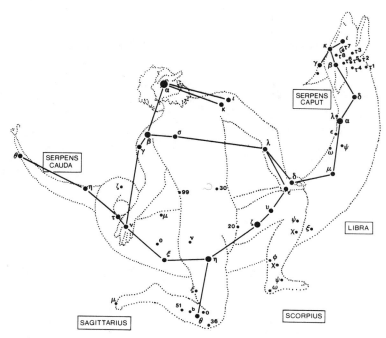

Figure 106. Ophiuchus and Serpens. The monster Tiamat, the Bitter Ocean, and Marduk, the Sea God, who finally killed Tiamat. (C36; Seneca, Roman, 1st Century A.D.)

between the demons of the dark and the deities of light—the battle between evil and good. From Tiamat's blood, skin and bones were made Heaven and Earth; the stars and constellations were created so that people could use them as indicators of the changing seasons.

The Abbé Poczobut of Wilna created the constellation Poniatowski's Bull in honour of Stanislaus Poniatowski, King of Poland (A.D. 1732–1798), using seven of the major stars in the area immediately east of Ophiuchus' right shoulder. An illustration of this constellation was made by the English astronomer John Flamsteed (Figure 107). It so happens that the seven major stars of the constellation form a small letter v, very much like the larger V of Taurus, the Bull. As a result, the constellation became known as Poniatowski's Bull. Flamsteed let the rear end of the Bull ramble into parts of Aquila, the Eagle, and the forelegs into parts of Scutum and Serpens Cauda.

Points of Interest in Ophiuchus

Ophiuchus is a rather sprawling constellation and covers a large area. However, assiduous watching and searching will eventually reveal the beauty of this magnificent hero. The head is in α-Ophiuchi, or Ras Alhague. On either side, and a little lower, we can find two pairs of stars

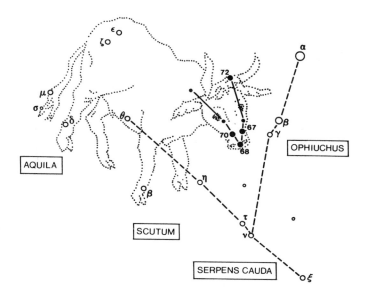

Figure 107. Ophiuchus. Poniatowski's Bull. (C35; Flamsteed, English, ca. A.D. 1729.)

which represent his shoulders. From there two straight lines depict the arms of the doctor. The serpent is seen in a curving meandering line of stars, the tail lying in the star θ-Serpentis, the body being gripped by Ophiuchus in ν- and δ-Ophiuchi, and the head swaying at shoulder level near Corona Borealis. δ-Ophiuchi, or Yed Prior, represents the left hand of the Serpent Bearer. α-Serpentis forms the heart of the serpent, and β-, γ-, κ-, ι-, ρ-Serpentis form the head of the serpent.

A glance at a star map will show the presence of a dense population of star clusters in Ophiuchus near the Milky Way. In 1604, a Nova blazed up in Ophiuchus which remained visible for some two years. This star can no longer be seen.

Hercules
Hercules, the Strongman

In mid-Summer, Hercules stands upside down, high in the sky, over the southern horizon (Figure 108). The head of Hercules, α- Herculis, or Ras Algethi, is close to Ras Alhague, the head of Ophiuchus. The shoulders of Hercules lie in β-, δ-Herculis, the waist has the two stars ζ-, ε-Herculis, the knees are in τ-, θ-Herculis, and the feet are in ι-, χ-Herculis. It is, like Orion, an enormous straggling constellation representing a man of great strength.

At first it is not so easy to find the outlines of Hercules, but with patience you will be able to locate him between the constellations of Draco, the Dragon, Corona Borealis, the Northern Crown, Ophiuchus, the Serpent Bearer, and Aquila, the Eagle.

Hercules was a child born from both godly and mortal blood. Hercules' father was the great Jupiter himself, who became attracted by the beauty of Alcmene, the wife of Amphytrion, a famous military leader in Thebes. One day, when Amphytrion was away at war, Jupiter announced himself, in the guise of Amphytrion, feigning a few hours leave. So Jupiter lay with Alcmene that night, and after the Moon had circuited the sky nine times, a son was born, called Hercules. Juno, Jupiter's wife, had not failed to notice the birth of this boy and suspected he might be one more product of her husband's infidelity. Consequently, she did everything within her power to make life difficult for Hercules. Her first act of vengeance was to send two snakes to attack him, but even as a baby, Hercules already displayed his enormous strength. He simply wrung their necks as if they had been toys.

When a young man, on one of his rambles through fields and woods, Hercules met two women called Pleasure and Virtue. Pleasure promised him a life of enjoyment, while Virtue promised him a life of hard toil but one which would be crowned ultimately by glory. Hercules decided to listen to Virtue. Before the promised glory could be his, however, he had to carry out many a difficult and sometimes virtually impossible task.

The legend of Hercules says that, as atonement for crimes he committed while under a spell of madness imposed by Juno, Hercules was placed in servitude to King Eurystheus, who ordered him to perform twelve labours. These labours required Hercules to combat ferocious animals. The twelve labours of Hercules often are seen in connection with the 12 signs of the zodiac.

The first monster that Hercules had to exterminate was the Nemean lion. This lion was alleged to be invulnerable so weapons were of no use

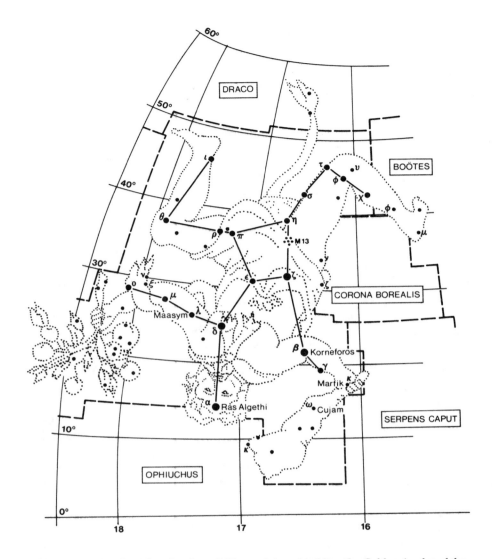

Figure 108. Hercules. Hercules, brandishing a club and holding the Golden Apples of the Hesperides. (C5; Royer, French, ca. A.D. 1679.)

against him. Hercules battled this lion for thirty days, then he finally managed to catch the lion in his arms and strangle it with his powerful grip. Hercules removed the skin and from it made a cloak which rendered him invulnerable.

The second task was the battle with the watersnake of Lerna, an enormous serpent with nine heads who had its lair in a marsh in the Peloponnesus. A glance at a planisphere will show that the next zodiacal constellation for the Sun to pass through, after Leo, is Virgo, the Virgin.

When the Sun sets under the western horizon with the stars of Virgo, we can just see the tail end of the Hydra disappear as well. This task also was to be a long battle of thirty days. The gruesome monster, with its nine heads, had one immortal head. Each of the eight heads that were not immortal would grow two new ones if decapitated. To make this task even more difficult for Hercules, Juno sent a huge crab to hinder Hercules. Hercules trampled the crab while he tackled the Hydra with a burning tree trunk and a sword. Every time Hercules cut off one of the Hydra's heads he scorched the stump with the burning wood, so that it could not grow two heads in its place. Finally, Hercules managed to subdue the Hydra, after which he soaked his arrows in its blood which made them deadly poisonous. Upon completing his second labour, Hercules had acquired all of his famous armour with which he is usually depicted—the lion's skin, the poisoned arrows and the club that he made from the tree trunk he had used to burn the Hydra's necks.

Next, Hercules was commanded to capture the boar of Erymanthus. This wild beast was alleged to have come down from Mount Erymanthus in Arcadia, and to have laid ruin to the vineyards in the surrounding countryside. Hercules had been ordered to bring this beast alive to Mycenae. To capture the boar, Hercules drove it into a snow bank where, after exhausting it, he caught it in a noose. The boar was taken triumphantly before King Eurystheus, who was so terrified at the sight of the struggling boar that he hid away in a tub in a cellar. King Eurystheus bid Hercules to display proof of his deeds outside the city gates in the future.

It is said that Chiron, the wise Centaur, instructed Hercules in how best to subdue the boar. When Hercules succeeded in capturing the boar, the Centaurs were so elated that they threw a feast for him. Much wine flowed that night. This orgy, however, ended in a fatal tragedy when Chiron was killed accidently.

The completion and celebration of Hercules' third task corresponds to the month of the wine harvest, when the Sun moves through the sign of the Crab.

Eurystheus next ordered Hercules to bring him the Ceryneian hind alive. The antlers of this deer were of gold and its hoofs were of brass. The animal belonged to Artemis, the Goddess of the Hunt. After a year of effort, Hercules finally captured the hind on the banks of the Ladon River. Artemis saw Hercules with her hind, stopped him, and demanded an explanation. Hercules explained that he was obeying the command of Eurystheus. Satisfied with Hercules' explanation, Artemis allowed him to proceed on the condition that he release the hind once Eurystheus had seen it. So ended Hercules' fourth task.

A glance at a planisphere will show Cassiopeia very low in the northern sky when the Sun enters the stars of Scorpio, the Scorpion. The W of Cassiopeia is likened to the antlers of the hind. The fact that Scorpio is the background constellation to the Sun in its trek through the zodiac indicates that this is the season of the hunt. After a year has passed, Cassiopeia again returns to the low position in the north. The capture of the hind on the banks of the Ladon is represented by the fact that the W of Cassiopeia lies in the Milky Way, here seen as the Ladon River.

Hercules' next task involved the Stymphalian birds which infested the lake of Stymphalus in Arcadia. These were man-eating monsters with claws and beaks of brass and feathers which they shot out as arrows. Hercules scared them by rattling brazen cymbals which made them fly up from the lake. Hercules shot some of the birds with his poisoned arrows. The other birds flew away and settled on the island of Aretias in the Black Sea, from where they were chased by the Argonauts.

The planisphere again depicts the heavenly reenactment of this episode quite clearly. When the Sun moves through the stars of Sagittarius, the Archer, the three birds—Aquila, the Eagle, Cygnus, the Swan, and Vega, the Vulture—fade from the sky behind the light of the mighty Sun.

The sixth task required of Hercules was the cleaning of the stables of King Augeas. King Augeas was a descendent of Sol, the Sun God, and Nuctea, the longest night. (This, of course, means that the Sun has reached its lowest point in the zodiac at the Winter Solstice. Some 2,000 years ago this solstice occurred against the background stars of Capricorn, the Seagoat.) Augeas lived in Elis, where he had 3,000 head of cattle. The stables of Elis were filthy with dung which had not been removed for years. Hercules had the unpleasant task of devising some means of cleaning these stables in only one day. If he should succeed, Augeas promised to give Hercules one tenth of the herd as a token of gratitude. Hercules managed this almost impossible task by diverting the flow of two rivers—Alpheus and Pineus. The thundering waters of these two rivers came rushing onwards and cleaned the stables out, making every cowshed as clean as new. Augeas, however, did not adhere to his part of the bargain. Augeas maintained that he could not really give Hercules the promised cattle because Hercules actually had been working for Eurystheus. Years after this encounter, Hercules punished Augeas for his dishonesty by slaying him and all of his sons.

The planisphere depicts this labour quite clearly. When Capricorn is setting in the west, the river Eridanus and the stream of Aquarius flow down.

The seventh task for Hercules was to capture the Cretan bull. The legend says that Neptune had sent a bull up from the waters of the sea to ransack the island of Crete. (The planisphere shows that when the Sun moves through Aquarius, the Water Carrier, Taurus, the Bull, is just coming up over the eastern horizon.) Neptune had sent this bull because Minos, the King of Crete, had not fulfilled his obligation to make ritual offering to the gods. Crete was terrorised by the bull. Minos appealed for help, so Hercules was sent to capture the bull and bring it back alive to Eurystheus. Nobody but Hercules dared to approach the bull. Hercules captured, bound, and tamed the animal. Hercules crossed the sea on the back of this bull, then threw it across his shoulder and carried it to Eurystheus. Upon seeing the mad looking bull from Crete, Eurystheus took such a fright that he ordered its release. Free again, the animal wandered all through the Peloponnesus and infested the countryside around Marathon before it was eventually slain by Theseus.

The eighth task of Hercules was to capture the horses of Diomedes, the son of Ares. Diomedes was King of the Bistones in Thrace. All strangers who landed in Diomedes' country were bound and thrown to the horses, who ate them alive. Hercules, with a few helpers, managed to drive these horses to the sea, but King Diomedes heard about this and rallied his army to combat Hercules. The Bistones came rushing and a battle ensued, but the mighty Hercules slew his attackers one after the other. At last Hercules caught Diomedes himself, and threw him to his own horses. The horses ate Diomedes and immediately became tame. Hercules then took the horses to Eurystheus. Eurystheus, again, was scared of the animals and he ordered them to be released in the woods where, later, they were torn to shreds by the hungry wolves.

The planisphere shows the Sun entering the stars of the Fishes. Above is the Horse, Pegasus, which represents the horses of Diomedes.

Hercules' ninth task was to collect the girdle of Hippolyte, the Queen of the Amazons, in Cappadocia. Hippolyte possessed a regal girdle, a magnificent piece of craftsmanship given to her by Ares. Admete, the daughter of King Eurystheus, had her heart set on this girdle and Hercules was given the task of fetching it for her. Hercules was received in peace by the Amazons and it looked like an easy task as Hippolyte was even agreeable to giving the girdle to Admete. But Juno, Jupiter's wife, was furious and spread the rumour among the Amazons that Hercules had come to abduct their queen. Infuriated, the horsewomen mounted their steeds and attacked Hercules who, thinking that they had betrayed him, slew them one by one. He even had to kill Hippolyte. He took the girdle and set out on his return journey, but did not immediately go home. In passing, he called on Laomedon in Troy, who was in great distress because he had to sacrifice his daughter Hesione to a sea monster to pacify Jupiter. This is very much the same theme as we can read about under Perseus and Andromeda. Hercules killed the lurching monster and rescued the girl. Laomedon, who had promised to give Hercules some horses which Laomedon had received from Jupiter in exchange for his son Ganymede, refused to give him this reward. Thereupon Hercules, who was in great haste to return to Eurystheus with the girdle, threatened Laomedon with future vengeance. The legend says that Hercules later waged war against Laomedon, captured and burnt the city, and slew the king and all of his sons.

The planisphere shows how the Sun enters the Ram. Andromeda is Hippolyte, the Amazon queen, who is always shown attached to Pegasus, symbolising the horsewomen. As in the story of Perseus, the monster Cetus lurches low over the horizon, and when Hercules rises over the eastern horizon, Cetus goes down in the west which represents the defeat of the monster. The girdle of Hippolyte can be seen in the string of faint stars which, in the Andromeda story, depicts the shackles with which she is bound to the rocks.

The 10th task of Hercules was to capture the oxen of Geryon, the son of Chrysaor and the ocean nymph, Callirhoe. Geryon was a giant with mighty wings and parts of three bodies, a combination of human, goat, and ram. The shepherd Eurytion guarded the oxen with the help of his two-headed dog Orthrus, an offspring of Echidna and Typhon. Hercules, in quest of these oxen, roamed far and wide through Europe and planned to cross the waters separating Spain from North Africa. To remind himself where this crossing point was on his return journey, he marked the spot with two huge boulders—the Pillars of Hercules—which we can see today as the rocks of Gibraltar. Hercules had not yet decided how he would negotiate the crossing, and he could not see the other side very well because the Sun was shining straight into his eyes. In his anger he fired an arrow at the Sun who marvelled at his courage. The Sun sent his personal boat, which he used to cross the waters from west to east, to carry Hercules across the straits. Hercules arrived in Erythea, where he slew Eurytion and Orthrus and drove off Geryon's cattle.

Menoetius, the shepherd of the herds of Pluto, heard about Hercules' acts in Erythea and sent word to Geryon. Geryon hurried in pursuit of Hercules but, following an intense battle, was felled by the arrows of Hercules. Hercules, however, was not yet quite safe. One night, when he was on his way home with the cattle, Cacus, a fire-breathing giant, arose from a hole in the Earth and stole the most exquisite animals from the herd. To fool Hercules, Cacus dragged the cattle into his cave tail first so that their hoof marks would point away from his hide-out. The bellowing of the stolen herd, however, was answered by the remaining oxen and this led Hercules to Cacus' hide-out. Hercules jumped through an opening in the top of the cave and overpowered Cacus in a fury of flames. Hercules recovered the stolen cattle and, finally, delivered the oxen safely to King Eurystheus, who sacrificed them to Juno.

The planisphere shows this episode. When the Sun enters the stars of Taurus, the Bull, Auriga with the Goats stands high above, whereas Orion and his Dogs stand below the Sun. These characters represent the giant Geryon, with his shepherd Eurytion and his two-headed dog (Sirius and Procyon). Hercules' crossing of the Straits of Gibraltar in the Sun's boat is seen when the Sun sets in the evening over the western horizon and the stars of the Beaker (boat) come up in the east. The evil Cacus is represented by Scorpius, the Scorpion, who rises with Hercules in the east and, when he is defeated, sets before Hercules in the west.

Hercules' 11th task was to fetch the hellhound Cerberus. This was considered the most difficult of the 12 tasks. Guided by Mercury and Minerva, Hercules descended into the Underworld, where Pluto was king. Hercules set free various people who were serving sufferance and pain in the Underworld, and he even wounded Pluto himself. Finally, Hercules obtained permission from Pluto to take Cerberus to the Upperworld if he could master the brute. By sheer muscular strength Hercules strangled Cerberus and dragged him by the scruff of the neck to the Upperworld (Figure 109). Hercules showed Cerberus to King Eurystheus who, as happened several times before, was frightened with the proof of the completed task. Eurystheus ordered Cerberus to be sent back to the Underworld.

The planisphere shows that the Sun now enters Gemini, the Twins, which also represent Mercury and Minerva. The Milky Way is prominent

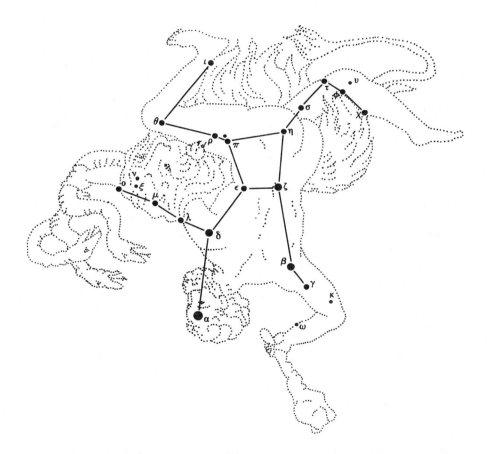

Figure 109. Hercules. Hercules wrestling with Cerberus, the Hellhound of Hades. (C6; Hevelius, Polish, ca. A.D. 1690.)

in the sky and represents the river Styx of the Underworld. Cerberus is, of course, Sirius, the Great Dog. When the Sun is in Gemini, Sirius also stands above the horizon in the daytime sky, and so cannot be seen, meaning that Cerberus has been brought to the Upperworld and returned to the Underworld.

The last task of Hercules was that of fetching the Golden Apples of the Hesperides. These apples had been given to Juno by Gaia, the Goddess of the Earth, when Juno married Jupiter. If Hercules could secure these apples he would be a free man. He set out and reached the place where Atlas carried the vault of Heaven on his shoulders. An oracle had told Hercules that only Atlas was able to enter the garden of the Hesperides, where the apple tree stood guarded by Ladon, the monster-dragon. So Hercules asked Atlas if he would be good enough to fetch the apples for him in return for which he—Hercules—would temporarily take the burden of the heavens on his shoulders. Atlas eyed the strong Hercules, then handed over the heavenly globe and set out to fetch the apples. When Atlas came back, however, he decided to leave Hercules toiling with the heavenly globe and enjoy some freedom himself. But Hercules was not going to give in so easily. He asked Atlas to take the load for just a second so that he could adjust a cushion on his shoulder. As soon as the globe of Heaven was again on Atlas' shoulders, Hercules was off with the golden apples (Figure 108). These were placed before King Eurystheus, who dedicated them to Minerva, who, in turn, finally restored them to their rightful owner, Juno.

The planisphere shows the Sun in Cancer, the Crab, which is the holy animal consecrated to Juno. The dragon, Ladon, stands high in the zenith when the Crab sets in the west. The three tail stars of the Great Bear are the golden apples. Hercules culminates high in triumph and becomes a free man. Boötes is seen as Atlas.

There are many stories in addition to the ones related above which depict Hercules in all his heroic splendour. Hercules married the beautiful Deianeira. One day Hercules and Deianeira came to the ford of a river where a Centaur was the ferry boatman who had the right to take people across. The Centaur first took Deianeira in his boat. In midstream the Centaur attempted to do violence to her, but Hercules, from the riverbank, shot him with a poisoned arrow. The dying Centaur told Deianeira to take some of his blood and keep it as an antidote. Should Hercules ever become unfaithful to her, then the Centaur's blood would restore her husband's fidelity. In one of the many battles in which Hercules got involved, he captured a beautiful girl, Iole, and took her as prisoner of war and destined her as a bride for his son. But Deianeira, seeing how beautiful Iole was, thought that Hercules was in love with Iole and she remembered the words of the Centaur. Deianeira impregnated one of Hercules' robes with a mixture of the blood of the Centaur. When the Hercules put on the robe, the poisonous blood began to devour his skin. In agony he tore off the robe, but in doing so he tore off pieces of flesh. The poor agonising Hercules prayed to Jupiter to deliver him from the pain. A great cloud descended from the sky. The vault of Heaven reverberated, full of fire, as the thunderbolts flashed. Hercules was lifted to the celestial sphere, and welcomed by the immortals, where we can still see the brave hero among the stars.

Points of Interest in Hercules

When Hercules culminates in the Summer, ι-Herculis, one of his feet, is high overhead. Directly opposite, 40° downwards, we find α- Herculis, or Ras Algethi, "the Head of Hercules." This star is a double, the primary being yellow and its companion blue. The period of the variable primary is about 120 days.

The most well known feature in this constellation, however, is the star cluster M13, near the star η, just by one of the sides of the square forming Hercules' body. This cluster is hardly visible to the naked eye, and even through a telescope of moderate aperture it is only a hazy speck with a bright nucleus. With the great modern telescopes, however, we can see an immense ball of stars, dense in the centre and thinning out towards the edges.

According to early estimates, M13 is so far away that it would take light travelling at 186,000 miles per second some 45,000 years to reach us. Investigations by Harlow Shapley indicated that this cluster was about 120,000 light years away, whereas recent measurements give 21,000 light years as its distance from Earth. Quite a difference! The cluster is estimated to contain millions of stars. Many of these stars have been examined; some are variables, as explained under Perseus.

The star λ-Herculis is important because the great Sir William Herschel forecast that the entire solar system was moving in a direction which had its apex near this star. Modern data have moved the apex of this movement nearer Vega in the Lyre, but even so Herschel's observation was a great contribution to astronomy. This drift of our solar system takes us millions of miles nearer to Vega than we were a year ago. So our Earth really performs a multitude of movements without our being aware of them. Firstly, it rotates around its own axis which causes the stars to rise and set; secondly, it revolves around the Sun which gives us our seasons; thirdly, the Earth wobbles, which gives the precession of the equinoxes and the change of Pole star; and fourthly, the Earth also partakes in a mad race through space with the Sun and the other planets, sweeping up cosmic dust on the way. Our movement is therefore a highly complicated spiral-shaped journey through space. Where will it lead us? What will journey's end be? What shall we find when one day we do arrive there? These remain physical and philosophical questions which astronomy endeavours to answer.

Corona Borealis
The Northern Crown

East of Boötes is an exquisite circlet of stars known as Corona Borealis, the Northern Crown (Figure 110). One star in this group outshines all the others; situated about halfway along the curve, this star is α-Coronae Borealis, Gemma or the Gem Star, also called Alphecca, "the Bright Dish," in ancient Arabia. Arabs and other Eastern people also called this constellation the Beggar's Bowl (Figure 111B).

The ancient Greek story of Ariadne's crown is perhaps the most fitting one for the constellation. Ariadne was the daughter of Minos, King of the island of Crete in the Mediterranean Sea. Minos also had a son named Androgeos, but Androgeos was killed in battle against the Athenians. After his son's death, Minos imposed a levy on the Athenians, who every year had to deliver to him seven young men and seven maidens. These youths were sacrificed as food for the Minotaur, which was locked up in a labyrinth. Once inside the labyrinth, nobody could ever find a way out.

Obviously this heavy punishment riled the Athenians. On the occasion of the third year of this levy, Theseus, the young son of King Aegeus, offered his services in attempting to free the Athenians of this tribute. Theseus told his nation that he would attempt to kill the Minotaur if he

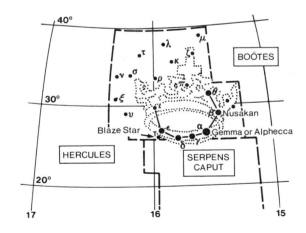

Figure 110. Corona Borealis. The Northern Crown. (F7; Hyginus, Roman, ca. A.D. 1.)

were allowed to go as one of the party of fourteen boys and girls. Theseus' father was at first very upset and opposed to this plan, but in the end he agreed provided that Theseus promised to hoist a white sail on the returning ship if he should be victorious.

The sad day of departure came, and the boat with the black sail of sorrow set forth with the fourteen boys and girls on board. Amongst them was Theseus. Upon arriving in Crete, Theseus managed to obtain an audience with King Minos. Minos agreed that the punishment of the Athenians would be considered fulfilled if Theseus slew the Minotaur. It so happened that Theseus met the king's daughter, Ariadne. Theseus deeply impressed her, and she decided to help him carry out his dangerous mission. Ariadne gave Theseus a reel of yarn which he was to unwind as he entered the labyrinth. This yarn would lead Theseus back to the entrance after he had dealt with the Minotaur. Theseus accepted Ariadne's help with gratitude, entered the dark maze of the deadly labyrinth, and came upon the monster who did not expect such a courageous youth. Usually people who saw the monster were stricken with fear and were easy prey, but this time the monster had met a hero who did not appear to be afraid in the least. A furious battle ensued, ending when Theseus ran his sword through the Minotaur. Theseus then found the way out of the labyrinth by tracing back the unwound yarn, and thanked Ariadne for her assistance. With the Minotaur dead, Athens was freed from the awful levy imposed by Minos. Overjoyed, all the people danced the Geranos, a dance with very complicated foot movements and figures symbolising Theseus' movements through the winding corridors of the labyrinth.

Meanwhile, Ariadne had fallen in love with Theseus and was to return with him to Athens to become his wife. It was a long journey, so Theseus decided to make a stop at Naxos, the island devoted to the Wine God, Bacchus. Bacchus, on discovering his guests, was so overcome with the beauty of Ariadne that he wished her to become his own wife. He ordered Theseus to leave the island without Ariadne noticing his departure. Theseus did not dare to argue with a god, and so he sailed away from Naxos. But in his great sadness, Theseus forgot to change the black sail for the white as he had promised his father he would do in the event he was successful in his fight against the Minotaur.

When Theseus' father saw the ship approach with the black sail still at the mast he could only think that his son was dead. In despair, Aegeus threw himself from the rock on which he was standing and fell to his death in the sea which, ever since, has been called the Aegean Sea.

When Ariadne awoke and found that she was left alone on the island she became frightened and shouted for help. Then Bacchus appeared and tried to calm her. He managed to persuade her to believe that Theseus was not worth crying for because he had proved himself a worthless hero by abandoning her on the island. Bacchus went on to

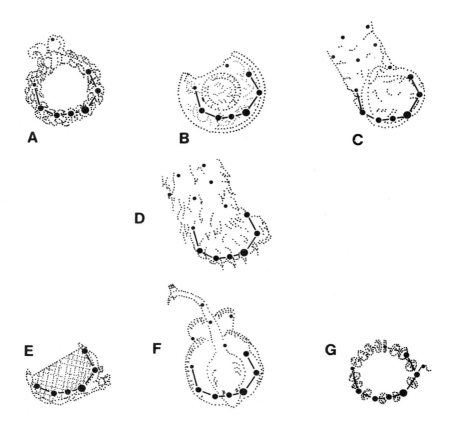

Figure 111. Corona Borealis. A. A laurel wreath. (F3; Bode, German, ca. A.D. 1800.) **B.** A beggar's dish: Middle East (F10). **C.** The Boot of Kilu: Koryak; Siberia (F11). **D.** The Polar Bear's Paw: Chukchee; Siberia (F12). **E.** The Fishing Net: Caroline Islands (F13). **F.** A fish: Borneo (F14). **G.** Koan-so, the Money String (Staal, British, A.D. 1986.)

say that he, himself, would like to marry her. Ariadne, however, was disillusioned with mortal men, and she did not believe that Bacchus was really a god. If he could prove that he was, she promised to reconsider his request. Bacchus laughed and took off the golden crown he always wore on his head saying that this tiara would be her wedding present. To show the whole world how beautiful he thought she was, Bacchus tossed the crown into the heavens. There the crown would shine forever as twinkling stars, with the star Gemma, in the front of the tiara, reminding mankind of Ariadne, the most beautiful queen mortals have ever known—so beautiful that even a god would not think it below his dignity to take her as his wife. Ariadne at last consented to become Bacchus' wife, after which she received godly immortality which allowed her to live on Olympus with all the other gods. We can still see the crown, designed by Venus, the Goddess of Love, and fashioned by the deft hands of Pluto, the God of the Underworld, as that dainty circlet of gems called Corona Borealis.

To the Chinese, Corona Borealis represented the money string Koan-so, with which coins were tied together (Figure 111G). There were holes in the coins through which the string was then threaded. Before money coins were used the Chinese had shells with pearls which they threaded together. Other Chinese names for this constellation were Lien-so, the Garland; Lien-ying, the Endless Enclosure; T'ien-lao, the Celestial Prison; and T'ien-wei, the Celestial Jail. In the latter asterism, the star η-Coronae Borealis represented the door of the prison. People liked it when the door was wide open! α-Coronae Borealis was the jailer.

Points of Interest in Corona Borealis

Apart from the occasional meteor between April and June which may be seen to streak from the neighbourhood of Gemma, there is nothing very noteworthy for the sky scanner in this constellation.

T-Coronae Borealis is an irregular variable star which in May 1866, blazed up from a star which could not be seen with the naked eye to one of the second magnitude. This star then faded, to be seen only through a good telescope when fluctuations in its brightness occurred. This star again flared up in February, 1946, this time to the third magnitude. T-Coronae Borealis is sometimes referred to as the "Blaze Star." With the aid of a good telescope, T-Coronae Borealis can be found just below the star ε-Coronae Borealis in the Crown.

Sagittarius
The Archer

Although the true meaning of Sagittarius is Archer, this constellation is usually depicted as a combination of a horse and a man, the rear part being the horse and the front part the man. The man is always armed with a bow and an arrow (Figures 112, 113). Unfortunately, there are two such horsemen in the stars—Sagittarius and Centaurus. This circumstance leads to confusion in the use of the name Centaur; Sagittarius is sometimes called Centaur, but Centaur is never called Sagittarius.

Sagittarius and Centaurus have a totally different meaning, however. Sagittarius is a more warlike character, a hunter, whereas the Centaur of the skies—Chiron—is the wise and kind personification of wisdom, strength and the art of medicine. Of the two constellations, Sagittarius was known first to the people of the Mediterranean region. Centaur

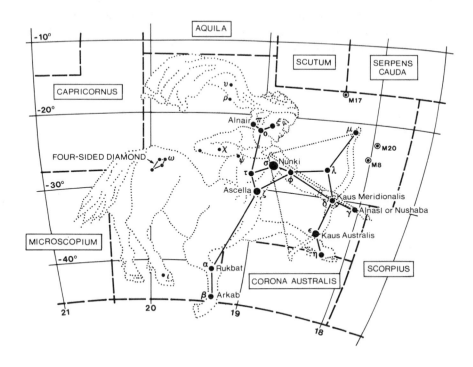

Figure 112. Sagittarius. Sagittarius, the Archer. (D31; al-Sufi, Persian, 10th Century A.D.)

could not have been seen well in its entirety from the Mediterranean countries.

The Sun passes through Sagittarius at the time of the hunt. Sagittarius has his arrow pointing to Antares, the heart of Scorpius, the Scorpion. Legend says that Sagittarius avenged Orion by slaying the Scorpion with one arrow shot. As a bull killer, we can follow Sagittarius in the sky around May and June. When the horntip of Taurus, the Bull, vanishes below the northwestern horizon, the first stars of Sagittarius come up in the southeast.

A star map shows that Sagittarius lies for the greater part in the Milky Way. This has a philosophical meaning. Our Milky Way system is a large disc-shaped city of stars in which the Sun is only an insignificant star. However, for us on the Earth, who derive warmth from this star, the Sun is of great importance. Any disc must have a centre, and for a long time astronomers have searched for the exact position of this centre of the Milky Way. Even ancient astronomers were aware of the fact that the Milky Way was a gathering of millions of stars. But more than twenty centuries had to elapse before these early thoughts were verified! It is now certain that the centre of the Milky Way lies in the direction of Sagittarius, and it could be interpreted that Sagittarius has tried to tell us the way to this centre as he points with his arrow in that direction.

The stars of the human part of Sagittarius (the stars σ-, τ-, ζ-, φ-, λ- and μ-Sagittarii) look exactly like a ladle. As this ladle lies close to, and with its handle in, the stream of the Milky Way, it is often called the Milk Dipper. σ-Sagittarii is also called Nunki, and the most southerly star of

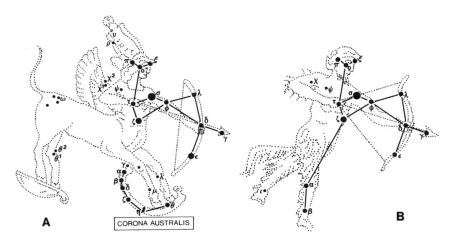

CORONA AUSTRALIS

A   B

Figure 113. Sagittarius. A. The Winged Archer standing with front feet in a Nile River boat (Corona Australis), after an illustration in the Denderah zodiac of ancient Egypt (D25). **B.** A Silenus, a Centaur that walked upright on two legs. (D32; Baeda, English, 7th–8th centuries A.D.)

the bow, the star ε-Sagittarii, is called Kaus Australis. The head is represented by ξ-, o- and π-Sagittarii, whereas the arrow is formed by σ-, φ-, δ- and γ-Sagittarii. Unfortunately, Sagittarius travels very low across the southern horizon and is difficult to see from across much of the Northern Hemisphere, but it can be traced during June, July and August if observed from a dark vantage point in the middle or lower latitudes.

The Chinese see two asterisms in Sagittarius—Ki-siou, the House of the Winnowing Tray or the House of the Manuring Tray, and Teou-siou, the House of the Bushel (Figure 114B). Ki-siou is the seventh house of the Blue Dragon of Spring, and refers to the Winnowing Tray used during the Autumn to clean the chaff from the various crops just harvested.

Teou-siou, the House of the Bushel, is the first house of the Black Tortoise of Winter, which follows the Blue Dragon in the sky. Rice and other harvest products brought to the granaries was measured by the bushel. Also, when in times of hardship during the Winter the emperor wished to mete out rations to the people, a bushel was used so that this could be done fairly.

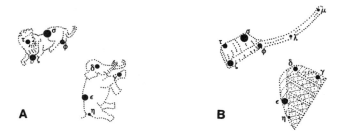

Figure 114. Sagittarius. A. A lion and elephant: Jaina; India (D34). B. Teou-siou, the House of the Bushel, and Ki-siou, the House of the Manuring Tray (D35).

Points of Interest in Sagittarius

The Milky Way seems to be richer and more dense in the neighbourhood of Sagittarius than in most other regions. This circumstance has inspired many literary allusions, such as:

Midst golden stars he stands refulgent now
And thrusts the Scorpion with his bended bow.

Sir John Herschel once said of the Milky Way that it resembled "stars seemingly flung down by the handfuls, with both hands at once." Aratus, in his *Phaenomena*, advised sailors:

But even in the previous month (November, when the sun enters Sagittarius) stormtossed at sea, when the sun scorches the Bow and the Wielder of the Bow, trust no longer in the night but put to shore in the evening.

Many nebulae and clusters are noticeable in Sagittarius. M8, a cluster visible to the naked eye, is located approximately 6° west of λ-Sagittarii in the bow. The popular name for M8 is the Lagoon Nebula. Slightly above M8 is M20, popularly known as the Trifid Nebula, a diffuse type of nebula with many dark rifts. Well north of the Trifid Nebula is the Horseshoe or Omega Nebula, M17, in the shape of an arched figure resembling the Greek capital letter Omega (Ω).

Capricornus
The Seagoat

Under Aries, the Ram, is the story of how the gods were taken by surprise by Typhon, the awful titanic demon. To save themselves from destruction they hurriedly changed into all varieties of animals. The God Pan, in the form of a goat, was playing his pipes during an afternoon rest along the bank of a river when he was startled by the sudden approach of Typhon. With no time to think and, in panic (a term derived from his name), Pan dived into the river and changed himself into a fish. Everything happened so quickly, however, that only Pan's rear end became a fish's tail. The front part remained unchanged—a goat with little horns and a little billy goat beard—and so the Capricorn came to be (Figure 115).

When Pan emerged from the water he noticed that Jupiter was in great trouble. Typhon had torn Jupiter's muscles out of his legs and arms and had thereby paralysed him. Pan immediately blew such an awful shrill and penetrating note on his pipes that he forced Typhon to flee in great haste. Mercury, the swift messenger with his winged sandals, came down from Olympus when he heard the whistle call of Pan to see what was the matter. When Mercury found Jupiter lying powerless on

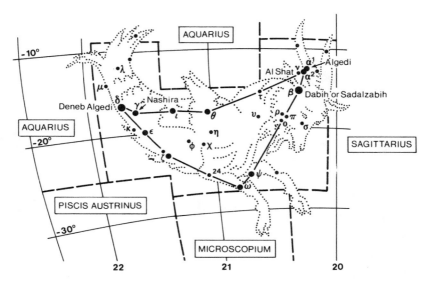

Figure 115. Capricornus. The Seagoat. (A42; Cicero, Roman, 1st Century B.C.)

216

the ground, he called for Pan's assistance. Together, they picked up the scattered remains of Jupiter's muscles and tied them carefully back in his arms and legs so that he could move once more. Jupiter quickly rose to Olympus, collected his deadly thunderbolts and pursued Typhon, who by now was gone. However, the sharp eyes of Jupiter spotted the evil demon. With one mighty swing of his godly arm, Jupiter hurled his largest thunderbolt toward Typhon. It hit Typhon with such force that it thrust him right back to his subterranean hide-out, where he slumped in a big heap and licked his wounds for a long time. Out of gratitude to Pan, whose presence of mind had saved him, Jupiter eternalised Pan in the stars as the constellation Capricorn (Figure 116).

Capricorn, lying between Aquarius and Sagittarius and consisting of faint stars only, tracks low above the southern horizon. At the end of July or the beginning of August, Capricorn can be seen at midnight due south. An easy way to locate Capricorn is to draw a line from Vega in the Lyre through Altair in the Eagle and on to the horizon. The faint stars of the head of Capricorn can be seen near where this line intersects the horizon.

Capricorn was, some two thousand years ago, the sign in the zodiac where the Sun would reach its lowest point in the sky during the Northern Hemisphere Winter. (Nowadays this point, which is called the Winter Solstice, lies against the background stars of Sagittarius.) In those far away days the symbol of the goat had a meaning. The Sun who, so it seemed, was on its way down forever, suddenly came to a standstill, lingered as if uncertain about what to do, then began to rise again. To ancient people this was a great moment which they called the birthday of the new unconquered Sun. There could not have been a better symbol for the rebirth of the Sun than a goat, especially a mountain goat, capable of jumping higher and higher from rock to rock.

Points of Interest in Capricorn

α-Capricorni, or Algedi, is actually two stars, α^1 and α^2. α^2 is about 100 light years distant, but α^1 appears to be about five times farther away. β-Capricorni, or Dabih, is also a double star which can be separated easily with an ordinary pair of field glasses. These two stars form the horns of the Goat. The colour of Algedi is yellow, and that of Dabih is bluish.

δ-Capricorni, or Deneb Algedi, "the Tail of the Goat," lies exactly at the tip of the tail of Capricorn. δ-Capricorni is always rememberd by astronomers as the star near which John Couch Adams (A.D. 1819–1892) of Cambridge University and Urbain Jean Joseph Le Verrier (A.D. 1811–1877) of France discovered simultaneously, in 1846, the planet now known as Neptune.

From 18–30 July a meteor stream called the Capricornids is visible, with its radiant point in α-Capricorni.

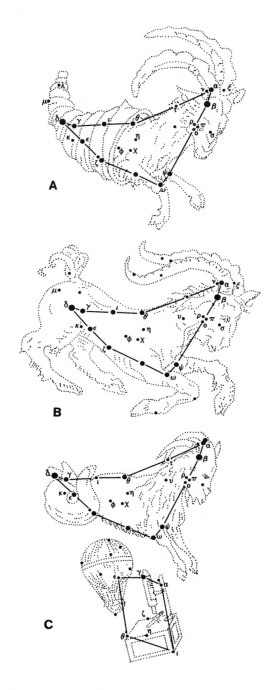

Figure 116. Capricornus. A. The Seagoat emanating from a large seashell. (A45; 15th Century.) **B.** The Ibex. (A46; Hyginus, Roman, ca. A.D. 1.) **C.** The Seagoat, the Microscope, and the obsolete constellation Globus Aerostaticus. (A48; Bode, German, ca. A.D. 1800.)

Scorpius
The Scorpion

Scorpius, the Scorpion, is a beautiful constellation that lies below Ophiuchus (Figures 117, 118). Scorpius is one of those constellations which always remains comparatively low above the southern horizon. Consequently, we cannot see this entire constellation from the middle and higher northern latitudes.

The heart of Scorpius is marked by the reddish star Antares. From this star three lines can be seen fanning out to three stars to the west which represent the claws of the animal. From Antares going southeastward one cannot miss that striking curve of stars which forms the tail of the

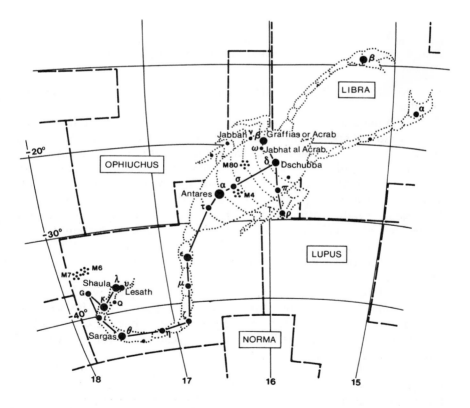

Figure 117. Scorpius. The Scorpion, with extended claws, as the constellation was recognized by the preclassical Greeks. (D36; Ptolemaeus, Greek, 2nd Century, A.D.)

219

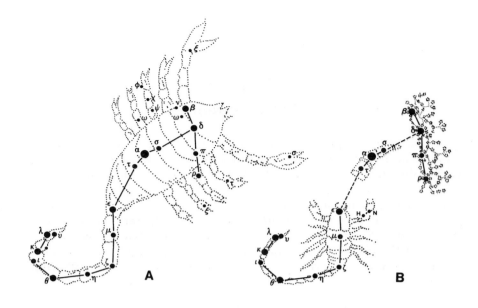

Figure 118. Scorpius. A. The Scorpion with shortened claws. (D37; Bode, German, ca. A.D. 1800.) **B.** The Scorpion with the Elephant Tusk and Diadem: Jaina, India (D38).

Scorpion, terminating in the poisonous upturned stinger, as if ready for an attack.

Scorpions are essentially creatures that frequent cracks, holes, and other secluded spots, and therefore are usually associated with acts of secrecy and evil. Scorpions also are active at night, a fact with symbolic meaning in popular astronomy. When the Sun passes through the stars of Scorpius, Winter commences bringing the long dark days of the cold and damp season. In previous months of the year the Sun has passed through Virgo, the Virgin, bringing the season of harvest, and Libra, the Scales, bringing the season for weighing and trading the gathered crops. In Winter, the grain lies stacked in barns and cellars, and it is in this season that vermin, amongst which may be counted the Scorpion, infest these stores.

If one looks on a star chart, the tail of the Scorpion will be seen to lie in a dark portion of the Milky Way. This signifies that the Scorpion lives in dark crevices. It was sometimes thought that the dark portion of the Milky Way was perhaps a crevice leading to the Underworld whence the Scorpion emerged.

Another story of the Scorpion is described in greater detail under Orion. It was Orion who boasted that he would exterminate all the animals on Earth, and was punished for his brazenness by the Goddess of Earth, Gaia, who sent a scorpion after him. A glance at a star map or planisphere will show how Orion disappears below the western horizon at the moment that Scorpius emerges over the eastern horizon. This movement represents the punishment of Orion, as he was bitten in his heel by the scorpion sent after him by Gaia. However, Orion is brought back to life by Ophiuchus, the Serpent Bearer, who gives him an antidote for the poison in his heel. Ophiuchus can be seen standing on top of the Scorpion when the latter sets in the west, which means that the vermin is trampled under Ophiuchus' feet. At the same time Orion comes up again in the east, recovered and healed. Jupiter punished Ophiuchus for his audacity in interfering with the lot of mankind, bestowed by the eternal gods, and sent Aquila, the Eagle, after him with one of his thunderbolts. When Ophiuchus sets in the west, the Eagle can be seen in a threatening position above Ophiuchus, symbolising that Ophiuchus is dying, mortally wounded by Jupiter's thunderbolt.

So the battle scene between Orion and the Scorpion can be followed day after day, season after season, year after year as an astronomical motion picture in the sky. This symbolises, of course, the eternal battle between light and dark. With the Sun in Scorpius, the Winter starts with its long dark days; with the Sun in Orion, the Summer has arrived with all its life-giving warmth. Orion represents life, the Scorpion represents death. The battle goes on and neither combatant is ever victorious. Although the animal is always seen as an evil creature—look how it crawls just as scorpions do, low over the horizon during May and June— the constellation itself is really exquisite and has a very good likeness to the animal it represents.

Once upon a time the Scorpion stretched its claws in an all-embracing curve to the stars of Libra, the Scales (Figure 117), about which we can still read in Ovid, who wrote:

In a wide curve of the skies he shines
And covers the space of two celestial signs.

But, nowadays, the stars of the Scales form a separate constellation.

The farther south one travels until reaching the middle latitudes of the Southern Hemisphere, the higher the Scorpion rises above the southern horizon. In doing so it seems that the Scorpion also loses its image of being an evil creature. From the Marshall Islands in the Pacific Ocean comes the myth of Dümur. The mother of all the stars is Ligedaner (Capella, in Auriga). Her oldest son is Dümur (Antares) and her youngest is Pleiades. Her sons came down from the vault of Heaven to visit their mother, who lived on the atoll Alinablab. While they were there, they suggested that he who was the first to reach a certain island somewhere in the East should be proclaimed King of the Stars.

The suggestion was agreed upon and all the sons busied themselves to get ready for the departure and their quest of the coveted kingship. The mother asked first of all that her eldest son should take her with him in his canoe. Dümur flatly refused, since his mother wanted to take many possessions the weight of which would impede the movement of his canoe. Then Ligedaner turned to each of her other sons only to discover that none of them would be willing to grant her request. Finally only the youngest son, Pleiades, was left. Pleiades did not object to his mother boarding his canoe or her bringing seven possessions. When the canoe had been lowered into the water, Ligedaner asked her son to load one object after the other in his canoe and gave him instructions as to where to place and fasten each one.

When all was ready, Pleiades started to row. One can imagine his surprise when the canoe shot forward with the greatest of ease, without his having to use the oars. The seven objects his mother brought turned out to be, in fact, previously unknown sail rigging. Driven by the wind the canoe overtook all the brothers' boats and in no time it closed in on Dümur's canoe. Dümur now ordered, on the strength of his right as the first-born son, that his youngest brother should hand over the canoe to him. With heavy heart Pleiades obeyed. However, Ligedaner now played a mean trick on her eldest son. She turned the canoe around and then jumped with Pleiades into the sea, taking with her the yardarm of the sail. And so they swam on to the island in the east.

In order to sail at all Dümur was forced to fasten the sail to his shoulders. This is why he has now a bent back. While Dümur tacked to get his canoe on course again, Ligedaner and Pleiades proceeded to their destination.

When Dümur finally reached the island and discovered that his youngest brother had become King of the Stars, he was so enraged that he wished never to see Pleiades again. This separation of Dümur and Pleiades can still be observed in the night sky. When Pleiades rises in the east, Dümur, or the star Antares, sets in the west. The bent back of Dümur can also still be seen in the curved line formed by the three stars σ-, α-, and τ-Scorpii and the line of fainter stars outlining his bent body (Figure 119).

The Dayak of Borneo, the Javanese, and the Balinese, all of whom live on islands in the Indonesian archipelago, see a palm tree in the stars of Scorpius (Figure 120A). The Javanese people see a hatchling goose in the curl of the stars of Scorpius' tail (Figure 120C). The bill fits in G-Scorpii. In conjunction with the previous constellation, the goose sits at the foot of the palm tree hatching out its eggs. Coconut palms are notoriously dangerous trees because the coconuts may suddenly part company with their stems. Anybody or anything unfortunate enough to be sitting under the tree when a coconut falls might easily be knocked unconscious. However, our goose sits at the lee side of the palm while the palm itself leans windward so that falling coconuts will not harm her.

The Maoris of New Zealand know Scorpius as Maui's fish hook. One day Maui was fishing with this hook (a jaw bone of his ancestress) when suddenly he felt it lodge in the bottom of the sea. He tugged and heaved

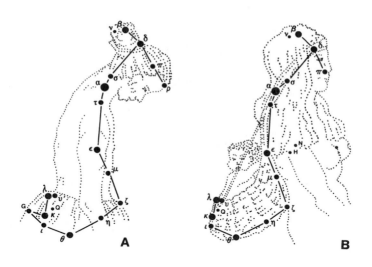

Figure 119. Scorpius. A. Dümur, oldest son of Ligedaner, mother of all the stars (D39). **B.** Mother with baby: Bakairi; South America (D40).

until finally the hook rushed up to the surface and lo . . . it brought up a huge fish-island. The island was green with grass. Trees were growing on the island. Men were hunting while women were cooking at their open fires. Maui warned his people not to harm the huge fish, but they did not listen and started hacking pieces out of it. This gave the island a serrated coast line. Finally the island broke into two islands, North and South Island—which we now know as New Zealand.

When the hook rushed up to the sea surface and broke free of the fish island, it had so much upward momentum that it shot right up into the sky. Today we see it as the stars of Maui's fish hook (Figure 120B).

The people living by Torres Strait, which separates the Cape York Peninsula of Australia and the island of New Guinea, saw the canoe of Tagai in Sagittarius and Corona Australis near the end of Scorpius' tail. This story tells that the crew sat in the middle of the canoe. The crew included the Usiam (stars of the Pleiades) and the Seg (the stars in alignment in Orion)—twelve men in all. They ate the food and drank the water which was stored aboard for the journey without asking permission from Tagai. Kareg, one of the men in the canoe, saw the others eat and drink the supplies, and he told Tagai, who came to the middle of the canoe with a rope. With it he strung the Usiam together and threw them overboard. Tagai was very angry and told Kareg that he was the only man who could stay in the canoe. Figure 120D shows a large object— probably the Usiam—hanging from a rope beneath the canoe. Nearby

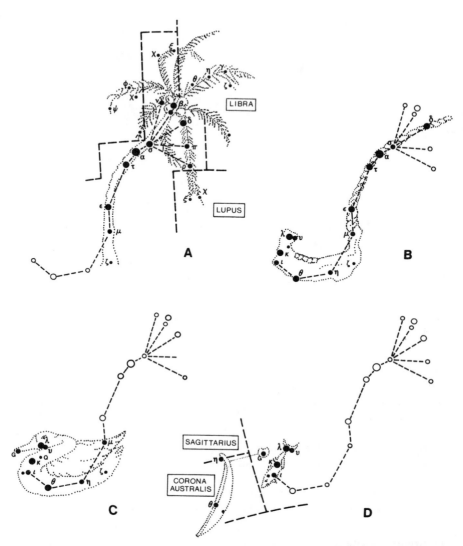

Figure 120. Scorpius. A. The Palm Tree: East Indies (D44). **B.** Maui's Fish Hook: Maori; New Zealand (D46). **C.** The Hatchling Goose: Java (D45). **D.** Tagai's Canoe: Torres Strait, Australia and New Guinea (D47).

is a suckerfish, possibly waiting to attach himself to the Usiam for a meal.

Other of the many asterisms known for Scorpius are shown in Figure 121.

Points of Interest in Scorpius

Antares is derived from the Greek words *Anti* and *Ares*—the "Rival of" or the "Equivalent of" Ares, the War God—on account of its reddish colour. Antares is a very large star, with a diameter about 300 times that

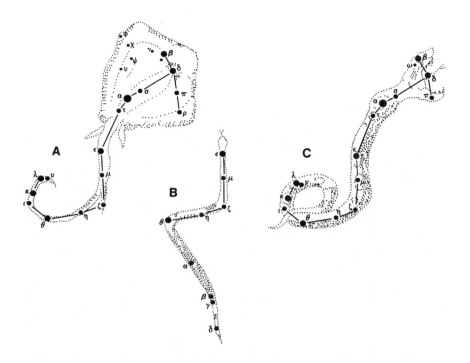

Figure 121. Scorpius. A. A ray: East Indies, western Pacific (D41). **B.** A serpent: Java (D43). **C.** The Great Serpent: Tukano, Kobeua, Siusi; Brazil (D42).

of the Sun, but with a reddish colour which indicates that the star is fairly cool (about 3,000° K). Antares is believed to be at a distance of about 522 light years from Earth. As Antares lies in the zodiac, it is often occulted by the passing moon, which is an interesting phenomenon to observe.

β-Scorpii, the upper claw of the animal, is a double star, white and purple in colour. δ-, π- and ρ-Scorpii form the other claw. σ- and τ-Scorpii flank Antares as bodyguards. ε-, μ-, ζ-, η-, θ-, κ-, and λ-Scorpii form the graceful curve of the tail. Above the star λ-Scorpii, in the tip of the stinger, are the two star clusters M6 and M7. Close to Antares is cluster M4, and about halfway on the line forming the top claw of the Scorpion (a line from α- to β-Scorpii) is found M80. All of these objects can be seen with field glasses or, better still, a small telescope which reveals hazy patches. Large telescopes resolve these patches into distinct star clusters.

Libra

The Scales

Libra, the Scales, is a constellation with an interesting and rather confusing history (Figure 122). Libra is one of the 12 signs of the zodiac, and was the last of these signs to be recognised. The constellation does not appear to have been known as such to preclassical astronomy in the Mediterranean region, and the stars of which it is composed were recognised as a distinct part of the extended Scorpion (Figure 117). When and where the separation of some of the claw stars of Scorpius took place in order to establish a separate constellation is not certain, but Allen, in *Star Names*, indicates that this could have occurred in Chaldaea. Knowing the present position of α-Librae, I asked the Zeiss Planetarium projector to determine when this star would have coincided with the Autumnal Equinox. The precession dial on this instrument indicated that the year would have been 1190 B.C. This, then, might be taken as the approximate time that Libra, the Scales, came into use since it is often considered a symbol of equinoctial equality. Classical Greek and Roman writers referred to the Scales as weighing the lengths of day and night at the Autumnal Equinox.

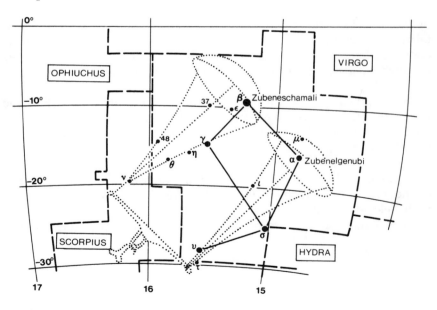

Figure 122. Libra. The Scales. (C26; al-Sufi, Persian, 10th Century A.D.)

That Libra was once part of Scorpion is evident from the names of the stars α- and β-Librae—respectively Zubeneschemali, "the Northern Claw," and Zubenelgenubi, "the Southern Claw." The Roman poet-astronomer Manilius said of Libra, when it was at the Autumnal Equinox:

Then day and night are weigh'd in Libra's scales
Equal for a while . . . .

The Roman poet Vergilius alluded to this too and gave some agricultural advice as well when he said:

When Astrea's balance, hung on high betwixt nights and days,
Divides the sky, then yoke your oxen, sow your winter grains
Till cold December comes with driving rains.

Sometimes the Scales are seen placed in the right hand of Virgo, who, personified as the Goddess of Justice, weighed the souls of men after death in order to determine whether they should go to the Elysian Fields of eternal happiness or be sent instead to places of punishment.

The English astronomer John Flamsteed used α- and β-Librae as his scale pan stars, but he made the scale beam point towards the north. He also added the Hermit Bird in the same location where the French astronomer Pierre Charles LeMonnier (A.D. 1715–1799) created the Solitaire (Figure 123). The latter was made up from the stars η-, 50-, 51-, 52-, 58-, 59-, 60-Hydrae and a few stars of the Centaur.

In more recent times an unknown illustrator placed Noctua, the Night Owl, in these stars. Some years ago I gave a lecture about obsolete constellations. At that time I had not seen Elijah Burritt's rendering of Noctua, so I made my own sketch of the Night Owl for use in the lecture (Figure 124). The constellations Hermit Bird, Solitaire and Noctua are not in use today.

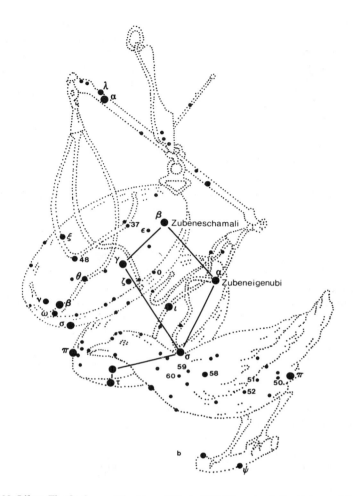

Figure 123. Libra. The Scales and the Hermit Bird. (C27; Flamsteed, English, ca. A.D. 1729.)

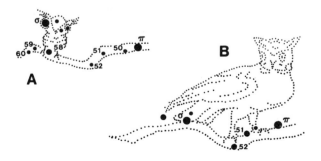

Figure 124. Libra. A. Noctua, the Night Owl. (Staal, British, A.D. 1986.) **B.** Noctua, the Night Owl, after an illustration in Elijah H. Burritt's *Atlas* accompanying his *Geography of the Heavens*, first published in 1833. (Staal, British, A.D. 1986.)

Ara

The Altar

Ara is the celestial Altar, perhaps representing the one created by the Olympic gods after they defeated the Titans. The Olympians needed an altar upon which to swear their allegiance to Jupiter and perform other mutual vows, so Ara was built—adorned with stars and filled with burning incense. The smoke coming from this altar was represented in the night sky by the soft whiteness of the Milky Way. The Altar has been positioned in various illustrations so that the flames and smoke rise toward the north in some and to the south in others (Figure 125).

Ara is located only a short distance above the southern horizon when it culminates, as seen from the southernmost United States. However, due to the unsteadiness of the atmosphere and the possible presence of clouds and haze it is very difficult to see this constellation even from most locations in the lower northern latitudes.

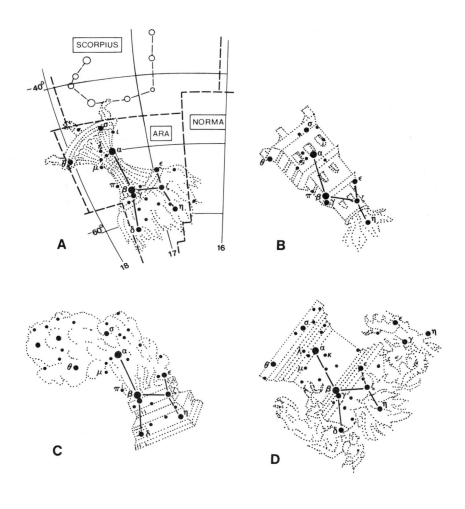

Figure 125. Ara. A. The Incense Altar, shown with flames rising southward. (A11; Bayer, German, ca. A.D. 1603.) **B.** The Lighthouse. (A12; Aratus, Greek, ca. 270 B.C.) **C.** A sacrificial altar with an animal offering. (A13; Blaeu. Dutch, 16th–17th centuries A.D.) **D.** An incense altar with devils around the flames. (A14; Hyginus, Roman, ca. A.D. 1.)

Corona Australis
The Southern Crown

In Ovid's *Metamorphoses*, Book III, is the story of how Bacchus was born from the seed of Jupiter and Semele. Juno, Jupiter's wife, had learned that willing Semele had grown big with the seed of generous Jupiter. So now Juno schemed to bring about Semele's downfall. Juno changed herself into the form of Semele's old nurse maid and confronted Semele with all sorts of seemingly well meant advice. Juno feigned that she did not believe that Semele carried Jupiter's child and she told Semele, "Next time you see him, ask him to appear before you as he would when he takes Juno into his arms."

Poor innocent Semele did just that. Jupiter was horrified by her request but he could not refuse. When he came to her bed, Semele could not take the full thrust of godly heat and love. She burned to ashes in Jupiter's quick embrace. The unborn child was ripped from its mother's womb and sewn into Jupiter's thigh. Ino, Semele's sister, tended the child after it was born. The baby was named Bacchus, and was destined to become the God of Wine.

When "twice-born" Bacchus had grown into manhood he placed a wreath in the stars to honour his mother, Semele. This is what we know today as Corona Australis, the Southern Crown (Figure 126). Corona Australis also has been seen as a wreath, perhaps a victor's wreath.

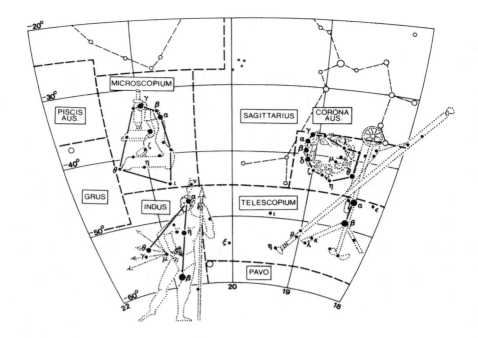

Figure 126. Corona Australis, Telescopium, Microscopium and Indus. The Southern Crown and Telescope (E2; La Caille, French, 18th Century A.D.); and Microscope and Indian (Staal, British, A.D. 1986.)

Telescopium, Microscopium and Indus
The Telescope, the Microscope and the Indian

The Abbé Nicolas Louis de La Caille created Telescopium to commemorate the invention of the telescope. This constellation overlaps a little with neighbouring Sagittarius, Ophiuchus, Corona Australis and Scorpius (Figure 126). In some old atlases this constellation was called Tubus Astronomicus.

The creation of the constellation Microscopium is also credited officially to La Caille. Like many other constellations created during the 17th and 18th centuries, Microscopium was created to commemorate the scientific progress that was occurring in Western Europe during the period (Figures 116, 126).

An obsolete constellation called Neper, the Auger or Borer, by some accounts was located near, and perhaps included, the stars of Microscopium. By other accounts, however, Neper was considered to be a predecessor of Monoceros, the Unicorn, located in a part of the sky distant from Microscopium.

The German astronomer Johann Bayer created the constellation Indus, the Indian (Figure 126). Indus is believed to have been placed in the southern skies as a memento of the American Indians which Magellan and other explorers discovered during their travels in the Western Hemisphere. In particular, Indus could commemorate the Indians of Tierra del Fuego and Patagonia.

Constellations Around The Celestial Poles

Six constellations are located above declination 60° North, including Cepheus, Cassiopeia, Ursa Minor, Ursa Major, Draco, and Camelopardus. In contrast the area around the South Celestial Pole is crowded with some 14 constellations, including Tucana, Hydrus, Dorado, Musca, Volans, Crux, Circinus, Norma, Triangulum Australe, Chamaeleon, Apus, Mensa, Octans and Carina of Argo Navis.

Four of the northern polar constellations already have been described. Draco and Camelopardus, however, remain to be discussed. The constellations of the southern polar region, largely unknown to Europeans until the 15th Century A.D., do not have many stories to tell. During the early voyages of discovery different sailors claimed certain areas of the sky and placed the tools of their trade in these stars. Some birds and animals discovered during the Age of Exploration also have found a place of honour in the stars around the South Celestial Pole.

Camelopardus
The Giraffe

Camelopardus, the Giraffe, was identified in outline form by the German astronomer Jakob Bartsch (or Bartschius) in A.D. 1614. Bartsch said that this constellation represented the camel that brought Rebecca to Isaac. The shape of the constellation and its many stars (spots) led Johannes Hevelius to formally name it Camelopardus, meaning "Camel-Leopard" or "Spotted Camel" (Figure 129). This constellation has since become known as the Giraffe.

Camelopardus comprises several extremely faint stars scattered from near Polaris to Perseus and Auriga. The Giraffe is difficult to trace because it has only four stars of magnitudes 4 and 4.5. The remaining stars are all of magnitudes 5 and 6. A clear, dark moonless night is required to see this constellation.

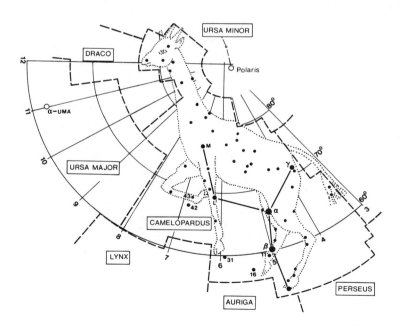

Figure 129. Camelopardus. The Giraffe. (A30; Hevelius, Polish, ca. A.D. 1690.)

Tucana
The Toucan

Toucans are interesting birds with extremely large and colourful beaks. The large colourful beak serves not only for feeding but also functions as a social signal. It is not surprising that the conspicuous, colorful toucan found a place of honour in the southern skies after early explorers found and admired these curious and beautiful birds.

There is no Classical mythology as such about this constellation. Johann Bayer published this constellation as Toucan. Later the name was Latinised to Tucana in keeping with the custom of giving the constellations Latin names. The English called the bird the Brazilian Pye. Another name used is Anser Americanus, the American Gans. In Dutch, Gans means Goose, and it is therefore rather a mixed honour for the bird to have himself described with so many illustrious names in different languages.

The Toucan sits on the Small Magellanic Cloud (Figure 130). However, because the Toucan lies high in the southern sky, sometimes the bird will be sitting upright in the sky and sometimes he will be upside down.

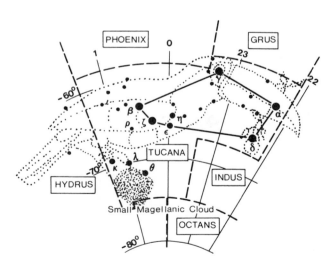

Figure 130. Tucana. The Toucan. (JS83; Staal, British, A.D. 1986.)

Hydrus
The Male Watersnake

Hydrus appears to be a creation of Johann Bayer (Figure 131). Hydrus was created as a male companion for Hydra, the Female Waterserpent. Legend says that in order for Hydrus to pay a visit to Hydra, he had to swim all the way up the river Eridanus, cross overland below Orion, and then swim across the River of Heaven (The Milky Way) before he could reach his amour.

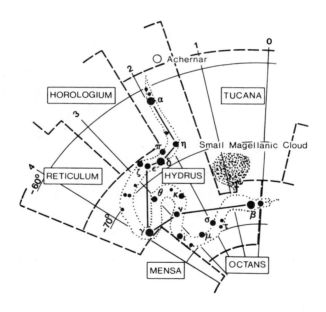

Figure 131. Hydrus. The Male Watersnake. (JS44; Staal, British, A.D. 1986.)

Dorado and Volans
The Gold Fish and the Flying Fish

Dorado, the Gold Fish, was created by Johann Bayer in 1603 based on information provided by European sailors who had been on voyages to the southern part of the Western Hemisphere. Dorado is usually translated as Goldfish or Gold Fish. Dorado, however, does not refer to the little golden fish commonly kept in household aquariums or garden ponds, but rather to members of the dolphin (fish, not mammal) family Coryphaenidae, which are found in many tropical seas. Dolphins, also known as Pompanos, can be large; they sometimes exceed five feet in length. These fish are also colorful, and have attracted attention as curiosities because they appear to change colours. Dolphins are very fast swimmers and frequently leap out of the water to catch flying fish. No wonder this playful fish, large numbers of which gamboled in and out of the water alongside ships, made sailors feel that their presence was a good omen for the journey. Sailors traditionally refrained from catching dolphins for food even though the flesh is delicious. On older star maps Dorado is sometimes shown as a swordfish but this is not a correct representation of the constellation.

Volans, the Flying Fish, also was introduced by Johann Bayer. The official name of this constellation is Piscis Volans, the Flying Fish, but astronomers today usually refer to it as Volans. Volans was placed in the stars of the southern circumpolar region presumably after sailors that had participated in the voyages of discovery and exploration reported seeing flying fish (Figure 132). Appropriately, Volans adjoins Dorado; Pompano often feed on schools of flying fish.

Points of Interest in and near Dorado

The South Ecliptic Pole lies in the head of Dorado (Figure 132). The Dutch globe maker Willem Jansson Blaeu called this point Polus Doradinalis.

Ferdinand Magellan (A.D. ?1480–1521) was a Portuguese navigator who commanded the first expedition that sailed around the world and thereby proved that the Earth was round. Magellan did not live to see the end of the expedition; he was killed by tribesmen in the Philippine Islands. Of the five ships that started the expedition, only one returned to Spain, arriving in St. Lucar on 6 September 1522 under the command of Juan Sebastian del Cano. Of the original 240 men who embarked on the expedition, only 17 returned. During the journey, the Magellan expedition saw the two misty patches we now know as the Clouds of

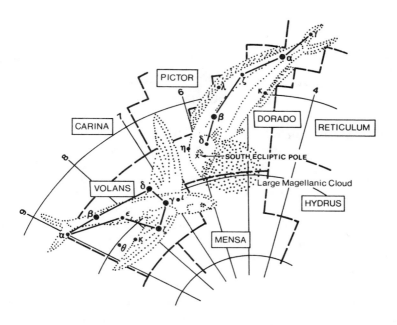

Figure 132. Dorado and Volans. Dorado, the Gold Fish, and Volans, the Flying Fish. (JS34 and JS88; Staal, British, A.D. 1986.)

Magellan, or the Magellanic Clouds, in the region of the South Celestial Pole.

The Small Magellanic Cloud in Tucana is an irregular galaxy visible to the unaided eye. Its neighbour, some 22° distant in the constellation Dorado, is the Large Magellanic Cloud. The small cloud is about 196,000 light years distant from Earth, and the Large Magellanic Cloud is about 168,000 light years away. The two systems seem to be connected by a bridge of gas, stars and clusters. The large cloud also contains the famous Tarantula Nebula (NGC 2070) and the most luminous star known, S-Doradus.

Musca

The Southern Fly

Musca, or Musca Australis, is the Southern Fly. This constellation was envisioned by sailors during the early voyages of discovery. Initially recognised as a bee, this constellation was given its modern name about 1752 by La Caille (Figure 133). The name of the constellation suggests that there must be a Northern Fly too. And indeed there was—Musca Borealis—but this unfortunately has become obsolete (Figure 133). The main stars of Musca Borealis are the stars numbered 33-, 39-, 41- and 45-Arietis. Since Musca Borealis is now obsolete, the suffix Australis is no longer needed for the southern constellation and astronomers today refer to the Southern Fly as simply Musca.

There are two stories of Greco-Roman age about a gadfly which might relate to Musca Borealis. The first one is that of Bellerophon who, rushing towards Mount Olympus on the winged horse Pegasus, tried to enter the domain of the heavenly gods. Jupiter, angered by this temerity, sent a gadfly which stung Pegasus. As the horse reared, Bellerophon was thrown off and fell to the Earth where, broken in spirits, he wandered a lonely man until his death.

The other story is that of Io, who was great with child by Jupiter. To conceal Io from Juno, Jupiter changed the poor girl into a heifer. She wandered and roamed through Europe, the Levant, and finally arrived in Egypt and Ethiopia. All the while she was closely watched by the one hundred eyes of Argus until Jupiter sent Mercury to lull Argus into a deep sleep with his magic flute. Once asleep, Mercury severed Argus' head from his body. Juno then sent a gadfly who mercilessly pursued Io. In Ethiopia, Jupiter put an end to Io's suffering by letting her have her human form back again. Io thereafter gave birth to Jupiter's son, Epaphus.

Crux
The Southern Cross

The Southern Cross has been romanticised in music with the song *Under the Southern Cross* ("No other love have I"). As a result, this constellation has gained a reputation for conjuring up thoughts of romantic tropical nights in balmy southern climes. However, the would-be traveler may be in for a disappointment, especially if he happens to be familiar with our cross in the Northern Hemisphere. The Southern Cross is a small cross made up of very bright first and second magnitude stars (Figure 134). Early sailors looked upon this cross as a good omen sent to guide them through unknown waters.

The Southern Cross as such was not known to the ancients during the time of Ptolemaeus who, for instance, used these bright stars to mark the rear legs of the Centaur. Recognition of the stars of Crux Australis as a separate constellation dates at least from 1592, when the English globe maker 'Emerie Mollineux illustrated it. Jakob Bartsch drew it separately in 1624, and the French astronomer Augustin Royer—who is usually credited with defining it—had represented the Southern Cross as a separate constellation by 1679. This constellation is known today as simply Crux.

A great variety of other objects has been seen in the stars of Crux by people of widely dispersed cultures (Figures 135–137).

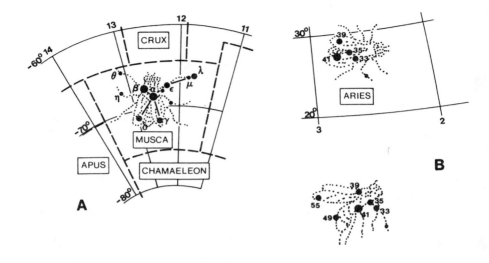

Figure 133. Musca. A. The Southern Fly. (JS57A; Staal, British, A.D. 1986.) **B.** Musca Borealis, the Northern Fly, and Vespa, the Wasp, or Apis, the Bee, all obsolete constellations in Aries. (JS57B, C; Staal, British, A.D. 1986.)

Figure 134. Crux. The Southern Cross. (F25; Blaeu, Dutch, 16th–17th centuries A.D.)

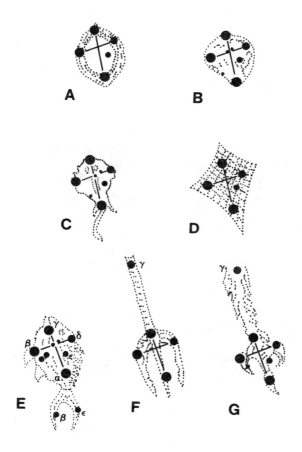

Figure 135. Crux. A. Mandorla, the Almond, a name given to the Southern Cross by Amerigo Vespucci (F26). **B.** A knee cap or knee protector: Solomon Islands (F29). **C.** A ray: East Indies, Brazil (F27). **D.** A net for catching Palolo worms: Solomon Islands (F30). **E.** A fish: Samoa, Marshall Islands (F28). **F.** Tagai's Fishing Spear: Torres Strait, Australia (F31). **G.** The Eagle's Foot: Aranda, Loritja; central Australia (F32).

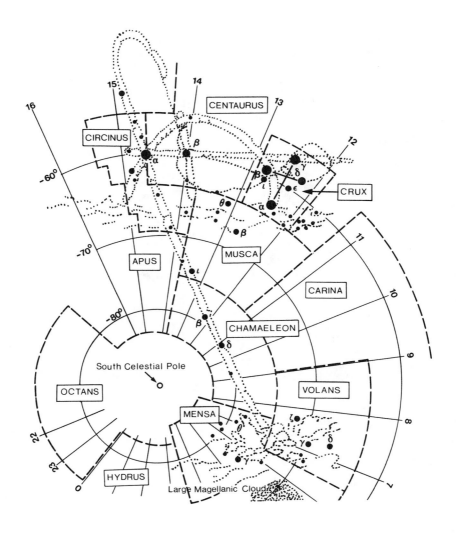

Figure 136. Crux. The Bird Snare: Bakairi; central Brazil (B24).

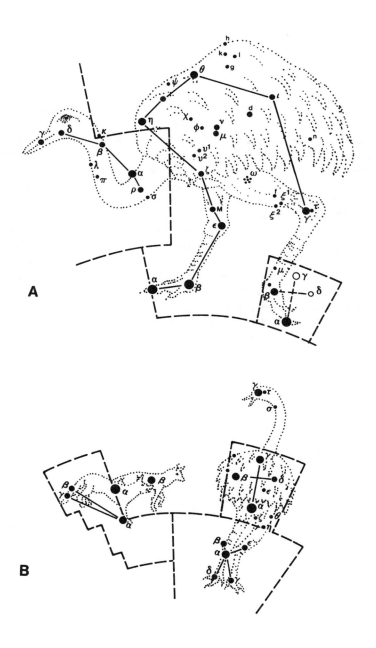

Figure 137. Crux. A. The Great Rhea: Bororo; Brazil (B25). **B.** A rhea under attack by two dogs: Mocovi; Argentina (B26).

Apus
The Bird of Paradise

There is no known Classical mythology about Apus, the Bird of Paradise. Europeans were introduced to the Birds of Paradise for the first time in 1522, for skins of some of these birds were among the natural curiosities on board the sole surviving ship of the Magellan expedition when it returned to Spain. The beauty of these skins, and others collected later, impressed the Europeans and led to the development of an appealing, if grossly inaccurate, folklore about the birds. It is not surprising therefore that this colourful bird found a place of honour in the stars of the southern skies. Johann Bayer is usually identified as the originator of this constellation, although he attributed its formation to European navigators of the early part of the 16th Century. Bayer originally published the Bird of Paradise in 1603 on his planisphere of new southern constellations (Figure 138).

The stars of Apus are not very conspicuous. α-, β-, γ-, δ-Apodus, all of magnitude 4, are the brightest stars in the constellation. Apus is approximately 13° from the South Celestial Pole. On older maps one may find the name Avis Indica, the Indian Bird, used for this constellation.

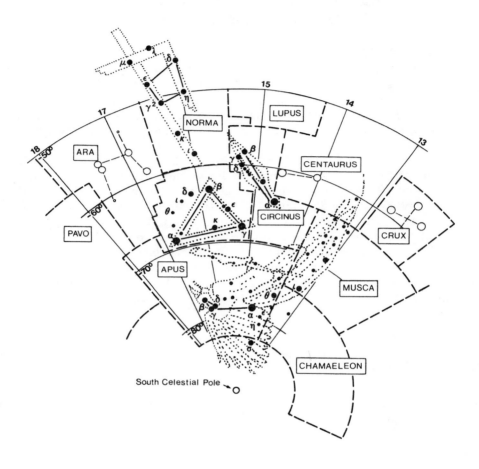

Figure 138. Apus, Circinus, Norma and Triangulum Australe. The Bird of Paradise, the Drawing Compass, the Carpenter's Square, and the Southern Triangle. (Apus: JS3; Staal, British, A.D. 1986; others: E3; La Caille, French, 18th Century A.D.)

253

Circinus, Norma and Triangulum Australe
The Drawing Compass, the Carpenter's Square and the Southern Triangle

The Abbé Nicolas Louis de La Caille created the constellation Circinus, the Drawing Compass. The drawing compass was used by carpenters and navigators on ships during the early voyages of discovery. Perhaps La Caille wished to eternalise this tool of exploration and discovery in the stars of the southern skies. The stars of Circinus are not very conspicuous. α-Circini, magnitude 3, is the pivot of the two legs of the compass.

Norma, the Carpenter's or Set Square, is yet another tool which ship's carpenters carried with them during the early voyages of discovery. The official name of this constellation is Norma and Regula, the Carpenter's Square and Ruler, but today astronomers refer to it only as Norma. This constellation is also attributed to La Caille.

It appears that Johann Bayer first published a description of Triangulum Australe, the Southern Triangle, in his *Uranometria* in 1603. The triangle is another of those tools used by carpenters and navigators.

Circinus, Norma and Triangulum Australe are illustrated in Figure 138.

Pavo

The Peacock

Pavo is the Peacock. Although in mythology the Peacock dates back to ancient times, as a constellation it is actually fairly new, having been introduced by Johann Bayer. Bayer placed the Peacock near the stars of the South Celestial Pole (Figure 139).

We return again to the story of Argus with the hundred eyes who had been ordered by Juno to guard Io, who—pregnant with Jupiter's child—had been changed into a heifer by Jupiter. Jupiter asked Mercury if he could help release Io from her plight. Agreeing to do so, Mercury disguised himself as a shepherd's boy and made friends with Argus. Mercury played his pipes and talked like a metronome for hours on end. Slowly, a soporific drowsiness began to fall upon the hundred eyes, and Argus was lulled into a deep sleep. As soon as Argus was asleep, Mercury hacked the bent neck of the demon, and so Argus perished. Thereafter, Juno took all of Argus' eyes and placed them in the tail feathers of her favourite bird, the peacock.

Another story involves Argos—the builder of the ship Argo, made famous by the journey of the Argonauts. When Argo died, Juno changed him into a peacock and placed him in the southern sky not far from his ship.

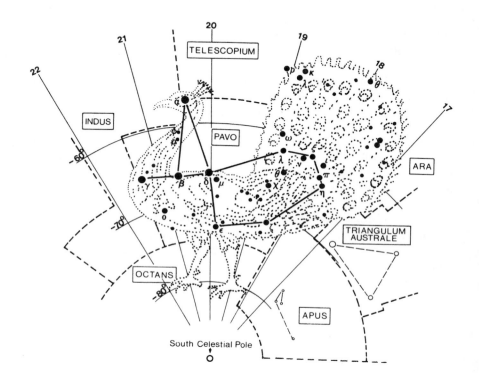

Figure 139. Pavo. The Peacock. (D11; Blaeu, Dutch, 16th–17th centuries A.D.)

Octans

The Octant

The Abbé Nicolas Louis de La Caille created this faint constellation in the region of the sky near the South Celestial Pole around 1752 (Figure 140). John Hadley had invented the octant in 1730 and, in his honour, this constellation is sometimes known as Octans Hadleianus, but modern astronomers refer to it only as Octans. The octant was the forerunner of the sextant. The frame of an octant has a top angle of 45° (one eighth of a circle, hence octant). The improved sextant has a frame angle of 60° (one sixth of a circle, hence sextant).

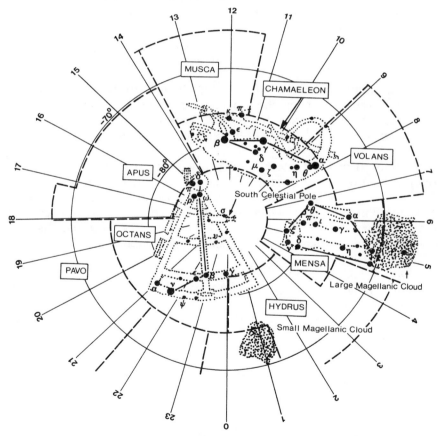

Figure 140. Octans, Mensa and Chamaeleon. The Octant, Table Mountain, and the Chameleon. (JS59, 54, 23; Staal, British, A.D. 1986.)

Octans is the constellation *par excellence* of the southern polar region. At the crest of the southern dome of Heaven and scattered around the South Celestial Pole are the stars of Octans. These stars, however, are very faint—so faint in fact that the casual observer might get the impression that the area of the South Celestial Pole is fairly dark and devoid of stars. ν- Octantis, at magnitude 3.8, is the brightest star in the constellation.

Is there a South Celestial Pole star? Yes there is, namely σ-Octantis. Unfortunately, this star is so faint (magnitude 5.46) that it is quite useless as a navigational star. Had this star been as bright as Polaris in the Northern Hemisphere, then there would have been a South Celestial Pole star only 58' of arc away from the South Celestial Pole. Due to precession, σ-Octantis will move slowly away from the true South Celestial Pole. In the year A.D. 2000, σ-Octantis will be about 1° from the South Celestial Pole.

There is not much mythology attached to this barren region of the sky. Aratus brushed the South Celestial Pole region aside because it could not be seen:

> . . . stars in other parts are drawn across the heavens always through all time continually. But the axis shifts not a whit, but unchanging is forever fixed, and in the midst it holds the earth in equipoise and wheels the heavens itself around. On either side the axis ends in two poles, but thereof the one is not seen, whereas the other faces us in the North high above the ocean.

In Book II of Ovid's *Metamorphoses*, we can read about the famous ride of Phaethon. In this story, Phaethon asked his father, Helios, the Sun God, if he could drive the Sun Chariot for one day. Helios tried to dissuade Phaethon because he knew the boy could not possibly control the four fiery horses. When Phaethon rejected this warning, the Sun God gave him all sorts of advice, including the following:

> Do not take the direct road through the Five Zones of the sky, but cut obliquely in a wide arc within the three zones, skirting South Heaven and Far North.

Mensa
Table Mountain

Mons Mensae means literally "Mountain of the Table," hence Table Mountain. This constellation was formed by the Abbé Nicolas Louis de La Caille and named after the famous landmark at the southern tip of Africa. Today astronomers refer to this constellation simply as Mensa, the Table (Figure 140).

This landform has a mesa-like top, each side of which is flanked by a peak which the locals call "Devil's Peak" and "Lion's Head." The flat top is some 3,566 feet above sea level. When early sailors approached the southern tip of Africa they could see Table Mountain from far away. If the mountain was clear of clouds, the sailors anticipated good weather ahead. Dense clouds over the mountain was an omen of bad weather to come. When Dutch sailors used to see these clouds hanging over the mountain, they would say *"De tafel is gedekt,"* which means "The table is laid." The Dutch and Germans call the mountain Tafelberg.

Sinbad the Sailor thought that Table Mountain was a huge magnet which could pull his dhows into the abyss. Bartholomeu Dias, the first European to sail to the southern tip of Africa, saw in Table Mountain an anvil where the storm deities fashioned storms and gales. Consequently he called the region *Cabo Tormentoso,* "Cape of Tormenting Storms." It was King John of Portugal who later named the region the Cape of Good Hope. Sir Francis Drake said that the Cape of Good Hope region was the most stately and fairest cape he saw in his entire circumnavigation of the Earth.

In spite of the fame of its namesake, the stars of Mons Mensae are extremely dim, ranging from magnitudes 5 to 6. Close by is the Large Magellanic Cloud, which symbolises the table cloth that may soon be spread over the mountain. While living in Johannesburg, the author tried often to spot the stars of Mensa but with very little success because Johannesburg, like any other large city, has too much light and air pollution. But when on tour in Krüger National Park, the famous wildlife reserve, I managed to see most of the stars of Mensa. Sunset at this latitude is rapid and darkness is complete in about 15 minutes. After cooking our evening meal barbecue style, which the locals call *braaivlees* (*braai;* to fry or roast; *vlees;* meat), we used to lounge in deck chairs and scan the heavens. On one of these occasions I had the good fortune to locate most of the elusive stars of Mensa. The Large Magellanic Cloud is an easy guide for finding Mensa.

Chamaeleon
The Chameleon

Johann Bayer was the first to describe and illustrate Chamaeleon. There is no classical mythology connected with this small constellation. When European seafarers of the 15th Century saw the stars of the Southern Hemisphere for the first time, they placed numerous new constellations in the sky commemorating their trades and professions or newly discovered birds and animals. The power of the chameleon to camouflage itself against its surroundings, and to change colours seemingly at will, must have fascinated these early voyagers. The sailors assigned unpredictability and fickleness to the chameleon (Figure 140).

Sun, Moon, Milky Way and Shooting Stars

Just as myths and legends developed around the constellations, so did they develop around other permanent celestial bodies and transient events. The dynamic daily cycles of the Sun and the Moon were easily observed, readily predictable and obviously important events that lent themselves to interpretation by early man. Likewise, the Milky Way, a prominent and always visible feature in the heavens—and the regularly occurring but somewhat less predictable meteors—lent themselves to use in stories involving the patterns and actions taking place on the celestial dome.

Helios and Phaethon
Helios, the Sun God and Phaethon, his Son

The Sun has been, still is, and for a long time will be the most important star to mankind as it is the source of the light and heat that supports all life on Earth.

The following version of a story involving the Sun dates from the days of the Roman civilization when one of Rome's greatest poets, Ovid, lived and wrote his *Metamorphoses*. In *Metamorphoses*, Ovid managed to record the Sun saga with extraordinary colour and vivacity. The following rendition of this story is taken from *Metamorphoses*.

A long time ago lived a youth called Epaphus and it was said that his father was none other than Jupiter, the highest of all Olympic gods. In the same time also lived another youth, Phaethon, whose mother was Clymene and whose father was the Sun God, Helios.

Fate would have it that these two young men came to quarrel one day about the authenticity of their descent. After a lot of bickering and teasing, Epaphus insulted Phaethon by telling him that he was not at all from godly blood; that if he were, he had better prove it.

Deeply hurt, Phaethon went to his mother, Clymene, and told her about the discord. Of course, Phaethon asked his mother for proof that he was in fact conceived from godly blood. Clymene could confirm this with her own words, but could she give tangible evidence? No. How could she, a mortal woman, give such proof? She said to him, "There is only one possibility of finding out, Phaethon. Go to your godly father and ask him for proof. I can only tell you this: look up at the Sun. I swear by that radiant light, which can see and hear us, that you are indeed the son of Helios. If I should speak a lie, then may my eyes see that light for the last time. It is not very difficult to find your father's house. Yonder where he commences his steep path in the morning—there is his palace, closely bordering the Earth. If you feel inclined, then go to him and question him yourself."

When Phaethon heard his mother speak so encouragingly, he jumped up in high spirits. Already he saw in his mind's eye the picture of his father's palace in Heaven. He did not hesitate. At once he began his long journey and travelled through far away countries, first through the land of the Ethiopians, and much later through the empire of the Indians. Finally, he reached the spot his mother had pointed out to him. From here he could see the glittering outlines of his father's palace in the far distance.

Dazzled by the light that reflected from the Sun's palace, he saw the royal sanctuary with its high columns which radiated the purest gold in imitation of the flames of the Sun. The roof was covered with gleaming ivory. The double doors which opened outwards shone with a silvery light. Indeed the product of the artist's hand surpassed the purity of the materials from which the palace was made.

Vulcan, the Smith of the Underworld, had adorned both doors of the Sun's palace with the most elaborate chiselwork. On one side of the doors he had created the sea encircling the continents and, above it, the high rising heavens. In the sea one could see the sea gods who, in conformance with their domain, had adopted a dark blue colour. Here sat Triton, with the horn of a large shell, and Proteus, who could change himself into all kinds of shapes. Here also could be seen Aegeon who contended with the enormous whale. Elsewhere were the Sea Goddess Doris with her daughters—some swimming around, others combing entangled seaweeds from their hair, and yet others riding around on fishes.

On another part of the door could be observed the Earth, which harboured the people and their houses, the forests, the wild animals, and the rivers, along with nymphs and other Earth gods. Above the Earth was the sky, glittering with stars. Cleverly fashioned on the right wing door were six zodiac signs and, on the left door, another six.

All this Phaethon saw from a distance. Then he began to ascend the slowly rising path that led to the palace. When Phaethon arrived at the portals, he resolutely entered and directed his footsteps towards the throne where his father sat. He could not, however, resist the glare coming from the Sun God.

There was Helios, draped in a purple garment and seated on his throne which flickered with clear emeralds. On his left and right stood the goddesses of the Day, the Month, the Year, and the Century. The Hours stood equally spaced in a row and beside them was the fresh new Spring, girdled with a wreath of Spring flowers. Then followed the airily dressed Summer Goddess, who wore a wreath of grain; the Autumn Goddess who looked dirty and messy like trampled grapes; and the icy cold Winter Goddess whose hair was covered with snow.

Then suddenly the Sun God saw the youth who, looking around with hestitation, was frightened amidst his new surroundings. Helios addressed the youth. "What reasons have brought you here? Why have you come to this stronghold? I know who you are, Phaethon, my son, whose fatherhood cannot be denied."

Phaethon, gladdened by these words, shed his fear and spoke. "O Light, which is familiar to the whole world. You, my father, Helios. If you allow me to make use of your name and if Clymene my mother has not lied under false pretenses, give me a pledge, which will make it truly obvious and credible that I spring from you. Take away this uncertainty from my heart."

The father, who saw that his son could not endure the light of his beaming wreath of sunrays, took it off and told Phaethon to come nearer. After they had greeted each other by embracing, Helios spoke. "You do not deserve that people should say that you do not spring from my blood. Your mother has at any rate told you your real descent quite truthfully. And in order that there shall not be any further doubt in your heart you may ask me for any pledge you wish and carry that with you as proof. And in order that you will know that I do not give idle promises, may Vulcan in the Underworld, by whom all the gods pledge their oaths, be witness of my promise."

No sooner had Helios spoken than Phaethon asked him for the use of his Sun Chariot for one day and to be allowed to steer the winged horses. Terrified, his father looked at him, already regretting his hastily spoken promise. But sworn by the Underworld, he could not go back on his word. While he shook his radiant head three or four times he spoke.

"Reckless has been my promise. O, if I were only free to take back my words, I confess my son, this is the only thing I would deny you, if I could do so now. I am, however, free to dissuade you. What you desire is not without danger. You ask for a great favour, Phaethon, which does not suit your age nor your strength. Your fate is that of a mortal, but what you ask is something that is not becoming to a mortal. In your ignorance you ask for something that even the other gods would not be granted by divine law. Everybody may fancy what he likes. Nobody, however, but I can steer the fiery Sun Chariot. Even the Ruler of High Olympus, Jupiter himself, who with terrible fists casts the flickering thunderbolts, is not capable of driving this chariot. And who is mightier than Jupiter? And this is only considering the chariot that makes it an inhuman task. Now I shall also describe to you the difficulties of the route you have to follow.

"The beginning of the road rises steeply. It is with great difficulty, even in the early morning when they are still fresh and strong, that my fiery steeds struggle up along this path. In the middle of the sky the road is highest, and it happens only too often even to myself that I am overtaken by a shudder when I see from this high position the sea and lands below me, and my heart beats within my chest with a terrible fear. Then, as the road descends steeply, it is necessary to have a steady hand to drive.

"Even Tethys, the Goddess of the Sea, who receives me in the evening in her cooling waves after completion of my daily task, is as a rule anxious lest I should tumble down head over heels once I have arrived at this part of my route. Add to this that the heavens are dragged forwards in perpetual revolution and that the stars are also carried forward with it. I set myself vigorously against this so that the frantic speed with which the heavens rotate and drag everything with them cannot get hold of me as I drive upwards against the steep rotation of the skies.

"Assume that you are allowed to take the chariot. What will you do? Will you be able to encounter the rotating Pole without being dragged away by the spinning heavenly axis? Perhaps you are already imagining that you will see over there the holy woods and cities of the gods and the temples copiously laden with gifts. But it will not be like that. No, the route goes through ambushes and past animals of all shapes. And even if you do manage to keep on the right course, and are not lured onto the wrong track, you will still have to pass through the horns of Taurus, the Bull, who will stand unfriendly towards you. You will have to pass the Archer who always has his bow ready for the attack, the fierce jaws of the Lion, the Scorpion who has its claws curved in wide twisting coils, and the Crab who stretches out its pincers just on the other side of the road. Also you will not find it easy to control my horses, who are animated by the fire that burns in their chests and which they breathe out of their noses and ears. They only barely obey me once their fiery minds are inflamed and their necks strain against the bridles.

"So, my son, be careful, so that I shall not become the instigator of a calamity, and listen to my advice. Change your mind while there is still time. Ask me another pledge by which you may know that you are a son of my blood. Am I not giving you a certain pledge by my fears and do I not prove to be your father by my paternal concern for you? Look, behold my face. O, how I wish you could direct your eyes into my heart to perceive the worries I suffer for you. Look around at all the rich things the heavens, Earth and sea possess and ask as much as you like of these beautiful things. You will not be denied anything.

"Renounce however that one thing which in reality is a punishment and not an honour. A punishment, Phaethon, you ask as proof of your descent. What use is it to embrace me with your loving arms, O foolish child? Have no doubt you will have what you desire. I swear this by the waters of the river Styx in the Underworld. But ask me something more sensible."

With these warnings Helios finished his advice to his son. Phaethon, however, resisted his father's pleading and stuck to his once made proposition, burning with eagerness to mount the Sun Chariot. With a deep sigh Helios took his son to the high Sun Chariot, a present and work of art from Vulcan. The axle, the carriage poles, and the rims of the wheels were made of gold, while the spokes were made of silver. Topazes and other gems were placed in a row over the yoke; these reflected the sunlight of the approaching Sun God.

And while Phaethon, full of proud courage, admired the work of Vulcan, Aurora, Goddess of the Early Dawn, started opening the purple double doors towards the yellow glow in the east. Likewise, she opened the doors to the heavenly halls which were strewn with the most fragrant roses. On seeing this, the stars faded away and fled from the firmament, while Lucifer, sometimes also called Venus, "the Last One," covered their retreat. As soon as the Sun God saw that all of the stars had disappeared, that the Earth and the vault of Heaven had begun to glow in a reddish colour, and that the sickle of the barely visible Moon had begun to fade, he ordered the goddesses and guardians of the correct time intervals and the archways to the heavens to harness the horses to the Sun Chariot. Quickly the goddesses complied with his wishes and led the fiery steeds, who had been fed with juicy ambrosia, away from their high troughs and fitted them with their gnawing bits.

Then Helios covered the limbs and body of his son with a holy ointment to ensure that he could resist the heat of the flames. Next he put the wreath of Sunbeams on his head and, with a premonition of sorrow, he spoke. "If at least you will listen to these warnings of your father, make very little use of the goad but pull the reins firmly all the more. The steeds will rush forward on their own incentive and it really is very difficult to curb their speed. Also you may not pass through the five zones of Heaven. Your route goes right between them in an inclined direction and wide arc. Be content with three zones and stay away from the South Pole and the Great and Little Bear who are neighbours of the icy north winds. Along this path be your road. You will clearly see the tracks of the wheels which I have left behind from my previous journeys. Take care that the heavens and the Earth be provided equally with heat and warmth. Therefore do not go too high nor too low with the chariot. If you go too high you will burn the heavenly palaces, and if you go too low you will scorch the Earth. It is safest for you to adhere to the middle path. Do not veer too much to the right, because there you will find the coiling Dragon, neither turn too much to the left because you will get too near to the glittering Altar, low by the horizon. Guide your path just between the two. The rest I commend to the Goddess of Fortune, whom I hope will look after you better than you do after yourself. But look, while I have been standing here talking, the Goddess of the Night has made off to the extreme west. Now we must not hang back any longer. Heaven and Earth desire your light. Already dawn is breaking in the east as the Goddess Aurora rushes in front of you, and the dark flees away. Get hold of the reins or, better still, if you would like to change your mind, then make use of my advice instead of the Sun Chariot, while you can, and as long as you do not stand yet on the so eagerly desired Sun Chariot which may lead you to perdition. Let me give the light to the Earth, so that you may see it without danger to yourself."

Phaethon, however, had no intention of changing his mind and jumped on the chariot which hardly responded to the burden of his youthful body. Proudly he stood on top. Jubilant, he accepted the reins and thanked his father who parted with the bridle against his will.

Meanwhile, the four winged horses, Pyrois, Eous, Aethon and Phlegon filled the air with their neighing, and as they did so they breathed direfully and kicked impatiently with their hooves against the bolts of the doors of their stables. After Tethys, ignorant of the fate that her grandson would meet, had pushed the bolts away and thus opened the door to the road to the infinite expanse of Heaven, the horses stormed forwards and, galloping furiously, parted the clouds that were standing in their way. Gliding on their wings, they even overtook the East Wind, which had risen earlier from the same quarter of the heavens.

But their burden was light, so light that the horses of the Sun God could not even feel it. They also noticed that the yoke did not press so much as it normally would. They therefore lurched the carriage from one end to the other and made the maddest and wildest capers as if they had no driver at all—as if the chariot were totally empty. When the horses of the Sun God could still feel no restraint, they darted forwards galloping disorderly and leaving the path which they normally followed.

Phaethon was frightened; he no longer knew how to handle the horses and he had lost track of the correct route. Nor could he, had he known the right road to follow, have controlled the horses.

Now, for the first time, the Great Bear and Little Bear were warmed by the hot sunbeams. The bears tried in vain to immerse themselves in the sea—a recourse which was forbidden to them. The Polar Dragon, located between the Great Bear and Little Bear, who before was stiff with cold and therefore not feared by anybody, now became inflamed into a fury never previously known. And Boötes, who usually goes to rest rather late at night, hurried away from the heat hastily and in confusion.

As soon as the unfortunate Phaethon saw from the high heavens how the sinking Earth beneath him receded, he became pale with terror. His knees buckled from a suddenly rising fear. A dark shadow of dread muffled his eyes amidst so much glare of sunshine. Already Phaethon wished he had never touched the horses of his father. He also regretted that he had wished to know the identity of his father.

What was he to do? A great part of his route already lay behind him, but a much larger part still lay before him. In his mind he measured both parts, and one minute he looked forwards to the west, which according to his fate he would never reach, and then he cast his eyes to the east where he had started his journey. He could not now go back. Being no longer capable of thinking, or of knowing what to do, he grew numb with fear, and forgetting to pay out the reins, was incapable of drawing the horses back. He could not even remember the names of the horses.

He saw all kinds of animal shapes amid the stars. There was the place where the Scorpion coiled its two claws in a big arc, and, together with its tail, stretched itself out over two constellations. As soon as the youth saw this creature, moist with dark oozing venom, threatening to wound him with its curved stinger, he became terrified by the sight and let go of the reins. As soon as the horses noticed that the reins lay loose on their backs and that nobody controlled them anymore, they tore through the unknown regions of the sky wherever their tempestuous impulses led them.

There they went without any order. They crashed against the stars fixed high in Heaven, and dragged the chariot behind them in all directions. One minute they careered up high, the next they went low down by the Earth along a steeply dipping path. And, in amazement, the Moon Goddess saw the horses of her brother pass below hers, while the clouds were starting to burn with the scorching heat. Already the Earth was touched by the fire in its highest places, and she became bone dry with great cracks in her surface after all her moisture had evaporated. The grass burned to grey mass. The trees perished with their leaves and branches joined in the conflagration. The fields, withered by the heat, furnished fuel for their own perdition. But this was not the worst.

Big cities perished, walls and all. Fires laid whole countries, with their people, to ash, and woods and mountains burned. Then Phaethon saw that the Earth was burning on all sides and he could not stand such terrific heat. He inhaled through his mouth, got the hot air inside his lungs like the inside of a furnace, and felt his chariot start to burn. No longer could he resist the hot axle and the flying sparks, and he was shrouded in swirling smoke which whirled around him on all sides. No more did he know where he went or where he was, surrounded as he was by a pitch black darkness. He was dragged from side to side by the horses who now moved just to please themselves.

It was said that the Ethiopians begot their dark skin at this time, after the heat had drawn their blood to the outer skin. Also, it was believed that the deserts of the world came into existence because of Phaethon. Brooks and springs, and large and small rivers became small insignificant streams and eventually showed their naked dry channels. The Earth split open on all sides, and through the fissures the light beams penetrated to the Underworld to the great consternation of the God of the Underworld and his wife. Because in this realm of the dead there was never any light, but only misty, hazy and sombre surroundings, which the souls of the deceased haunted in equally vague and transparent attire. Also the seas shrank. What only a while ago had been sea—where the waves played their frisky games—became dry and turned to plains of sand.

Mountains which before were covered by the deep sea now appeared. The fishes looked for great depths, and the dolphins, who usually jumped up from the sea full of frolic, no longer dared to come above the waves. The dead bodies of suffocated seals floated around on the waves. Even Nereus and his daughters, the Nereids, so it was said, kept well hidden away in the deepest parts of their holes where the water had already started to become tepid. Neptune had tried to stretch his arms out above the seas but could not stand the heat of the fire. The Goddess of the Earth, surrounded by the sea and with the waters of all the sources now gathered in her lap, was withered up to her neck. She lifted up her head and, trying to shield her eyes from the heat of the Sun with her hands, spoke.

"If this is what pleases you and if this is what I deserve, why do you hesitate any longer, O highest of all the gods? Why don't you cast your thunderbolts? If I have to perish by fire then let me die by your fire and ease my death with the knowledge that you are the instigator of it all. Behold my singed hairs, and how many ashes and cinders there are on my face and mouth. Is this what I have deserved? Is this the thanks I get for all my fertility and readiness to put up with the wounds which the curved ploughshares inflict on me and with which I let myself be tortured all through the year so that I can feed the herds and the human beings? And I supply the gods and your altars with incense. May it be so. Assume that I do deserve this, but what have my waters and what has your brother Neptune in the depths of the sea done to endure all this? Why do his waters shrink, those which became his domain according to divine fate? If you cannot be moved by your own brother, nor by me, then at least have mercy upon your own heavens.

"Just look around you. Both Poles are already smoking, and when the flames have eaten through these, the heavenly palaces will collapse. See how Atlas struggles to keep the slippery axis upright? If the seas and the lands and your heavenly palaces perish then we shall return to the age old chaos. Snatch the flames away if there is anything left to be saved, and take care that the Universe remains."

These words Gaia, the Goddess of the Earth, spoke. She could not say anything more as the smoke completely choked her. The Almighty Father, Jupiter, called all the gods of Heaven and him who had entrusted the Sun Chariot to Phaethon to witness the situation for themselves. Jupiter said that if no help were forthcoming everything in the world would perish in one terrible conflagration. Jupiter then went to his high castle whence he used to spread out the clouds over the Earth, rumble his thunder and cast his thunderbolts. But he no longer possessed any clouds which he could send to cover the Earth, nor had he any rains left which he could send down from the highest heavens to extinguish the fire.

Jupiter was left with but one choice. Taking careful aim by directing the shaft along his right ear, Jupiter thundered in his fury and tossed his lightning bolt at Phaethon. The lightning bolt hit its target and Phaethon was knocked out of the Sun Chariot. In doing this, Jupiter took Phaethon's life and extinguished the fires which were burning all around.

The horses jumped frantically aside and, having made all kinds of capers, they tore themselves away from beneath the yoke and left the broken reins dangling behind them. Here lay the harness, there the smashed wheels and yonder the axle which was torn away from the carriage pole. Parts of the Sun Chariot lay scattered all around.

Phaethon tumbled head over heels down to Earth, shooting to the ground like a falling star with a long trailing tail. Far away from his homeland, the river Eridanus caught Phaethon, its waters rinsing his scorched face. The Naiades of the stream buried his body, still smoking from the three-pronged thunderbolt, and erected a monument on which they wrote, "Here rests Phaethon, who steered his father's Sun Chariot, and although he did not manage to complete the journey, it was a great enterprise in which he perished."

The Sun God, deeply saddened by the fate that had befallen his son, hid his face for one day behind a cloud. Phaethon's mother, Clymene, uttered laments and, robbed of her senses, set out to find the body of her son. She finally found it on the banks of a strange river. Here she sat by the gravestone shedding tears and pressing her breasts against the chilly stone in the hope that she could still warm her poor dead child.

Thus came the end of Phaethon, who paid dearly for his presumptuousness. In the heavens we can still see the Milky Way—the scorched path of Phaethon's catastrophic ride.

Selene, or Luna
The Moon Goddess

Selene was the sister of Helios, the Sun God. Every evening when Helios dipped his tired horses in the refreshing waves of the ocean, Selene used to take over to give light during the hours of darkness. Although we know now that the Moon is but a barren world with a very old and withered face, poets like to describe her as the Queen of Night. Ancient people thought of her as a most beautiful goddess clad in flowing robes, wearing a radiant tiara, who drove a chariot pulled by shiny horses.

Selene's beauty did not remain unnoticed by Jupiter, and he succeeded in attracting her into one of his many escapades of love. Consequently, Selene became the mother of three daughters by Jupiter. The Nemean Lion was also a creation of Jupiter and Selene. The Nemean Lion used to live on the Moon. It fell to Earth as a shooting star where, eventually, it was slain by Hercules.

Selene, however, was very much attracted by a youth called Endymion, who became King of Elis in the Peloponnesus. One day while Endymion was resting in the mountains after a strenuous hunting expedition, Selene saw him and could not resist stealing a kiss from him while he slept. Endymion saw this in his dreams. When he awoke, Endymion asked Jupiter for eternal youth and immortality, which Jupiter gave him under one condition—that he would remain eternally asleep. Selene is said to have come ever since during the night to have a look at her sleeping lover and to steal another kiss. Perhaps this is symbolic of the inevitable influence the Moon still seems to have on amorous affairs of mortals.

Another story is sometimes related to Io, the daughter of King Inachus. In the story of Taurus, Jupiter changed himself into a white bull and carried off Io to Crete where he became her lover. In the Moon story Jupiter is supposed to have come down in a cloud and slept with Io. In this disguise he hoped that his jealous wife Juno would not notice his escapade, but the all-seeing Juno became suspicious and found out. She asked Jupiter, who had quickly changed Io into a white heifer, to give the heifer to her as a present. As soon as Juno received this gift, she placed the animal under the guard of Argus, the giant with one hundred eyes. The eyes of Argus are symbolic of the star-studded heavens. Io is made to roam far and wide before she is restored again to a human being, a fate reflected in the wanderings of the Moon, night after night, among the stars of different constellations. In the morning when Hermes, or Mercury, the swift Messenger of the Gods, manages to lull the giant

Argus to sleep, he swiftly cuts off the head and all of the one hundred eyes close, symbolising the disappearance of stars in the morning light. The figure of the young crescent Moon depicts the maiden Io after she was changed into a white heifer.

Sometimes it is said that the Moon has 28 lovers. This is symbolic of the journey the Moon makes through the heavens when she passes through the 12 constellations of the zodiac and the neighbouring stars of other constellations. The number 28 roughly indicates the number of days required for the Moon to complete one revolution around the Earth.

Via Lactea
The Milky Way

During dark Summer evenings, the Milky Way can be seen as a luminous band oriented in a more or less north-south direction. During Autumn the same silvery sash lies more nearly in an east-west direction. The Milky Way is the extremity of our galaxy, a disc-shaped island of stars. The Milky Way has a diameter of some 100,000 light years. Our star, Sun, and its retinue of planets lie about 20,000 light years from the edge, and about 30,000 light years from the centre, of the galaxy. Had our Sun with its planets attained a position away from the plane which can be imagined through the edge of the Milky Way, we would be able to see that the Milky Way looks like a giant catherine wheel with a glowing dense central core whence whirling arms of stars, gas and dust clouds spiral outwards. Unfortunately, however, Sun and its planets lie in the plane of the galaxy and, from our infinitesimally small vantage point called Earth, we look as it were, from along one spoke of the wheel towards the center or rim of the wheel. As we do this our line of sight passes through layer after layer of stars. These stars appear to crowd together so densely at such enormous distances that, with the naked eye, we cannot see them any more as single stars but, instead, as a mixture of silvery light. This mixture forms that exquisite sash of light, irregular in shape, varying in light and veiled with dark clouds of gas and dust. Just as we can only see half the total sky and its stars, so can we only see half of this gigantic Milky Way at any one time.

To ancient people the Milky Way was always seen as something like a road, river, tree, bridge or similar symbol of unity in connection with the passage from life to death. In the story of Helios, the Sun God, we can read how the trail of burning cinders left by Phaethon came to be identified as the Milky Way.

Another interesting story of the Milky Way involves Jupiter. A son was born to Jupiter from his union with Alcmene, a mortal woman. Jupiter secretly laid this son—Hercules—beside his wife Juno in order that the child could feed from her godly breasts and thus receive immortality. The sturdy baby suckled the godly bosom so powerfully that a great deal of the precious milk spilt and sprayed over the heavens. This spray formed the Milky Way. Stray droplets landed on the Earth and became the flowers now known as lilies.

For many ancient people the Milky Way was the road taken by the souls of the dead on their long and weary trek to Heaven. Some American Indians held this view of the Milky Way and believed that the bright stars in it were the camp fires where the souls could warm themselves and rest. Nordic people believed the Milky Way to be the road along which the Walkiries took the dead warriors to Walhalla.

In other instances the Milky Way was seen as the seam where the heavens were joined together. Through the tiny stitch holes the lights of the palaces of the gods could be seen faintly, shimmering as a luminous sash.

In China and Japan, the Milky Way is viewed as a river along which the disembodied wraiths swim towards the Land of Peaches. The stars are like the elusive "silver fish." When the Moon is shining the stars of this river become invisible because they are frightened by the Moon which, in crescent shape, looks very much like a fisherman's hook.

The Milky Way often was seen as a heavenly representation of a river known on Earth. When viewed this way, the Milky Way was usually imagined to be connected to some mysterious unknown part of the earthly river's origin. In Egypt the Milky Way was seen as the Nile, in Italy the Po, in India the Ganges, and in China the Chang Jiang. The Greeks had a river called the Styx, across which the ferry boatman, Charon, transported the souls of the dead to the Underworld.

Perhaps the most unromantic analogy of all comes from Britain. Here, the Milky Way is referred to as Watling Street after the old Roman road that was built to allow Caesar's legions to move from London to Chester.

In the Middle Ages the Milky Way was seen as the bridge between Heaven and Earth down which angels could descend, or ascend, either to comfort those still alive on earth or to pester the earthlings. And so we can see how in various stories, poltergeists, witches on broomsticks and ghosts joined the traffic to and fro from Earth to Heaven, along the gleaming Road of the Sky.

Shooting Stars
Meteors

Ancient people had no knowledge of the exact nature of meteors. We know now that the luminous, short-lived streaks which we see in the night sky are caused by small particles of cosmic debris which enter our atmosphere at terrific speed. In their descent through the atmosphere they begin to glow and then, usually, disintegrate. While passing through the atmosphere, they leave behind luminous trails. We recognise these particles of debris and their trails as shooting stars.

To the ancients the stars were seen as many holes in the dome of Heaven behind which could be seen the fires in the palaces of the gods. When the gods sometimes became a little bored with their luxurious life and they wanted some amusement, they used to throw little pieces of coal from their fires through these holes to see if they could hit the Earth. These little pieces of coal were seen on Earth as shooting stars.

Epilogue

So—we have traveled far and wide, round the horizon, right to the ceiling of Heaven. In this journey I have tried to capture not only the beauty of the stars but also to sharpen your awareness and imagination so that you may come to know the stars as your friends and recognise some of their stories in the night sky as they trek past you during the years, acting out their eternal scripts on the great heavenly stage.

The mythology of the stars with its celestial actors has stood the test of time. Other things may have changed or long since disappeared to be left only as memories, but the stars have been shining in recognised patterns for many thousands of years and will continue to do so for many generations yet to come.

Astronomers still use the constellation names and they still like to refer to some of the more well-known stars by their ancient Greek or Arabic names. To them, however, such names may be just a convenience to denote a reference point, to hang a label regarding a spectral class, or to associate a star type with certain known astrophysical conditions. If the amateur astronomer and star lover, after reading this book, feels inclined to know a little more about the heavens from the scientific point of view, then I may count this as my reward for having opened the gates for you by means of the stories of the stars, to the most noble of sciences— Astronomy. If, however, you do not feel so inclined, then at least I hope that the beauty of the stars may hold your attention and interest for many night watches to come.

Though my soul may set in darkness
It will rise in perfect light;
I have loved the stars too fondly
To be fearful of the night.

An old astronomer
to his pupil, Galileo

Appendix I
The Greek Alphabet

Letter Name	Upper Case Letter	Lower Case Letter	Transliteration to English
Alpha	A	α	A, a
Beta	B	β	B, b
Gamma	Γ	γ	G, g
Delta	Δ	δ	D, d
Epsilon	E	ε	Ē, ē
Zeta	Z	ζ	Z, z
Eta	H	η	E, e
Theta	Θ	θ	Th, th
Iota	I	ι	I, i
Kappa	K	κ	K, k
Lambda	Λ	λ	L, l
Mu	M	μ	M, m
Nu	N	ν	N, n
Xi	Ξ	ξ	X, x
Omicron	O	o	O, o
Pi	Π	π	P, p
Rho	P	ρ	R, r; rh
Sigma	Σ	σ, ς	S, s
Tau	T	τ	T, t
Upsilon	Y	υ	U, u
Phi	Φ	φ	Ph, ph
Chi	X	χ	Kh, kh
Psi	Ψ	ψ	Ps, ps
Omega	Ω	ω	O, o

Appendix II
The Constellations in Alphabetical Order

No.	Latin Name	Genitive Case	English Name	Abbreviation	Key Figure
1	Andromeda	Andromedae	Andromeda	And	1
2	Antlia	Antliae	Air pump	Ant	90
3	Apus	Apodis	Bird of paradise	Aps	138
4	Aquarius	Aquarii	Water carrier	Aqr	19
5	Aquila	Aquilae	Eagle	Aql	96
6	Ara	Arae	Altar	Ara	125
7	Aries	Arietis	Ram	Ari	16
8	Auriga	Aurigae	Charioteer	Aur	39
9	Boötes	Boötis	Bear driver	Boo	81
10	Caelum	Caeli	Burin	Cae	50
11	Camelopardus	Camelopardalis	Giraffe	Cam	129
12	Cancer	Cancri	Crab	Cnc	75
13	Canes Venatici	Canum Venaticorum	Hunting dogs	CVn	81
14	Canis Major	Canis Majoris	Greater dog	CMa	43
15	Canis Minor	Canis Minoris	Lesser dog	CMi	43
16	Capricornus	Capricorni	Seagoat	Cap	115
17	Carina	Carinae	Keel	Car	51
18	Cassiopeia	Cassiopeiae	Cassiopeia	Cas	4
19	Centaurus	Centauri	Centaur	Cen	93
20	Cepheus	Cephei	Cepheus	Cep	4
21	Cetus	Ceti	Sea monster	Cet	14
22	Chamaeleon	Chamaeleontis	Chameleon	Cha	140
23	Circinus	Circini	Drawing compass	Cir	138
24	Columba	Columbae	Dove	Col	52
25	Coma Berenices	Comae Berenices	Berenice's hair	Com	79
26	Corona Australis	Coronae Australis	Southern Crown	CrA	126
27	Corona Borealis	Coronae Borealis	Northern crown	CrB	110
28	Corvus	Corvi	Crow, raven	Crv	85
29	Crater	Crateris	Beaker	Crt	85
30	Crux	Crucis	Southern cross	Cru	134
31	Cygnus	Cygni	Swan	Cyg	95
32	Delphinus	Delphini	Dolphin	Del	102

No.	Latin Name	Genitive Case	English Name	Abbreviation	Key Figure
33	Dorado	Doradus	Gold fish	Dor	132
34	Draco	Draconis	Dragon	Dra	127
35	Equuleus	Equulei	Little horse	Equ	104
36	Eridanus	Eridani	River Eridanus	Eri	45
37	Fornax	Fornacis	Furnace	For	48
38	Gemini	Geminorum	Twins	Gem	41
39	Grus	Gruis	Crane	Gru	25A
40	Hercules	Herculis	Hercules	Her	108
41	Horologium	Horologii	Pendulum clock	Hor	49
42	Hydra	Hydrae	Watersnake (female)	Hya	85
43	Hydrus	Hydri	Watersnake (male)	Hyi	131
44	Indus	Indi	Indian	Ind	126
45	Lacerta	Lacertae	Lizard	Lac	23A
46	Leo	Leonis	Lion	Leo	53
47	Leo Minor	Leonis Minoris	Lesser lion	LMi	53
48	Lepus	Leporis	Hare	Lep	30
49	Libra	Librae	Scales	Lib	122
50	Lupus	Lupi	Wolf	Lup	93
51	Lynx	Lyncis	Lynx	Lyn	74
52	Lyra	Lyrae	Lyre	Lyr	98
53	Mensa	Mensae	Table mountain	Men	140
54	Microscopium	Microscopii	Microscope	Mic	126
55	Monoceros	Monocerotis	Unicorn	Mon	43
56	Musca	Muscae	Southern fly	Mus	133
57	Norma	Normae	Carpenter's square	Nor	138
58	Octans	Octantis	Octant	Oct	140
59	Ophiuchus	Ophiuchi	Serpent bearer	Oph	105
60	Orion	Orionis	Orion	Ori	30
61	Pavo	Pavonis	Peacock	Pav	139
62	Pegasus	Pegasi	Winged horse	Peg	11
63	Perseus	Persei	Perseus	Per	9
64	Phoenix	Phoenicis	Phoenix	Phe	28
65	Pictor	Pictoris	Painter's easel	Pic	50
66	Pisces	Piscium	Fishes	Psc	21
67	Piscis Austrinus	Piscis Austrini	Southern fish	PsA	26
68	Puppis	Puppis	Stern	Pup	51
69	Pyxis	Pyxidis	Mariner's compass	Pyx	91
70	Reticulum	Reticuli	Net	Ret	49
71	Sagitta	Sagittae	Arrow	Sge	96
72	Sagittarius	Sagittarii	Archer	Sgr	112
73	Scorpius	Scorpii	Scorpion	Sco	117
74	Sculptor	Sculptoris	Sculptor	Scl	27

No.	Latin Name	Genitive Case	English Name	Abbreviation	Key Figure
75	Scutum	Scuti	Shield	Sct	101
76	Serpens	Serpentis	Serpent	Ser	105
77	Sextans	Sextantis	Sextant	Sex	92
78	Taurus	Tauri	Bull	Tau	30
79	Telescopium	Telescopii	Telescope	Tel	126
80	Triangulum	Trianguli	Triangle	Tri	22A
81	Triangulum Australe	Trianguli Australis	Southern triangle	TrA	138
82	Tucana	Tucanae	Toucan	Tuc	130
83	Ursa Major	Ursae Majoris	Great bear	UMa	58
84	Ursa Minor	Ursae Minoris	Little bear	Umi	71
85	Vela	Velorum	Sail	Vel	51
86	Virgo	Virginis	Maiden	Vir	84
87	Volans	Volantis	Flying fish	Vol	132
88	Vulpecula	Vulpeculae	Little fox	Vul	102

Appendix III
Greek and Roman Gods and Goddesses
A Selected List of Associated Deities Mentioned in This Book

Greek Deity	Roman Deity	Role or Affiliation
Aphrodite	Venus	Goddess of love and beauty.
Apollo	Apollo	God of light, music, healing and prophecy.
Artemis	Diana	Goddess of light and the hunt.
Asclepius	Aesculapius	God of healing.
Athene	Minerva	Goddess of wisdom and womanly arts.
Demeter	Ceres	Goddess of grain.
Dionysus	Bacchus	God of the vine and wine.
Eos	Aurora	Goddess of the dawn.
Eros	Cupid	God of love.
Hades/Pluto	Pluto/Dis	Keeper of the Underworld.
Hephaestus	Vulcan	God of metalworking and/or fire.
Hera	Juno	Queen of the deities.
Hermes	Mercury	God of travelers, commerce, dreams and flocks; messenger of the gods.
Pan	Faunus	God of nature, pastures, and woodlands.
Persephone	Proserpina	Wife of Hades.
Poseidon	Neptune	God of earthquakes and the sea.
Rhea	Ops	Great Mother; goddess of earthly productivity.
Zeus	Jupiter	King of the deities.

Appendix IV
Spectral Classes of Stars

Class	Color	Representative Temperatures	Some Stars of this Type
O	Blue-white	50,000° K	None visible to the naked eye
B	Blue	30,000° K	Achernar, Algol, Rigel
A	White	10,000° K	Sirius, Fomalhaut, Vega
F	White	7,000° K	Canopus, Procyon, Polaris
G	Yellow	6,000° K	Capella, Sun
K	Orange	5,000° K	Arcturus, Aldebaran, Pollux
M	Red	3,500° K	Betelgeuse, Antares, Mirach

Appendix V
Zeiss Planetariums Worldwide

City	Country	Inauguration Date	Model	Dome φ Meters	Feet	Seating Capacity
Amsterdam	Netherlands	8 Apr 1982	IV B	20.00	65.62	350
Athens	Greece	7 Jun 1966	IV	15.00	49.21	250
Atlanta	United States	3 Dec 1967	V	21.34	70.01	500
Bangkok	Thailand	18 Aug 1964	IV	20.00	65.62	463
Baton Rouge	United States	24 May 1967	III	18.30	60.04	248
Berlin	West Germany	27 Nov 1926	II	24.80	81.57	
		16 Jun 1965	V	20.00	65.62	330
Bochum	West Germany	6 Nov 1964	IV	20.00	65.62	248
Boston	United States	11 Jan 1971	VI	18.30	60.04	316
Boulder	United States	20 Sep 1975	VI	19.80	64.96	213
Buenos Aires	Argentina	19 Dec 1966	V	20.00	65.62	360
Caracas	Venezuela	24 Jul 1961	IV	20.00	65.62	327
Champaign	United States	Sep 1987	1015	15.00	49.22	
Chapel Hill	United States	10 May 1949	III	20.70	67.91	
		26 Mar 1969	VI	20.70	67.91	330
Chicago	United States	10 May 1930	II	20.70	67.91	
		26 Feb 1970	VI	20.70	67.91	392
Copenhagen	Denmark	Aug 1989	VI TD	23.00	75.46	280
Fort Lauderdale	United States	Dec 1987	1015	12.20	40.02	100
Guayaquil	Ecuador	25 Jul 1983	Vs	20.00	65.62	
Hamburg	West Germany	15 Apr 1930	II	20.60	67.59	
		12 Dec 1957	IV	20.60	67.59	300
		1983	VI	20.60	67.59	
Hong Kong	Hong Kong	7 Oct 1980	VI	23.00	75.45	365
Johannesburg	South Africa	12 Oct 1960	III	20.00	65.62	420
Kassel	West Germany	1989	1015 A	10.00	32.81	80
London	Great Britain	19 Mar 1958	IV	20.30	66.60	418
Los Angeles	United States	14 May 1935	II	22.90	75.13	
		30 Mar 1964	IV	22.90	75.13	663
Lucerne	Switzerland	1 Jul 1969	Vs	18.00	59.05	300
Mannheim	West Germany	22 Mar 1927	II	24.50	80.38	
			VI	20.00	65.62	280
Mexico City	Mexico	2 Jan 1967	IV	20.00	65.62	440
Milan	Italy	20 May 1930	II	19.60	64.30	
		7 Dec 1968	IV	19.60	64.30	307
Montreal	Canada	1 Apr 1966	V	20.00	65.62	400

City	Country	Inauguration Date	Model	Dome φ Meters	Feet	Seating Capacity
Morelia	Mexico	29 Sep 1975	IV	20.00	65.62	336
Munich	West Germany	21 Oct 1923	I	9.80	32.23	
		7 May 1925	I	9.80	32.23	
		7 May 1951	I	9.80	32.23	
		7 May 1960	IV	15.00	49.21	180
Münster	West Germany	13 Nov 1981	V	20.00	65.62	289
Nagoya	Japan	1 Nov 1962	IV	20.20	66.27	445
New York	United States	2 Oct 1935	II	22.80	74.80	
		29 Jan 1960	IV	22.80	74.80	
		2 Oct 1969	VI	22.80	74.80	763
Nuremburg	West Germany	10 Apr 1927	II	23.00	75.45	
		11 Dec 1961	III	18.00	59.05	
		30 Jan 1977	V	18.00	59.05	286
Osaka	Japan	13 Mar 1937	II	18.00	59.05	330
Philadelphia	United States	11 Jan 1933	II	20.00	65.62	
		18 Sep 1962	IV	20.00	65.62	400
Pittsburgh	United States	24 Oct 1939	II	20.00	65.62	490
Riyadh	Saudi Arabia	Dec 1987	VI A	20.00	65.62	
Rochester	United States	14 Sep 1968	VI	19.80	64.96	240
Rome	Italy	28 Oct 1928	II	19.00	62.34	387
Rosario	Argentina	1984	IV	22.00	72.18	500
São Paulo	Brazil	26 Jan 1957	III	20.00	65.62	374
Santiago	Chile	1984	VI	20.00	65.62	300
Stuttgart	West Germany	16 May 1928	II	24.70	81.03	
		22 Apr 1977	VI	20.00	65.62	277
Tokyo	Japan	2 Nov 1938	II	20.00	65.62	
		28 Mar 1957	IV	20.00	65.62	453
Vienna	Austria	7 May 1927	II	20.00	65.62	
		8 Jan 1930	II	20.00	65.62	
		20 Jun 1964	IV	20.00	65.62	240
Washington, D.C.	United States	4 Jul 1976		21.33	70.00	242
Winnipeg	Canada	17 May 1968	Vs	18.30	60.04	287
Yonkers	United States	Oct 1987	1015	12.00	39.36	132

Appendix VI
The Celestial Coordinate System

A spherical coordinate network exists by which the location of objects upon the celestial sphere can be described. This system is based upon east-west lines that lie upon or are parallel to the Celestial Equator and north-south lines that cross the Celestial Equator at right angles. The east-west coordinate values are called **right ascension (R.A.)** and the north-south coordinate values are called **declination**.

When used as a reference for celestial coordinates, the Celestial Equator is divided into degrees, minutes and seconds or, more often, hours, minutes and seconds. The full circumference of the Celestial Equator consists of 360°, or 24 hours; 1 hour of right ascension equals 15° of arc. Zero-hour right ascension lies at the point where the Vernal Equinox falls on the Celestial Equator, as well as at all points on a north-south line that passes through that point on the Celestial Equator. Right ascension increases to the east, passing—in hourly increments— from 0 to 1, 2, 3, . . . to 24, which is located in the same place as 0 (Figure 141).

Declination is measured in degrees of arc. Declination north of the Celestial Equator is positive, and declination south of the Celestial Equator is negative. The Celestial Equator is at declination 0°, while the North and South celestial poles are at declinations +90° and −90°, respectively.

A point upon the celestial sphere is defined with the identification of the right ascension and declination lines which intersect at the given point. In this book, each constellation is illustrated at least one time against a portion of the celestial coordinate network. Using the coordinates included on these illustrations, the location of the constellations upon the celestial sphere can be determined.

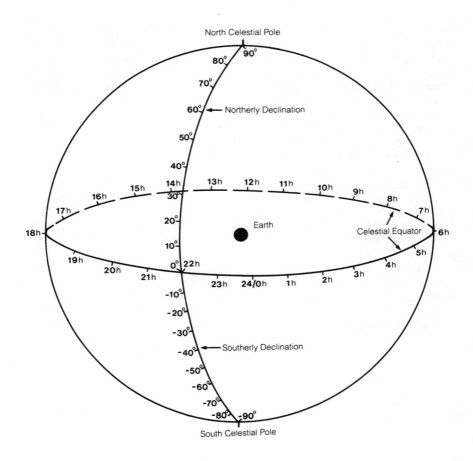

Figure 141. The celestial coordinate system.

288

Appendix VII
Star Maps

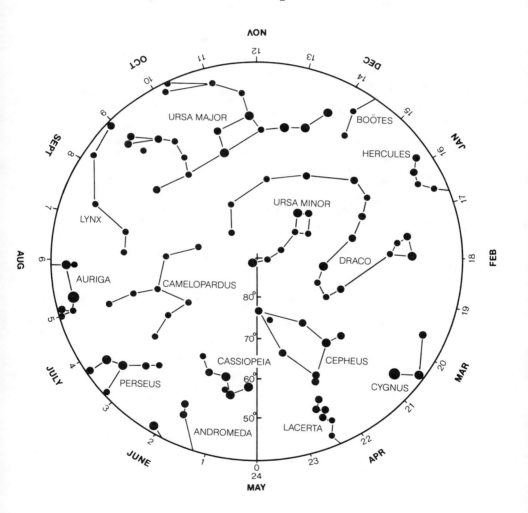

Figure 142. Constellations around the North Celestial Pole. Approximate orientation for 9 P.M. on the first day of any month may be determined by holding the chart so that the respective month is at the bottom of the chart.

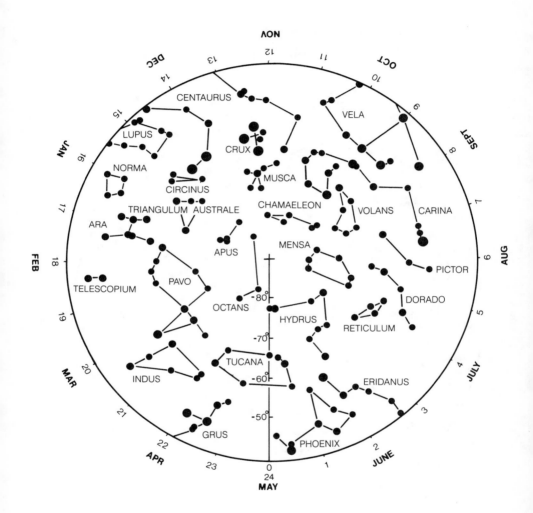

Figure 143. Constellations around the South Celestial Pole. Approximate orientation for 9 P.M. on the first day of any month may be determined by holding the chart so that the respective month is at the bottom of the chart.

290

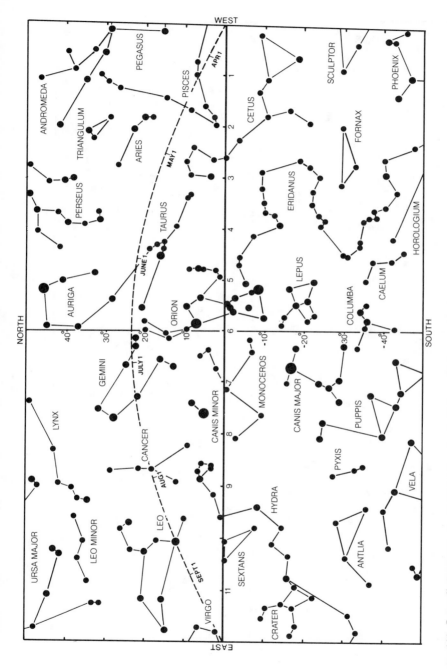

Figure 144. Constellations near the Celestial Equator: 0–12 hours R.A.

291

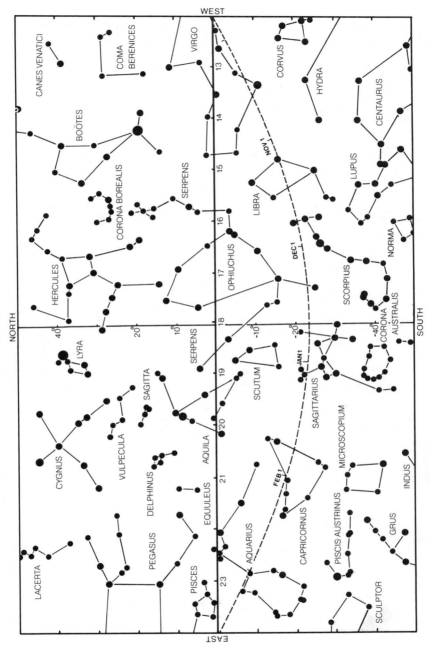

Figure 145. Constellations near the Celestial Equator: 12–24 hours R.A.

Index

Dictys 19, 20, 22
Die Gestirne 164
Dis 283
dolphin (fish) 244
Dolphin, the 189–191
Dorado 235, 244, 245
Doris 264
double cluster 23, 24, 26
Dove, the 110
Draco 235, 237, 238, 240
Draconids 240
Dragon, the 173, 237, 267, 268
Dragon Fish, the 33, 34
Drawing Compass 253
Dubhe 121, 152
Dümur 221–223
Dürer, A. 46, 47, 146, 179, 185

Eagle, the 173, 179, 182, 195, 202, 217
Egypt 36, 39, 74, 85, 158, 213, 246
Egyptian 8, 42, 54, 94, 126, 139, 140,
    145–147
Electra 75
Elis 79, 202, 272
Eltanin 240
Endymion 272
Enif 27, 29
Epaphus 74, 246, 263
equinoxes 207
Equuleus 194
Eratosthenes 141
Erichthonius 80
Eridanus 33, 59, 92–95, 175, 202, 243, 271
Erigone 152, 153
Eskimo 136
Ethiopia 7, 9, 14, 246
Euphrates River 9, 58
Europa 74
Euryale 61
Eurydice 184
Eurystheus 141, 199, 201–206
Eurythion 204

Fabricius, D. 34
Fatima 14
Faunus 283
Felis 163, 164
Firebird, the 58
Fishes, the 11, 177
fishing rod, the 53
Five Notables, the 83, 84
Flamsteed, J. 37, 40, 146, 153, 157, 185, 188,
    189, 197, 198, 227, 228
Flying Fish 244, 245
Fomalhaut 44, 54, 159, 284
Fornax 96, 97
Fou-youe 43, 44
Four Trenches, the 83, 84
Fraunhofer, J. von 25
Fraunhofer lines 25
Frog 147
Furnace, the 96

Gaia 61, 141, 195, 206, 220, 221, 237, 270
Ganymede 42, 179, 180, 203

Gemini 59, 82–84, 108, 205, 206
Geminids 84
Gemma 208, 210, 211
Geography of the Heavens 228
Germanicus 55
Geryon 204
Gibraltar 204
girdle of Hippolyte 203
Glaucus 27, 103, 162–164
Globus Aerostaticus 218
Gloria Frederica 50
golden apples 126, 141, 162, 168, 200, 206
golden fleece 82, 101, 103, 105, 106, 108
Gold Fish 244, 245
Goodricke, J. 25
Goose, the 193
Gorgon 8, 20, 21
gourds 190
Great Bear 111, 121, 122, 124–126, 128, 131,
    136, 137, 152, 206, 237, 267, 268
Great Dog 85, 206
Great Trench 23
Greenland 136
Grus 53
Guiana 30

Habrecht, I. 97
Hades 21, 83, 283
Hadley, J. 257
Hair of Berenices 149, 151
Hamal 41, 159
Hare, the 91
Harp, the 107, 183, 184
Heaped-up Corpses 23
Hebrew 128, 129
Heis, E. 121
Heliopolis57
Helios 92, 173, 175, 258, 263–267, 272, 274
Hell, M. 95
Helle 36, 37
Hellen 176
Hellespont 37
Hercules 93, 103, 107, 108, 114, 126, 145,
    160, 162, 170, 173, 180, 182, 199–207, 274
Hermes 64, 65, 272
Hermit Bird, the 227, 228
Herschel, J. F. W. 138, 207, 214
Hesiodus 75
Hesmut 140
Hesperides, the 20, 21, 126, 141, 142, 200,
    206, 237
Hevelius, J. 50, 51, 86, 120, 144, 154, 169,
    179, 188, 193, 205, 241
Hien-youen 117–119
Himalaya Mountains 90
Hind of Mount Ceryneia 201
Hindu 30, 31, 67, 68, 137, 165, 180
Hing-tchin 150
Hipparchus 139, 141, 146, 194
Hippocrene 27, 29
Hippodameia 79
Hippolyte 203, 204
Hippopotamus, the 139, 140
Ho 24
Homer 37, 125
Ho-niao 58
Honores Frederici 50, 51

Phylira 170
Pictor 99, 100
Pigeon 132
Pikolan 180,
Pillars of Hercules 204
Piranha, the 155
Pisces 10, 31, 33, 36, 45–47, 108
Piscis Austrinus 33, 42, 44, 54, 55
Pleiades 9, 25, 59, 221, 222
Pleiades, the 62, 67, 70, 74–76, 108, 126, 223
Plough, the 121, 126, 152
Pluto 142, 157, 158, 184, 204, 205, 211, 237, 283
Pneumatic Pump 97
Po River 92, 275
Poczobut, Abbé 197
Polaris 32, 34, 121, 135, 151, 152, 237, 284
pole star 31, 32, 111, 137, 207, 237
Pollux 82–86, 103, 105, 108, 159, 176, 284
Polydectes 19–21, 27
Polyidus 162–164
Polyphemus 38, 39
Poniatowski's Bull 197, 198
porpoise 17, 18
Poseidon 7, 64, 65, 189, 190, 283
Praesepe 148
Prajápati 67, 68
precession 31, 36, 45, 77, 207, 226
Procyon 85, 89, 162, 284
Prometheus 180, 182
Proserpina 111, 143, 157, 158, 283
Proteus 19, 22, 27, 264
Psalterium Georgei 95
Ptolemaeus, C. 114, 122, 141, 152, 154, 168, 170, 219, 247
Ptolemy 149
Pup, the 88
Puppis 101, 102
Pyramus 115, 149, 162
Pyxis 97, 168

Quetzalcoatl 134

Rain Dragon 117, 118
Ram, the 31, 32, 36, 41, 216
Ras Algethi 199, 207
Ras Alhague 197, 199
Raven, the 161
Regulus 2, 54, 113, 116, 119, 159
reindeer 17, 135, 136
Reticulum 97, 98
rhea 251
Rhea (asterism) 170
Rhea (goddess) 283
Rhomboidal Net 98
Rigel 61, 72, 92, 284
Rotanev 192
Royal Daughters, the 118, 119
Royer, A. 14–16, 50, 52, 200, 247

Sagitta 179, 182
Sagittarius 108, 173, 182, 202, 212–215, 223, 233
Saiph 61

Samoa 249
Samos 19
San-koung 150
Saturn 46
Saw Whet 132
Scales, the 32, 158, 173, 220, 221, 226–228
Scarabaeus 145–147
Sceptre and Hand of Justice 50, 52
Sceptrum Brandenburgicum 95
Scheat 27
Scorpius 109, 170, 195, 196, 201, 204, 213, 219, 221–225, 233
scorpion 61, 165
Scorpion, the 61, 62, 109, 173, 195, 196, 204, 213, 214, 219–221, 226, 227, 266, 268
Sculptor 56, 96, 151
Scutum 188, 197
Seagoat 202, 216, 218
Secchi, A. 164
Selene 272
Seneca 197
Serpens 195–197
serpent 225
Serpent, the 173, 195, 196, 198
Serpent Bearer 195, 196
Set 64, 140
Seven Ploughing Oxen, the 124
Sextans 169
Sextant, the 169
Shapley, H. 207
Shield, the 188
Shooting Stars 261, 276
Siberia 17, 116, 117, 135, 136, 191, 210
Sicily 48
Sileni 170, 213
Sirius 61, 67, 85, 87, 88, 206, 284
Sirrah 27
Situation of the Waters 83, 84
Siusi Indians 95, 116, 225
Sobieski, J. 188
Solitaire 227
Solomon Islands 249
South America 223
South Celestial Pole 92, 151, 233, 245, 252, 255, 257, 258, 287, 288
South Galactic Pole 151
Southern Camp Gate, the 12
Southern Cross 170, 247–249
Southern Crown 232
Southern Fish, the 53, 54
Southern Fly 246, 248
Southern Triangle, the 253
Spica 109, 157–159
Spotted Dog 86
Sse-tou 83, 84
Staal, J. D. W. 12, 23, 40, 44, 48, 52, 56, 70, 87, 94, 100, 110, 144, 161, 167, 168, 210, 228, 232, 242, 243, 245, 248, 253, 257
Stables of Augeas 202
Star Names 50, 193, 194, 226
Star of Bethlehem 46
Sterope 75
Sthenaboea 27
Stymphalian Birds 182, 202
Sualocin 192
Summer Solstice 114, 146
Summer Triangle 176, 181
Sun 284

NOTES